SOURCE READINGS IN $\mathcal{M}$USIC
HISTORY

SOURCE READINGS IN *M*USIC HISTORY

OLIVER STRUNK

EDITOR

Revised Edition

LEO TREITLER GENERAL EDITOR

VOLUME 7

The Twentieth Century

Edited by ROBERT P. MORGAN

 W · W · NORTON & COMPANY

New York · London

The text of this book is composed in Caledonia
with the display set in Bauer Bodoni and Optima.
Composition by the Maple-Vail Book Manufacturing Group
Manufacturing by Maple-Vail Book Manufacturing Group
Book design by Jack Meserole
Cover illustration by Mary Frank

The Library of Congress has cataloged the one-volume edition as follows:

Source readings in music history / Oliver Strunk, editor. — Rev. ed.
    / Leo Treitler, general editor.
        p.   cm.
    Also published in a 7 v. ed.
    Includes bibliographical references and index.
    ISBN 0-393-03752-5
    1. Music—History and criticism—Sources.   I. Strunk, W. Oliver
(William Oliver), 1901–   .   II. Treitler, Leo, 1931–   .
ML160.S89   1998
780'.9—dc20   94-34569
                                                        MN

ISBN 0-393-96700-X (pbk.)

W. W. Norton & Company, Inc., 500 Fifth Avenue, New York, N.Y. 10110
http://www.wwnorton.com

W. W. Norton & Company Ltd., 10 Coptic Street, London WC1A 1PU

1 2 3 4 5 6 7 8 9 0

FROM THE FOREWORD TO THE
FIRST EDITION OF *SOURCE*
READINGS IN MUSIC HISTORY

*T*his book began as an attempt to carry out a suggestion made in 1929 by Carl Engel in his "Views and Reviews"—to fulfil his wish for "a living record of musical personalities, events, conditions, tastes . . . a history of music faithfully and entirely carved from contemporary accounts."[1] It owes something, too, to the well-known compilations of Kinsky[2] and Schering[3] and rather more, perhaps, to Andrea della Corte's *Antologia della storia della musica*[4] and to an evaluation of this, its first model, by Alfred Einstein.

In its present form, however, it is neither the book that Engel asked for nor a literary anthology precisely comparable to the pictorial and musical ones of Kinsky and Schering, still less an English version of its Italian predecessor, with which it no longer has much in common. It departs from Engel's ideal scheme in that it has, at bottom, a practical purpose—to make conveniently accessible to the teacher or student of the history of music those things which he must eventually read. Historical documents being what they are, it inevitably lacks the seemingly unbroken continuity of Kinsky and Schering; at the same time, and for the same reason, it contains far more that is unique and irreplaceable than either of these. Unlike della Corte's book it restricts itself to historical documents as such, excluding the writing of present-day historians; aside from this, it naturally includes more translations, fewer original documents, and while recognizing that the somewhat limited scope of the *Antologia* was wholly appropriate in a book on music addressed to Italian readers, it seeks to take a broader view.

That, at certain moments in its development, music has been a subject of widespread and lively contemporary interest, calling forth a flood of documentation, while at other moments, perhaps not less critical, the records are either silent or unrevealing—this is in no way remarkable, for it is inherent in the very nature of music, of letters, and of history. The beginnings of the Classical

1. *The Musical Quarterly* 15, no. 2 (April 1929): 301.
2. *Geschichte der Musik in Bildern* (Leipzig, 1929; English edition by E. Blom, London, 1930).
3. *Geschichte der Musik in Beispielen* (Leipzig, 1931; English edition New York, 1950).
4. Two volumes (Torino, 1929). Under the title *Antologia della storia della musica della Grecia antica al' ottocento,* one volume (Torino, 1945).

symphony and string quartet passed virtually unnoticed as developments without interest for the literary man; the beginnings of the opera and cantata, developments which concerned him immediately and deeply, were heralded and reviewed in documents so numerous that, even in a book of this size, it has been possible to include only the most significant. Thus, as already suggested, a documentary history of music cannot properly exhibit even the degree of continuity that is possible for an iconographic one or a collection of musical monuments, still less the degree expected of an interpretation. For this reason, too, I have rejected the simple chronological arrangement as inappropriate and misleading and have preferred to allow the documents to arrange themselves naturally under the various topics chronologically ordered in the table of contents and the book itself, some of these admirably precise, others perhaps rather too inclusive. As Engel shrewdly anticipated, the frieze has turned out to be incomplete, and I have left the gaps unfilled, as he wished.

For much the same reason, I have not sought to give the book a spurious unity by imposing upon it a particular point of view. At one time it is the musician himself who has the most revealing thing to say; at another time he lets someone else do the talking for him. And even when the musician speaks it is not always the composer who speaks most clearly; sometimes it is the theorist, at other times the performer. If this means that few readers will find the book uniformly interesting, it ought also to mean that "the changing patterns of life," as Engel called them, will be the more fully and the more faithfully reflected. . . . In general, the aim has been to do justice to every age without giving to any a disproportionate share of the space.

It was never my intention to compile a musical Bartlett, and I have accordingly sought, wherever possible, to include the complete text of the selection chosen, or—failing this—the complete text of a continuous, self-contained, and independently intelligible passage or series of passages, with or without regard for the chapter divisions of the original. But in a few cases I have made cuts to eliminate digressions or to avoid needless repetitions of things equally well said by earlier writers; in other cases the excessive length and involved construction of the original has forced me to abridge, reducing the scale of the whole while retaining the essential continuity of the argument. All cuts are clearly indicated, either by a row of dots or in annotations.

Often, in the course of my reading, I have run across memorable things said by writers on music which, for one reason or another, were not suited for inclusion in the body of this book. One of these, however, is eminently suited for inclusion here. It is by Thomas Morley, and it reads as follows:

> But as concerning the book itself, if I had, before I began it, imagined half the pains and labor which it cost me, I would sooner have been persuaded to anything than to have taken in hand such a tedious piece of work, like unto a great sea, which the further I entered into, the more I saw before me unpassed; so that at length, despairing ever to make an end (seeing that grow so big in mine hands which I thought to have shut up in two or three sheets of paper), I laid it aside, in full determination to

have proceeded no further but to have left it off as shamefully as it was foolishly begun. But then being admonished by some of my friends that it were pity to lose the fruits of the employment of so many good hours, and how justly I should be condemned of ignorant presumption—in taking that in hand which I could not perform—if I did not go forward, I resolved to endure whatsoever pain, labor, loss of time and expense, and what not, rather than to leave that unbrought to an end in the which I was so far engulfed.[5]

OLIVER STRUNK
The American Academy in Rome

5. Thomas Morley, *A Plain and Easy Introduction to Practical Music,* ed. R. Alec Harman (New York: Norton, 1966), p. 5.

FOREWORD TO THE REVISED EDITION

Hiding in the peace of these deserts
with few but wise books bound together
I live in conversation with the departed,
and listen with my eyes to the dead.
—Francisco Gómez de Quevedo
(1580–1645)

*T*he inclusion here of portions of Oliver Strunk's foreword to the original edition of this classic work (to which he habitually referred ironically as his *opus unicum*) is already a kind of exception to his own stricture to collect in it only "historical documents as such, excluding the writing of present-day historians." For his foreword itself, together with the book whose purpose and principles it enunciates and the readings it introduces, comes down to us as a historical document with which this revision is in a conversation—one that ranges over many subjects, even the very nature of music history.

This principle of exclusion worked for Strunk because he stopped his gathering short of the twentieth century, which has been characterized—as Robert Morgan observes in his introduction to the twentieth-century readings in this series—by "a deep-seated self-consciousness about what music is, to whom it should be addressed, and its proper role within the contemporary world." It is hardly possible to segregate historian from historical actor in our century.

For the collection in each of the seven volumes in this series the conversation begins explicitly with an introductory essay by its editor and continues with the readings themselves. The essays provide occasions for the authors to describe the considerations that guide their choices and to reflect on the character of the age in each instance, on the regard in which that age has been held in music-historical tradition, on its place in the panorama of music history as we construct and continually reconstruct it, and on the significance of the readings themselves. These essays constitute in each case the only substantial explicit interventions by the editors. We have otherwise sought to follow Strunk's own essentially conservative guidelines for annotations.

The essays present new perspectives on music history that have much in common, whatever their differences, and they present new perspectives on the music that is associated with the readings. They have implications, therefore, for those concerned with the analysis and theory of music as well as for students of music history. It is recommended that even readers whose interest is focused on one particular age acquaint themselves with all of these essays.

The opportunity presented by this revision to enlarge the work has, of course, made it possible to extend the reach of its contents. Its broader scope reflects achievement since 1950 in research and publication. But it reflects, as well, shifts in the interests and attitudes that guide music scholarship, even changes in intellectual mood in general. That is most immediately evident in the revised taxonomy of musical periods manifest in the new titles for some of the volumes, and it becomes still more evident in the introductory essays. The collections for "Antiquity and the Middle Ages" have been separated and enlarged. What was "The Greek View of Music" has become *Greek Views of Music* (eight of them, writes Thomas J. Mathiesen), and "The Middle Ages" is now, as James McKinnon articulates it, *The Early Christian Period and the Latin Middle Ages*. There is no longer a collection for "The Classical Era" but one for *The Late Eighteenth Century*, and in place of the epithet "The Romantic Era" Ruth Solie has chosen *The Nineteenth Century*. The replacements in the latter two cases represent a questioning of the labels "Classic" and "Romantic," long familiar as tokens for the phases of an era of "common practice" that has been held to constitute the musical present. The historiographic issues that are entailed here are clarified in Solie's and Wye Jamison Allanbrook's introductory essays. And the habit of thought that is in question is, of course, directly challenged as well by the very addition of a collection of readings from the twentieth century, which makes its own claims to speak for the present. Only the labels "Renaissance" and "Baroque" have been retained as period designations. But the former is represented by Gary Tomlinson as an age in fragmentation, for which "Renaissance" is retained only *faute de mieux,* and as to the latter, Margaret Murata places new emphasis on the indeterminate state of its music.

These new vantage points honor—perhaps more sharply than he would have expected—Strunk's own wish "to do justice to every age," to eschew the "spurious unity" of a "particular point of view" and the representation of history as a succession of uniform periods, allowing the music and music-directed thought of *each* age to appear as an "independent phenomenon," as Allanbrook would have us regard the late eighteenth century.

The possibility of including a larger number of readings in this revision might have been thought to hold out the promise of our achieving greater familiarity with each age. But several of the editors have made clear—explicitly or implicitly through their selections—that as we learn more about a culture it seems "more, not less distant and estranged from ours," as Tomlinson writes of the Renaissance. That is hardly surprising. If the appearance of familiarity has arisen out of a tendency to represent the past in our own image, we should hardly wonder that the past sounds foreign to us—at least initially—as we allow it to speak to us more directly in its own voice.

But these words are written as though we would have a clear vision of our image in the late twentieth century, something that hardly takes account of the link, to which Tomlinson draws attention, between the decline of our confidence about historical certainties and the loss of certainty about our own identities. Standing neck-deep in the twentieth century, surrounded by uncountable numbers of voices all speaking at once, the editor of this newest selection of source readings may, ironically, have the most difficult time of any in arriving at a selection that will make a recognizable portrait of the age, as Morgan confesses.

Confronted with a present and past more strange and uncertain than what we have been pleased to think, the editors have not been able to carry on quite in the spirit of Strunk's assuredness about making accessible "those things which [the student] must eventually read." Accordingly, this revision is put forward with no claim for the canonical status of its contents. That aim has necessarily yielded some ground to a wish to bring into the conversation what has heretofore been marginal or altogether silent in accounts of music history.

The sceptical tract *Against the Professors* by Sextus Empiricus, among the readings from ancient Greece, is the first of numerous readings that run against a "mainstream," with the readings gathered under the heading "Music, Magic, Gnosis" in the Renaissance section being perhaps the most striking. The passage from Hildegard's *Epistle* to the prelates of Mainz in the medieval collection is the first of many selections written by women. The readings grouped under the reading "European Awareness of Other Musical Worlds" in the Renaissance collection evince the earliest attention paid to that subject. A new prominence is given to performance and to the reactions of listeners in the collection from the Baroque. And the voices of North American writers and writers of color begin to be heard in the collection from the nineteenth century.

There is need to develop further these once-marginal strands in the representation of Western music history, and to draw in still others, perhaps in some future version of this series, and elsewhere—the musical cultures of Latin America for one example, whose absence is lamented by Murata, and the representation of the Middle Ages in their truly cosmopolitan aspect, for another.

This series of books remains at its core the conception and the work of Oliver Strunk. Its revision is the achievement of the editors of the individual volumes, most of whom have in turn benefited from the advice of numerous colleagues working in their fields of specialization. Participating in such a broadly collaborative venture has been a most gratifying experience, and an encouraging one in a time that is sometimes marked by a certain agonistic temper.

The initiative for this revision came in 1988 from Claire Brook, who was then music editor of W. W. Norton. I am indebted to her for granting me the privilege of organizing it and for our fruitful planning discussions at the outset. Her thoughts about the project are manifested in the outcome in too many ways to enumerate. Her successor Michael Ochs has been a dedicated and active editor, aiming always for the highest standards and expediting with expertise the complex tasks that such a project entails.

Leo Treitler
Lake Hill, New York

CONTENTS

IV MUSIC, SOCIETY, POLITICS

V EXTENDING WESTERN MUSIC'S BOUNDARIES

VI CONCERT LIFE, RECEPTION, AND THE CULTURE INDUSTRY

VII PLURALISM

NOTES AND ABBREVIATIONS

Footnotes originating with the authors of the texts are marked [Au.], those with the translators [Tr.].

Omitted text is indicated by five spaced bullets (•   •   •   •   •); three spaced bullets (•   •   •) indicate a typographical break in the original.

THE
TWENTIETH
CENTURY

INTRODUCTION

*T*he richness and complexity of twentieth-century musical culture stems from many factors, the foremost being the volume and variety of the music itself. But another significant feature is the unusually large number of written documents available to us that relate to this music. In no previous epoch have we approached the copiousness of twentieth-century writing about music. All this material—whether its focus be current or past music, concert, vernacular, or folk music, and whether its perspective be analytical, historical, sociological, political, or reportorial—contributes to the music history of our age. The range and diversity of these writings mirror the range and diversity of the era's compositional styles and technical approaches. These two aspects join to create an overall image of both considerable vitality and considerable uncertainty. Whatever one thinks of twentieth-century musical culture as a whole (and it does not present a particularly neat picture), the very multiplicity of its compositional and critical artifacts gives expression to one of its most telling attributes: a deep-seated self-consciousness about what music is, to whom it should be addressed, and its proper role within the contemporary world.

The editor of a collection such as this, confronted with difficult decisions at every turn, must be relentlessly selective. I have generally, if not exclusively, favored writings by active participants in the musical developments of the time rather than by observers. More particularly, my choices reflect the tendency—noticeable in the nineteenth century but typifying the twentieth—of composers to write about their own work, the work of others, and music and musical life in general. Inevitably, significant areas of interest remain neglected. Especially regrettable is the limited representation of academic musical scholarship, whose impressive growth marks the period, and in particular the fields of music theory and analysis, whose characteristic documents are too technical and specialized for this collection.

The music of the twentieth century is stamped by two closely interconnected features. One is the pervasive interest among composers in creating music that is "new," which fosters an unprecedented emphasis on innovation and experimentation. This tendency, though generally characteristic of Western music, became so dominant as to assume an ideologically central position. The other, a direct outcome of the first, is the extraordinary diversity mentioned above—both of compositional styles and techniques and of attitudes about music and its range of uses. Entire musical cultures now coexist temporally and geograph-

3

ically, often in shifting alliances with one another, forming a vibrant whole to which a sizable portion of the world's population has almost immediate access.

This diversity helps account for the unusually large number of entries included here. The original intent—consistent with Oliver Strunk's own policy—was to present relatively long, essentially complete selections. It quickly became evident, however, that in order to give some sense of the scope of twentieth-century musical writing, it would be necessary to select many more items, and significantly shorter ones, than this policy allowed. Though I have chosen a core group of reasonably substantial readings, other entries, some no longer than a single page in length, have been included to indicate the range of issues encompassed during the period and the wealth of different, frequently opposing voices that have articulated them.

Diversity and multiplicity have raised issues of organization as well. After considerable experimentation I have settled on seven conceptual categories under which to order the readings. Inevitably, these disregard other important realms of interest, such as changing conceptions of musical genre, conflicting approaches to performance practice, and interactions between concert music and popular and vernacular musics. Moreover, the categories accommodate only uncomfortably certain entries that could easily fit under two or more headings. Nevertheless, such a framework is useful and even necessary for giving shape to these diverse contents.

The first and perhaps most basic category addresses changes in musical esthetics. During the first quarter of the century, in one of those epoch-defining shifts that have occasionally punctuated Western music history, the predominant nineteenth-century view of music as a spiritual, subjective, and highly individualized art gradually lost ground to a more materialist and objective one emphasizing craftsmanship and social function over transcendence and personal expression. Like all such changes, this one did not take place at once, nor did it coincide neatly with the turn of the century. The inherited view, a legacy of musical Romanticism, prevailed at least until World War I, though not without considerable modification, as in the esthetics of musical impressionism and expressionism, represented here by Claude Debussy and Arnold Schoenberg; and now in conjunction with significant countercurrents, such as the anti-esthetic position of Erik Satie. Even when the older view began rapidly losing favor in the years around the end of World War I, it did not entirely disappear but persisted side by side with the new one. Indeed, the relative merits of the two continued to be debated down to the end of the century, with the "Romantic" view even seeming to regain some momentum in the position of a composer such as George Rochberg.

The basic argument is mapped out in the first three readings. Schoenberg, writing before the onset of World War I, espouses an esthetic of unbridled intuitive creation and expression. Jean Cocteau and Igor Stravinsky, writing after the war, endorse a new kind of music more suitable to the modern age, distinguished by wit, detachment, and restraint. Something of the subsequent dialectic spun out of this opposition can be traced in the views of John Cage, Milton Babbitt, and Evan Ziporyn, who expand and further complicate the confrontation by introducing issues touching upon indeterminacy, integral serialism, and the idea of "world music."

A third significant esthetic position, formalism—the idea that musical significance derives primarily from internal compositional relationships rather than specific external reference—applies equally to both of these views. Though usually associated with the twentieth century, formalism was in fact originally linked with Romanticism, both conceptually and historically;[1] and it can be detected here in such diverse figures as Ferruccio Busoni and the early Schoenberg on one side, and Stravinsky and Babbitt on the other. Though formalism, linked to Romanticism, encouraged a belief in the "purification" of music through withdrawal from its social context (as Busoni seems to hold), it could equally foster tendencies toward social functionalism when associated with an objectivist-materialist position (as in Kurt Weill), thereby edging music back toward its pre-Romantic, contextual condition.[2]

Given their foundational nature, these esthetic matters are inseparable from questions of musical style and language. The abandonment by many composers of the relatively codified principles of common-practice (harmonic) tonality—tonal centricity, dominant-tonic cadential structure, triadic harmony, and the like—that had governed Western music for some two hundred years, drastically affected the way composers went about—and thought about—writing music. Traditional Western tonality, despite the very substantial differences in composers of dissimilar tastes, geographical regions, and cultural backgrounds, retained a central core of relationships throughout the nineteenth century. It represented a shared language that could be internalized by both composers and listeners, seeming thereby to become part of their very mental structure. This internalization fostered and, perhaps, even provided a necessary precondition for the Romantic belief that music resided in the human interior where it possessed the power to project humanity's innermost beliefs and deepest feelings.

When that common language was seriously called into question—as it was in the early years of the new century—without another compositional language emerging as a widely accepted alternative, the musical situation was fundamentally altered. Previously untapped areas of musical experience were suddenly made accessible and were actively explored. Although most composers in the

---

1. Even later, when nineteenth-century formalist thinking takes on a more rigorous and "scientific" tone (most notably in the writing of Eduard Hanslick), it departs from Romanticism not by rejecting musical "expressivity," or the idea that music is a "spiritual language," but by restricting what music expresses to strictly musical ideas, excluding emotions.
2. The importance of formalistic thinking in twentieth-century music is evident in many of the readings in this volume: from Stravinsky, Babbitt, and Stockhausen at one extreme to Xenakis, Ligeti, and Reich at the other. Even Cage could be included, since he believed that one way composers can allow sounds to "be themselves" is by ruling out human choice through the injunction of purely formal procedures, such as throwing dice or consulting the *I Ching*.

earlier years restricted themselves to using new kinds of nontriadic harmony and nonmetrical (additive) rhythm, the implications of the change were far more fundamental and far-reaching. Once the superstructure of traditional tonality had been compromised, its underlying foundation—the scalar system of twelve-tone equal tuning—was placed in jeopardy as well. As a consequence, not only could the familiar organizational principles associated with musical material be reconfigured, the very nature of that material became subject to reexamination.

The result, addressed in the second group of readings, was an unprecedented and ongoing expansion of sonic resources, which characterized the entire century from its outset. Busoni, writing in 1907, already proposes an augmentation of the basic pitch repertory through microtonal scale divisions and the use of new scalar types. From there it is but a short step to Luigi Russolo's 1913 manifesto calling for the adoption of a new type of sound material altogether: noise, rather than pure pitch. By the beginning of World War I the frontiers of music had thus been vastly extended, so that for many it must have appeared that the art was being transformed into something essentially different, providing a largely uncharted terrain of novel creative possibilities.

An ongoing challenge for composers was to cultivate and extend this newly acquired territory. Charles Ives responds by viewing musical relationships in a more "sculptural" or spatial mode and considers how sounds are altered by distance and direction. Both Edgard Varèse and Pierre Boulez, with the growing confidence produced by advances in science and technology, develop an idea introduced by Busoni: the invention and creative exploitation of new sound-producing instruments. For them, composers will achieve true liberation only when relieved of the limitations of traditional instruments, intended for older music and thus unsuited for the new. By mid-century Boulez even envisions machines capable of producing virtually any sound, a possibility that would at least partly be realized with developments in computer-generated sound, sampling, and sound modification.

The reevaluation of sound materials went hand in hand with a similarly fundamental exploration of compositional method, the third category in this collection. Confronted with the prospect of bringing order to these possibilities, composers sought new musical languages suitable for a greatly expanded sonic universe. It is symptomatic of the scope of this undertaking that, despite the utopian cast of Busoni's and Russolo's early appeals, no serious attempt was made during the first half of the century to formulate a synoptic method for ordering nonpitch sound as a central compositional ingredient. Even proposals for the systematic control of microtonal pitch divisions were rare and had little impact until later in the century. Within the framework of tempered tuning, however, systematic reformulations appeared relatively early, most notably in Schoenberg's twelve-tone system. Schoenberg provided a method for treating the total chromatic as a set of equally weighted elements placed in an ordered sequence and manipulated by serial transformations, a procedure completely bypassing the hierarchical structure that traditional tonality imposed on this material. Karlheinz Stockhausen, writing after the century's midpoint, further generalizes the serial principle, extending it to other components of sound, including duration, timbre, and amplitude, which he sees as emanating from a common physical source, the soundwave. Similar tendencies toward generalization are also expressed by Iannis Xenakis and György Ligeti, who shift emphasis away from the individual sonic components entirely and focus instead on large masses of sound intended to be perceived as global composites. Steve Reich, by comparison, seeking an alternative to the enormous complexity typifying post-tonal musical structures, suggests reducing the sound material to a minimum, thereby achieving a sort of tonal revolution in reverse.

Since these matters of compositional structure, sound material, and esthetic intent are critical elements in determining what makes twentieth-century music unique, they receive generous treatment here. Yet they cannot be considered in a vacuum, as if music were sealed off from the world at large. The erosion of harmonic tonality and its esthetic counterpart, expressive individualism, undermined the essential support for the Romantic view of music as "a world apart," located beyond the realm of everyday problems and concerns. Once music was no longer considered "pure," that is, constituted of an ephemeral material and framed by transcendent relationships handed down by nature (or God), it could be conceived more readily as a normal component of life—a human product capable of assuming social, political, and other practical functions.

This demystification of music, its rerooting in more common soil, is addressed in the fourth section, "Music, Society, Politics." It is most evident in efforts to exploit the social potential of music itself, either as an active agent of political regeneration, as envisioned by Kurt Weill, Cornelius Cardew, and—less openly—Sergey Prokofiev, or as a medium to be manipulated for oppressive control, as evinced in the Joseph Goebbels speech, the *Pravda* review, and Dimitri Shostakovich's description of the Soviet crackdown on composition. But the political face of twentieth-century music is no less recognizable in efforts to transform musical life—to democratize its institutions and practices, rendering them more accessible to previously excluded groups. Ethel Smyth details the benefits that would accrue if women achieved a more active role in performance organizations, and Eva Rieger argues for the unique qualities that women bring to musical composition. Marian Anderson tells of prejudices encountered and overcome by a black performer in mid-century America, and the black composers William Grant Still and Olly Wilson discuss the special challenges confronted by members of an ethnic minority in finding an authentic compositional voice.

The tendency toward inclusiveness in musical life is apparent not only in these extramusical domains but in music itself. A recurring feature in twentieth-century musical thought, considered in the fifth group of readings, is the conviction that Western music has reached a state of exhaustion and requires revitalization from without. The range of suggested sources is impressive: Claude Debussy recommends techniques borrowed from cinema and the music of non-Western cultures, Béla Bartók champions native folk music, Wanda Landowska turns to music from the past, and Harry Partch incorporates the microtonal pitch inflections of non-Western musical cultures. Darius Milhaud, rejecting all pretensions to transcendentalism, proposes a music so ordinary that one should not even notice it at all. And the scholar Bruno Nettl undertakes to interpret the Western musical enterprise from the perspective of an outsider, a detached observer who attempts to make sense of some of its most cherished—and thus least examined—beliefs.

The sixth section documents how concert life and the musical experience of listeners have been altered during the century, both by specifically musical issues—not least the great complexity of so many contemporary compositions—and by changing social and economic conditions. Alban Berg's description of Schoenberg's Vienna concert series for new music vividly betrays that music's isolation, its propensity to address a limited and specialized audience. Theodor W. Adorno analyzes the ways mass communication and commercialization affect musical culture and reception, a point that Lawrence Gilman's radio address serves to exemplify. Roland Barthes examines how the restructuring of musical experience has transmuted the listener from an active participant into a passive consumer, while Steven Connor argues that developments in audio and visual technology have blurred distinctions between musical "presentation" on the one hand and musical "reproduction" or "representation" on the other.

The final group of readings in this collection addresses the most definitive feature of current musical culture: its unparalleled variety, diversity, and culturally pluralistic makeup. Three earlier stages in the development of this state are documented here: Erik Satie lampoons the notion of the artist as prophetic genius, repudiating by implication the belief in a single privileged understanding of the art; Nadia Boulanger is concerned with cultivating the music of a non-European country; and Constant Lambert describes the fashion between the two world wars for creating new works out of simulations of older ones.

Leonard B. Meyer, viewing the matter in the 1960s, finds stylistic plurality so deeply ingrained in the musical culture of the time that he sees it as a permanent condition, allowing different styles to interact freely with one another without any definite sense of direction. For Umberto Eco plurality and instability also inhabit the individual work in much twentieth-century art, which sacrifices traditionally sanctioned qualities of self-sufficiency and closure for an open structure that is tolerant of multiple realizations. George Rochberg, viewing pluralism as a composer, articulates what is at once its cause and consequence: the impossibility of forging a stylistically unified language in an age in which the musical past is just as much with us as the musical present and thus becomes an essential component of the present.

Finally, Carl Dahlhaus addresses the single most encompassing question

raised by the current state of music: in the midst of such multiplicity and fragmentation, can one still speak of something called music at all in a fully inclusive sense, accommodating all of the myriad manifestations of today's musical
world? His response provides a fitting close to these introductory comments:
"One remains true to the idea of 'music' (in the singular) by relinquishing it as
a concept of substance in order to reinstate it as a regulative principle of mutual
understanding."

•   •   •

The original 1950 edition of Strunk's *Source Readings in Music History* had
no section devoted to the twentieth century. Professor Strunk, whom I knew
and greatly admired as a graduate student, did not even find it necessary to
explain this omission in his preface: twentieth-century music was, in the view
of most musicologists of the time, simply not considered an appropriate topic
for serious scholarly work. That attitude has changed dramatically in the
intervening years, to a point where twentieth-century studies may well command the field in the coming decades the way nineteenth-century studies have
during the previous ones.

Deciding what should be included in this collection thus takes on special
importance. That process, at once so stimulating and so frustrating, was greatly
facilitated by discussion and correspondence with friends and colleagues, with-
out whose counsel and sympathy I would not have undertaken the project.
Although I am unable to acknowledge all, I especially want to mention Joseph
Auner, Michael Beckerman, Peter Burkholder, Reinhold Brinkmann, Tom
DeLio, Christopher Hailey, Charles Hamm, Joseph Horowitz, Jeffrey Kalberg,
David Lewin, Karen Painter, Andrew Porter, Sally Reid, Lee Rothfarb, Michael
Tenzer, Judith Tick, and Gary Tomlinson. Ruth Solie, editor of the nineteenth-
century readings, was especially helpful; and my former colleague Stephen
Hinton, in addition to discussing various aspects of the project with me from
the beginning, provided translations for the Weill and Dahlhaus entries. Philip
Rupprecht and Julia Hubbert performed valuable service as successive
research assistants, advising on shape and content as well as tracking down
numerous details of fact and bibliography. Finally, Leo Treitler has overseen
this project from its inception with care and understanding, providing stimulating suggestions at every stage of the way. Although the result surely differs
from a twentieth-century reader he himself might have compiled, it is very
much the fruit of a most pleasant and beneficial collaboration.

$\mathcal{E}$STHETIC POSITIONS

1 Arnold Schoenberg

The Austrian composer Arnold Schoenberg (1874–1951) was among the most influential figures in twentieth-century music. These excerpts are from letters written to Ferruccio Busoni in 1909, after Busoni, a renowned composer, pianist, and conductor, had sent his younger colleague a transcription of one of Schoenberg's piano pieces, Op. 11, No. 2, intended to render the composition more "pianistic." Schoenberg not only rejects Busoni's notion of pianism as inappropriate to his own work but offers an impassioned statement describing the highly intuitive approach to artistic creation that he favored at the time. This compositional esthetic, a holdover from the nineteenth century, reached its most extreme formulation just as these letters were written—at the moment Schoenberg was breaking away from the tonally centric and harmonically triadic basis of traditional Western music.

Two Letters to Ferruccio Busoni
(1909)

Steinakirchen am Forst [August 1909]

•   •   •   •   •

I am writing in such detail because I want to declare my intentions (encouraged by your comment: my music affects you because you envisage something of the kind as the goal of our immediate developments).

I strive for: complete liberation from all forms

from all symbols

of cohesion and

of logic.

    Thus:

away with "motivic working out."

Away with harmony as

cement or bricks of a building.

Harmony is *expression*

and nothing else.

    Then:

Away with Pathos!

Away with protracted ten-ton scores, from erected or constructed

towers, rocks, and other massive claptrap.

My music must be

brief.

TEXT: *Ferruccio Busoni. Selected Letters,* ed. and trans. by Antony Beaumont (London: Faber & Faber, 1987), pp. 389, 392–97.

Concise! In two notes: not built, but *"expressed"*!!

And the results I wish for:

no stylized and sterile protracted emotion.

People are not like that:

it is *impossible* for a person to have only *one* sensation at a time.

One has *thousands* simultaneously. And these thousands can no more readily be added together than an apple and a pear. They to their own ways.

And this variegation, this multifariousness, this *illogicality* which our senses demonstrate, the illogicality presented by their interactions, set forth by some mounting rush of blood, by some reaction of the senses or the nerves, this I should like to have in my music.

It should be an expression of feeling,[1] as our feelings, which bring us in contact with our subconscious, really are, and no false child of feelings and "conscious logic."

Now I have made my confession and they can burn me. You will not number amongst those who burn me: that I know.

* * * * *

Steinakirchen am Forst, August 24, 1909

* * * * *

You must consider the following: it is impossible for me to publish my piece together with a transcription which shows how I could have done it *better*. Which thus indicates that my piece is *imperfect*. And it is impossible to try to make the public believe that my piece is *good*, if I simultaneously indicate that it is *not good*.

I could not do this—out of my instinct for self-preservation—even if I believed it. In this case I would either have to destroy my piece or *rework* it *myself*.

But now—please forgive my unrestrained frankness, just as I do not take yours amiss—*I simply don't believe it*. I firmly believe you are making the same mistake as every *imaginative* critic: you do not wish to put yourself in the writer's place but seek rather, in the work of another, yourself, *only yourself*. And that just isn't possible. An art which is at one and the same time its creator's and its appraiser's cannot exist. One of these has to give way, and I believe this must be the appraiser.

And your reasoning seems to me quite unsound, when you say that I shall become different but no richer by pointlessly doing without what is already established.

I do not believe in putting *new wine* into old bottles. In the history of art I have made the following antipodal observations:

1. Orig. "Sie soll Ausdruck der Empfindung sein." Allusion to Beethoven's comment about his "Pastoral" Symphony, "Mehr Ausdruck der Empfindung als Malerei" = more an expression of feeling than painting. [Tr.]

Bach's contrapuntal art vanishes when Beethoven's melodic homophony begins.

Beethoven's formal art is abandoned when Wagner introduces his expressive art.

Unity of design, richness of coloring, working out of minutest details, painstaking formation, priming and varnishing, use of perspective and all the other constituents of older painting simply die out when the Impressionists begin to paint things as they *appear* and not as they *are*.

Yes indeed, when a new art seeks and finds new means of expression, almost all earlier techniques go hang: seemingly, at any rate; for actually they are retained; but in a different way. (To discuss this would lead me too far.)

And now: I must say that I actually dispensed with more than just piano sound when I began to follow my instincts and compose *such* music. I find that, when renouncing an *art of form,* the architecture of the leading voice, the polyphonic art that Brahms, Wagner, and others brought to a high degree of perfection in the past decades—the little bit of piano sound seems a mere trifle. And I maintain: one must have grasped, admired, and marveled at the mysterious wonders of our tonal harmony, the unbelievably delicate balance of its architectural values and its cabbalistic mathematics as *I* have, in order to feel, when one no longer has need of them, that one requires new means. Questions of sonority, whose attraction ranks scarcely so high amongst the eternal values, are by comparison trivial.

Nevertheless, I take a standpoint in this question from which it is absolutely unnecessary to consider me a renouncer, a loser. Were you to see my new orchestral pieces, you would be able to observe how clearly I turn away from the full "God and Superman" sound of the Wagner orchestra. How everything becomes sweeter, finer. How refracted shades of color replace the former brilliant hues. How my entire orchestral technique takes a path which seems to be leading in quite the opposite direction to anything previously taken. I find this to be the natural reaction. We have had enough of Wagner's full, lush sonorities, to the point of satiation: "Nun laßt uns andere Töne anstimmen . . ."[2]

And now I must add that I feel myself justified in believing (I must repeat this) that my piano writing is *novel.* Not only do my feelings tell me so. Friends and pupils express the opinion that the sonorities of my piano writing are completely novel.

For me the matter is as follows:

I do not consider my piano texture the result of any sort of *incompetence,* but rather the expression of *firm resolve, distinct preferences and palpably clear feelings.*

What it *does not* do is not what it *cannot,* rather what it *will* not.

2. Intended as a quotation from Beethoven's Symphony No. 9. The actual words are: "O Freunde, nicht diese Töne! Sondern laßt uns angenehmere anstimmen . . ." ["O friends, not these sounds! Instead let us strike up more pleasing ones . . ."]. Schoenberg's words mean: now let us strike up other sounds. [Tr.]

What it does is not something which could have turned out differently, rather what it *had* to do.

Therefore it is distinctive, stylish, and organic.

• • • • •

I fear that a transcription, on the other hand, would either

introduce what I avoid, either fundamentally or according to my preferences;

add what I myself—within the limits of my personality—would never have devised, thus what is foreign or unattainable to me;

omit what I would find necessary, or

improve where I am, and must remain, imperfect.

Thus a transcription would be bound to do me violence: whether it helps or hinders my work.

In your pamphlet, which gives me uncommon pleasure and truly proves how the same thoughts can occur to different people at once, you write about transcription. I particularly agree with your thesis that all notation is transcription.[3] I argued similarly some years ago when Mahler was publicly attacked for changing Beethoven's orchestration. But again: whether one improves upon Beethoven's undoubtedly *old-fashioned* treatment of instruments and orchestration on account of undoubtedly superior *newer* instrumental techniques, or whether one improves upon my piano style with older techniques or, at any rate, techniques whose greater appropriateness has today not yet been established, there is no doubt at all that these are two different matters.

I can at present say this without your having to take it as any harsh criticism, because I have not yet seen your transcription. After all, your arrangement could always prove that I am mistaken. But also, apart from that, I am sure you will not take my vehemence amiss, I am certain, because your opinion of my work was otherwise neither harsh nor unfavorable.

Another point occurs to me which seems a suitable argument against you.

Do you really set such infinite store by perfection? Do you really consider it attainable? Do you really think that works of art are, or should be, perfect?

I do not think so. I find even God's works of art, those of nature, highly imperfect.

But I find perfection only in the work of carpenters, gardeners, pastry-cooks, and hairdressers. Only they produce that smoothness and symmetry which I have so often wished to the Devil. Only they fulfill every requirement one can expect of them, but otherwise nothing human or godlike in the world.

And if

Notation = Transcription = *Imperfection*

then also

---

3. Schoenberg's reference is apparently to the following statement from Busoni's *Sketch of a New Esthetic of Music,* trans. Theodore Baker (New York, 1911), as reprinted in *Three Classics in the Aesthetics of Music* (New York: Dover), p. 84: "Notation, the writing down of musical compositions, is above all an ingenious aid for pinning down an improvisation so that it can be brought to life again."

Transcription = Notation = *Imperfection.*
For if a = b and b = c, then also
   a = c.
Why then replace one imperfection with another?
Why eliminate that which perhaps contributes to the appeal of a work and substitute something added by a foreign hand?

Don't the characteristics of a man's personality also include his defects? Do these not have an effect, even if unbeautiful, then at least as contrast, like the basic color upon which the other shades are superimposed?

I have often thought that one should give Schumann's symphonies (which I believe you have greatly underestimated[4] and which I rate *far above* those of Brahms) a helping hand by improving the orchestration. The theoretical aspects were quite clear to me. This summer I spent a little time on this and—lost courage. For I can see exactly that wherever things misfire, something highly original was intended, and I lack the courage to replace an *interesting idea,* which has not been quite successfully carried out, with a *"reliable"* sonority. And with a true work of art, the imagination of an outsider can achieve no more than this! —

From a purely technical angle, I would like to ask you if you have perhaps taken too slow a tempo. That could make a great difference. Or too *little* rubato. I never stay in time! Never in tempo! —

Your "Outline for a New Esthetic of Music" gave me uncommon pleasure, above all on account of its audacity. Particularly at the beginning, there are a few powerful sentences, of compulsive logic and superlative acuteness of observation. I have also thought a lot about your idea of thirds of tones, though in a different way. But I had been thinking of quarter tones, am however now of the opinion that it will depend less on the construction than on other things. Moreover, one of my pupils[5] calculated, at my suggestion, that the next division of the octave with similar properties to our twelve semitone division would have to introduce 53 notes. If you adopt 18 thirds of tones, that would be approximately equal, for $3 \times 18 = 54$. But then the semitones would disappear completely.

Earlier I thought out the following method of notating quarter tones:

$c - \frac{1}{4}$ c $c + \frac{1}{4}$

< and > are
mathematical symbols.

---

4. In the *Sketch of a New Esthetic of Music* Busoni writes: "In general, composers have drawn nearest the true nature of music in preparatory and intermediary passages . . . " The passage is included in the Busoni excerpt found on p. 53.

5. This was the philosopher Dr. Robert Neumann, who studied with Schoenberg from 1907 to 1909. [Tr.]

However, I scarcely think that such attempts at notation will catch on; for I confidently hope that the notation of the future will be—how can I say: "wire-lesser."[6]

I also think differently about tonality—my music shows that. I believe: everything one can do with 113 keys[7] can also be done with 2 or 3 or 4: major-minor, whole-tone, and chromatic. Anyway, I have long been occupied with the removal of all shackles of tonality. And my harmony allows no chords or melodies with tonal implications any more.

Now to your questions.

To what extent I realize my intentions? Not as far as I would like to. Not one piece has yet satisfied me entirely. I would like to achieve even greater variegation of motifs and figures without melodic character; I would like to be freer and less constrained in rhythm and time signature; freer from repetition of motifs and spinning out of thoughts in the manner of a melody. This is my vision: this is how I imagine music before I notate = transcribe it. And I am unable to force this upon myself; I must wait until a piece comes out of its own accord in the way I have envisaged.

And thus I come to answer your other question: how much is intentional and how much is instinctive.

My only intention is

to have *no* intentions!

No formal, architectural, or other artistic intentions (except perhaps of capturing the mood of a poem), no esthetic intentions—none of any kind; at most this:

to place nothing inhibiting in the stream of my unconscious sensations. But to allow anything to infiltrate which may be invoked either by intelligence or consciousness.

If you knew how I have developed, you would have no doubts. But I have prepared myself for this question and am thus able to answer it. I knew one would question the naturalness of my intentions, precisely because they are natural. That one would find them formalized for the very reason that I avoid anything formal.

But when one sees how I have developed in stages, how I was long ago approaching a form of expression to which I now adhere freely and unreservedly, one would understand that nothing unorganic, no "cheap aestheticism,"[8] is involved, but that *compulsion* has produced these results.

As I am now fairly clear about the theoretical side, only those can scoff who

---

6. Orig. "drahtloser." Schoenberg presumably means that the communication should be more like a "wireless"—that is, as immediate and instantaneous as possible, and thus independent of any material connection (i.e., the "wire").

7. In the *Sketch of a New Esthetic of Music* Busoni writes: "I have made an attempt to find all the possibilities of arranging the seven-tone scale and have succeeded, by lowering and raising the intervals, in producing 113 different scales." See p. 56.

8. Orig. "nichts 'Verschmockt-Aesthetisches.'" [Tr.]

imagine the unconsciously creating artist to be a sort of half-cretin; and who cannot grasp that after unconscious creativity follows a period of *quiet clear-sightedness,* in which one renders account of one's situation.

As for the third piece,[9] which you do not care for at present, as can be inferred from your caustic criticism, I find it goes a considerable way beyond what was successful in the other two. At any rate, as far as the above-mentioned variegation is concerned. But also in the "harmony"—if one can speak so architecturally here—there seems to be something novel in it. In particular: something more slender, more linear.[10] But I also consider it unjust to expect that one can revolutionize music in three *different* ways in three little piano pieces. Does it not seem permissible, having departed so far from convention, to pause for a moment's breath, to gather new strength, before one rushes on? And is it not unjust to describe laconicism as a mannerism? Is formalism just as much a manner as pointillism or impressionism? Must one build? Is music then a savings bank? Does one get more when it is longer?

If I was wrong *there* to be brief, I have *amply* compensated for it in this *letter!* But there were indeed several things I wanted to say—that I could not express them more concisely can be blamed upon my technical shortcomings.

And finally: I hope my frankness does not annoy you, and that you maintain your interest in me.

Maybe you will find a formula, an explanation, through which I shall be able to publish my piece in your series.

Or perhaps you could publish all three and your paraphrase, with an explanation some other time??

In any case, I hope not to lose your good will if I now ask you to tell me whether you wish to play the pieces. For, clearly this would mean an enormous amount to me.

One other curious thing, to close: before composing these piano pieces, I had wanted to contact you—knowing of your predilection for transcriptions—to ask if you would take one of my chamber or orchestral works into your repertoire, transcribed for piano solo.

Curious: now we come into contact again through a transcription! Was I misunderstanding a message from my subconscious, which made me think of you in the context of a transcription?

This has just occurred to me!

9. Schoenberg had completed only the first two of the Three Piano Pieces Op. 11 when he originally sent them to Busoni. The third was sent later, shortly before this letter was written.
10. Orig. "manches dünnere, zweistimmigere." [Tr.]

2 Jean Cocteau

The French writer and filmmaker Jean Cocteau (1889–1963) was a leading figure in *l'esprit nouveau,* "the new spirit" that emerged in French art and culture
at the close of World War I. Erik Satie's 1917 ballet *Parade,* for which Cocteau
supplied the story, Picasso the costumes and sets, and Leonid Massine the cho-
reography, played a major role in defining that spirit; and Cocteau's essay "Cock
and Harlequin," published in 1918, was written while still under the influence
of this collaboration. To replace the intuitive, subjective, and individualistic
esthetic of Romanticism, which in his view was equally present in the music of
both Wagner and Debussy, Cocteau argues for something more in tune with his
idea of French culture: a simpler and more popular, "everyday" music, inspired
by the music hall, cabaret, café concert, and circus. Cocteau's aphoristic writing
style—curt, crisp, hard-edged, and without transition—perfectly mirrors that
new esthetic, so strikingly different from the one expressed by Schoenberg in
the previous entry.

FROM Cock and Harlequin
(1918)

The bad music which superior folk despise is agreeable enough. What is
disagreeable is their good music.

Beware of the paint, say certain placards. I add: Beware of music.

Look out! Be on your guard, because alone of all the arts, music moves all
around you.

Musicians ought to cure music of its convolutions, its dodges and its tricks,
and force it as far as possible to keep *in front of the hearer.*

A POET ALWAYS HAS TOO MANY WORDS IN HIS VOCABULARY, A
PAINTER TOO MANY COLORS ON HIS PALETTE, AND A MUSICIAN
TOO MANY NOTES ON HIS KEYBOARD.

ONE MUST SIT DOWN FIRST; ONE THINKS AFTERWARDS.

This axiom must not serve as an excuse to those who are always sitting down.
A true artist is always on the move.

Picturesqueness, and especially exoticism, are a handicap to musicians, and
cause them to be misunderstood.

•   •   •   •   •

TEXT: *Cock and Harlequin,* trans. by Rollo H. Myers (London: Faber & Gwyer, 1926), pp. 11, 15–
17, 18–26, 32–33.

SATIE VERSUS SATIE. The cult of Satie is difficult because one of Satie's charms is that he offers so little encouragement to deification.

One often wonders why Satie saddles his finest works with grotesque titles which mislead the least hostile sections of the public. Apart from the fact that these titles protect his works from persons obsessed by the sublime, and provide an excuse for the laughter of those who do not realize their value, they can be explained by the Debussy-ist abuse of "precious" titles. No doubt they are meant as a good-humored piece of ill-humor, and maliciously directed against "Lunes descendant sur le temple qui fut," "Terrasses des audiences du Clair de lune" and "Cathédrales englouties."[1]

The public is shocked at the charming absurdity of Satie's titles and system of notation, but respects the ponderous absurdity of the libretto of *Parsifal*.

The same public accepts the most ridiculous titles of François Couperin: "Le ti-toc choc ou les Maillotins" "Les Culbutes Ixcxbxnxs" "Les coucous bénévoles," "Les Calotins et Calotines ou la pièce à trétous," "Les vieux galants et les Trésorières surannées."[2]

The impressionist composers cut a pear into twelve pieces and gave each piece the title of a poem. Then Satie composed twelve poems and entitled the whole "Morceaux en forme de poire."

Satie acquired a distaste for Wagner in Wagnerian circles, in the very heart of the "Rose-Croix."[3] He warned Debussy against Wagner. "Be on your guard," he said. "A scenery tree is not upset because somebody comes on to the stage." That is the whole aesthetic of *Pelléas*.

Debussy missed his way because he fell from the German frying pan into the Russian fire. Once again the pedal blurs rhythm and creates a kind of fluid atmosphere congenial to *short-sighted* ears. Satie remains intact. Hear his *Gymnopédies* so clear in their form and melancholy feeling. Debussy orchestrates them, confuses them, and wraps their exquisite architecture in a cloud. Debussy moves further and further away from Satie's starting point and makes everybody follow in his steps. The thick lightning-pierced fog of Bayreuth becomes a thin snowy mist flecked with impressionist sunshine. Satie speaks of Ingres: Debussy transposes Claude Monet *à la Russe*.

1. Cocteau refers to titles of three of Debussy's piano pieces: "Et la lune descend sur le temple qui fût" ("And the Moon Descends on the Temple that was"), "La terrasse des audiences du clair de lune" ("The Terrace of Audiences by the Light of the Moon"), and "La cathédrale engloutie" ("The Sunken Cathedral").
2. Couperin's titles might be translated as: "The Tick-Tock Shock, or the Maillotins" (there is uncertainty as to who the "Maillotins" were); "The Somersaults of the Jxcxbxnxs" (Jxcxbxnxs = Jacobines); "The Complacent Cuckolds"; "The Calotins and Calotines, or the Piece for Buffoons" (the "Calotins" were members of a satirical institution founded at Versailles in 1702 by courtiers and young officers to mock the solemn atmosphere of the court; the humorous pamphlets they issued were called "calotines"); "Aging Suitors and Fading Charmers."
3. A mystical religious sect, modeled on the secret societies of the Middles Ages, which Satie joined in 1891.

·   ·   ·   ·   ·

Satie teaches what, in our age, is the greatest audacity, simplicity. Has he not proved that he could refine better than anyone? But he clears, simplifies, and strips rhythm naked. Is this once more the music on which, as Nietzsche said, "the spirit dances," as compared with the music "in which the spirit swims"?

Not music one swims in, nor music one dances on; MUSIC ON WHICH ONE WALKS.

·   ·   ·   ·   ·

The Impressionists feared bareness, emptiness, silence. Silence is not necessarily a hole; you must use silence and not a stop gap of vague noises.

BLACK SHADOW. Black silence. Not *violet* silence, interspersed with *violet shadows.*

YOUTHFULNESS. Nothing is so enervating as to lie and soak for a long time in a warm bath. Enough of music in which one lies and soaks.

Enough of clouds, waves, aquariums, watersprites, and nocturnal scents; what we need is a music of the earth, every day music.

Enough of hammocks, garlands, and gondolas; I want someone to build me music I can live in, like a house.

A friend tells me that, after New York, Paris houses seem as if you could take them in your hands. "Your Paris" he added "is beautiful because she is built to fit men." Our music must also be built to fit men.

Music is not all the time a gondola, or a race horse, or a tightrope. It is sometimes a chair as well.

A Holy Family is not necessarily a holy family; it may also consist of a pipe, a pint of beer, a pack of cards, and a pouch of tobacco.

In the midst of the perturbation of French taste and exoticism, the café-concert remains intact in spite of Anglo-American influence. It preserves a certain tradition which, however crapulous, is none the less racial. It is here, no doubt, that a young musician might pick up the lost thread.

·   ·   ·   ·   ·

The music hall, the circus, and American Negro bands, all these things fertilize an artist just as life does. To turn to one's own account the emotions aroused by this sort of entertainment is not to derive art from art. These entertainments are not art. They stimulate in the same way as machinery, animals, natural scenery, or danger.

·   ·   ·   ·   ·

CONCERNING A CERTAIN ACROBATIC TENDENCY. Our musicians have avoided the Wagnerian torrent on a tightrope, but a tightrope cannot be considered, any more than a torrent, as a respectable mode of locomotion.

MUSICAL BREAD is what we want.

For the last years Chardin, Ingres, Manet, and Cézanne have dominated European painting, and the foreigner comes to us to put his racial gifts to school with them. Now I declare that French music is going to influence the world.

In *Parade* I attempted to do good work, but whatever comes into contact with the theater is corrupted. The luxurious setting characteristic of the only European impresario who was sufficiently courageous and sufficiently interested to accept our work, circumstances in general, and fatigue, made me unable to realize my piece which remains, as it stands, in my opinion, an open window through which may be had a glimpse of what the modern theater ought to be.

The score of *Parade* was meant to supply a musical background to suggestive noises, e.g., of sirens, typewriters, airplanes, and dynamos, placed there like what Georges Braque so aptly calls "facts." Material difficulties and hurried rehearsals prevented these noises from materializing. We suppressed them nearly all. In other words, the piece was played incomplete and without its principle *clou*.

* * * * *

Sick to death of flabbiness, fluidity, superfluity, frills, and all the modern sleight-of-hand, though often tempted by a technique of which he knows the ultimate resources, Satie voluntarily abstained, in order to "model in the block" and remain simple, clear, and luminous. But the public hates candor

Each of Satie's works is an example of renunciation.

The opposition put forward by Erik Satie consists in a return to simplicity. Moreover, that is the only possible kind of opposition in an age of extreme refinement. The good faith of the critics of *Parade*, who thought that the orchestral part was a mere din, can only be explained by the phenomenon of *suggestion*. The word "cubism," wrongly applied, *suggested* an orchestra to them.

The Impressionist musicians thought the orchestra in *Parade* poor, because it had no sauce.

* * * * *

Impressionism has fired its last fine fireworks at the end of a long fête. It is up to us to set the rockets for another fête.

One does not blame an epoch; one congratulates oneself on not having belonged to it.

To be on one's guard against a decadent movement is not to deny the individual value of its artists.

Impressionism is a reaction from Wagner. The last reverberation of the storm.

The impressionist school substitutes sunshine for light, and sonority for rhythm.

Debussy played in French, but used the Russian pedal.

"What a crowd of false disciples there is around a Picasso, a Braque, a Stravinsky, or a Satie, who discredit them!" Such is the opinion of the impressionist. No doubt he forgets the Autumn Salon, and Mélisande's hair splitting.

Pelléas is another example of music to be listened to with one's face in one's hands. All music which has to be listened to through the hands is suspect. Wagner is typically music which is listened to through the hands.

One cannot get lost in a Debussy mist as one can in a Wagner fog, but it is not good for one.

3 Igor Stravinsky

Although the Russian composer Igor Stravinsky (1882–1971) had already established a major reputation before World War I, he significantly redefined his style, adopting a manner after the war that came to be known as "neoclassicism." Partly influenced by contemporary trends in French music (compare the previous essay by Jean Cocteau), Stravinsky began cultivating objectivity and restraint, distinctly departing from the flamboyance shown in much of his earlier work. The following excerpts from a series of lectures delivered at Harvard University in 1946 address a number of esthetic and technical matters relevant to his new approach: preference for what Stravinsky here calls "ontological" time over the dynamic, "psychological" time of musical Romanticism; the redefinition, as opposed to the rejection, of tonal centricity; an emphasis on technique over inspiration; and the need to set limits.

FROM *Poetics of Music*
(1946)

More complex and really fundamental is the specific problem of musical time, of the *chronos* of music. This problem has recently been made the object of a particularly interesting study by Mr. Pierre Souvtchinsky, a Russian philosopher-friend of mine. His thinking is so closely akin to mine that I can do no better than to summarize his thesis here.

Musical creation appears to him an innate complex of intuitions and possibil-

TEXT: *Poetics of Music,* trans. by Arthur Knodel and Ingolf Dahl (Cambridge, Mass.: Harvard University Press, 1947), pp. 29–32, 34–38, 50–51, 63–65. Reprinted by permission of the publisher.

ities based primarily upon an exclusively musical experiencing of time—
chronos, of which the musical work merely gives us the functional realization.

Everyone knows that time passes at a rate which varies according to the
inner dispositions of the subject and to the events that come to affect his consciousness. Expectation, boredom, anguish, pleasure and pain, contemplation—all of these thus come to appear as different categories in the midst of
which our life unfolds, and each of these determines a special psychological
process, a particular tempo. These variations in psychological time are perceptible only as they are related to the primary sensation—whether conscious or
unconscious—of real time, ontological time.

What gives the concept of musical time its special stamp is that this concept
is born and develops as well outside of the categories of psychological time as
it does simultaneously with them. All music, whether it submits to the normal
flow of time, or whether it disassociates itself therefrom, establishes a particular
relationship, a sort of counterpoint between the passing of time, the music's
own duration, and the material and technical means through which the music
is made manifest.

Mr. Souvtchinsky thus presents us with two kinds of music: one which
evolves parallel to the process of ontological time, embracing and penetrating
it, inducing in the mind of the listener a feeling of euphoria and, so to speak,
of "dynamic calm." The other kind runs ahead of, or counter to, this process.
It is not self-contained in each momentary tonal unit. It dislocates the centers
of attraction and gravity and sets itself up in the unstable; and this fact makes
it particularly adaptable to the translation of the composer's emotive impulses.
All music in which the will to expression is dominant belongs to the second
type.

This problem of time in the art of music is of capital importance. I have
thought it wise to dwell on the problem because the considerations that it
involves may help us to understand the different creative types which will concern us in our fourth lesson.

Music that is based on ontological time is generally dominated by the principle of similarity. The music that adheres to psychological time likes to proceed
by contrast. To these two principles which dominate the creative process correspond the fundamental concepts of variety and unity.

All the arts have recourse to this principle. The methods of polychromatics
and monochromatics in the plastic arts correspond respectively to variety and
unity. For myself, I have always considered that in general it is more satisfactory
to proceed by similarity rather than by contrast. Music thus gains strength in
the measure that it does not succumb to the seductions of variety. What it loses
in questionable riches it gains in true solidity.

Contrast produces an immediate effect. Similarity satisfies us only in the long
run. Contrast is an element of variety, but it divides our attention. Similarity is
born of a striving for unity. The need to seek variety is perfectly legitimate, but
we should not forget that the One precedes the Many. Moreover, the coexis-

tence of both is constantly necessary, and all the problems of art, like all possible problems for that matter, including the problem of knowledge and of Being, revolve ineluctably about this question, with Parmenides on one side denying the possibility of the Many, and Heraclitus on the other denying the existence of the One. Mere common sense, as well as supreme wisdom, invite us to affirm both the one and the other. All the same, the best attitude for a composer in this case will be the attitude of a man who is conscious of the hierarchy of values and who must make a choice. Variety is valid only as a means of attaining similarity. Variety surrounds me on every hand. So I need not fear that I shall be lacking in it, since I am constantly confronted by it. Contrast is everywhere. One has only to take note of it. Similarity is hidden; it must be sought out, and it is found only after the most exhaustive efforts. When variety tempts me, I am uneasy about the facile solutions it offers me. Similarity, on the other hand, poses more difficult problems but also offers results that are more solid and hence more valuable to me.

•   •   •   •   •

Consonance, says the dictionary, is the combination of several tones into an harmonic unit. Dissonance results from the deranging of this harmony by the addition of tones foreign to it. One must admit that all this is not clear. Ever since it appeared in our vocabulary, the word dissonance has carried with it a certain odor of sinfulness.

Let us light our lantern: in textbook language, dissonance is an element of transition, a complex or interval of tones which is not complete in itself and which must be resolved to the ear's satisfaction into a perfect consonance.

But just as the eye completes the lines of a drawing which the painter has knowingly left incomplete, just so the ear may be called upon to complete a chord and coöperate in its resolution, which has not actually been realized in the work. Dissonance, in this instance, plays the part of an allusion.

Either case applies to a style where the use of dissonance demands the necessity of a resolution. But nothing forces us to be looking constantly for satisfaction that resides only in repose. And for over a century music has provided repeated examples of a style in which dissonance has emancipated itself. It is no longer tied down to its former function. Having become an entity in itself, it frequently happens that dissonance neither prepares nor anticipates anything. Dissonance is thus no more an agent of disorder than consonance is a guarantee of security. The music of yesterday and of today unhesitatingly unites parallel dissonant chords that thereby lose their functional value, and our ear quite naturally accepts their juxtaposition.

Of course, the instruction and education of the public have not kept pace with the evolution of technique. The use of dissonance, for ears ill-prepared to accept it, has not failed to confuse their reaction, bringing about a state of debility in which the dissonant is no longer distinguished from the consonant.

We thus no longer find ourselves in the framework of classic tonality in the scholastic sense of the word. It is not we who have created this state of affairs, and it is not our fault if we find ourselves confronted with a new logic of music that would have appeared unthinkable to the masters of the past. And this new logic has opened our eyes to riches whose existence we never suspected.

Having reached this point, it is no less indispensable to obey, not new idols, but the eternal necessity of affirming the axis of our music and to recognize the existence of certain poles of attraction. Diatonic tonality is only one means of orienting music towards these poles. The function of tonality is completely subordinated to the force of attraction of the pole of sonority. All music is nothing more than a succession of impulses that converge towards a definite point of repose. That is as true of Gregorian chant as it is of a Bach fugue, as true of Brahms's music as it is of Debussy's.

This general law of attraction is satisfied in only a limited way by the traditional diatonic system, for that system possesses no absolute value.

There are few present-day musicians who are not aware of this state of affairs. But the fact remains that it is still impossible to lay down the rules that govern this new technique. Nor is this at all surprising. Harmony as it is taught today in the schools dictates rules that were not fixed until long after the publication of the works upon which they were based, rules which were unknown to the composers of these works. In this manner our harmonic treatises take as their point of departure Mozart and Haydn, neither of whom ever heard of harmonic treatises.

So our chief concern is not so much what is known as tonality as what one might term the polar attraction of sound, of an interval, or even of a complex of tones. The sounding tone constitutes in a way the essential axis of music. Musical form would be unimaginable in the absence of elements of attraction which make up every musical organism and which are bound up with its psychology. The articulations of musical discourse betray a hidden correlation between the *tempo* and the interplay of tones. All music being nothing but a succession of impulses and repose, it is easy to see that the drawing together and separation of poles of attraction in a way determine the respiration of music.

In view of the fact that our poles of attraction are no longer within the closed system which was the diatonic system, we can bring the poles together without being compelled to conform to the exigencies of tonality. For we no longer believe in the absolute value of the major-minor system based on the entity which musicologists call the *c*-scale.

The tuning of an instrument, of a piano for example, requires that the entire musical range available to the instrument should be ordered according to chromatic steps. Such tuning prompts us to observe that all these sounds converge towards a center which is the *a* above middle *c*. Composing, for me, is putting into an order a certain number of these sounds according to certain interval-relationships. This activity leads to a search for the center upon which the series of sounds involved in my undertaking should converge. Thus, if a center is given, I shall have to find a combination that converges upon it. If, on the other hand, an as yet unoriented combination has been found, I shall have to determine the center towards which it should lead. The discovery of this center suggests to me the solution of my problem. It is thus that I satisfy my very marked taste for such a kind of musical topography.

The superannuated system of classic tonality, which has served as the basis for musical constructions of compelling interest, has had the authority of law among musicians for only a short period of time—a period much shorter than is usually imagined, extending only from the middle of the seventeenth century to the middle of the nineteenth. From the moment when chords no longer serve to fulfill merely the functions assigned to them by the interplay of tones but, instead, throw off all constraint to become new entities free of all ties— from that moment on one may say that the process is completed: the diatonic system has lived out its life cycle. The work of the Renaissance polyphonists had not yet entered into this system, and we have seen that the music of our time abides by it no longer. A parallel progression of ninth-chords would suffice as proof. It was here that the gates opened upon what has been labeled with the abusive term: *atonality*.

The expression is fashionable. But that doesn't mean that it is very clear. And I should like to know just what those persons who use the term mean by it. The negating prefix *a* indicates a state of indifference in regard to the term, negating without entirely renouncing it. Understood in this way, the word *atonality* hardly corresponds to what those who use it have in mind. If it were said that my music is atonal, that would be tantamount to saying that I had become deaf to tonality. Now it well may be that I remain for a considerable time within the bounds of the strict order of tonality, even though I may quite consciously break up this order for the purposes of establishing a new one. In that case I am not *a*tonal, but *anti*tonal. I am not trying to argue pointlessly over words: it is essential to know what we deny and what we affirm.

•   •   •   •   •

Most music-lovers believe that what sets the composer's creative imagination in motion is a certain emotive disturbance generally designated by the name of *inspiration*.

I have no thought of denying to inspiration the outstanding role that has devolved upon it in the generative process we are studying; I simply maintain that inspiration is in no way a prescribed condition of the creative act, but rather a manifestation that is chronologically secondary.

Inspiration, art, artist—so many words, hazy at least, that keep us from seeing clearly in a field where everything is balance and calculation through which the breath of the speculative spirit blows. It is afterwards, and only afterwards, that the emotive disturbance which is at the root of inspiration may arise—an emotive disturbance about which people talk so indelicately by conferring upon it a meaning that is shocking to us and that compromises the term itself. Is it not clear that this emotion is merely a reaction on the part of the creator grappling with that unknown entity which is still only the object of his creating and which is to become a work of art? Step by step, link by link, it will be granted him to discover the work. It is this chain of discoveries, as well as each individual discovery, that give rise to the emotion—an almost physiologi- cal reflex, like that of the appetite causing a flow of saliva—this emotion which invariably follows closely the phases of the creative process.

All creation presupposes at its origin a sort of appetite that is brought on by the foretaste of discovery. This foretaste of the creative act accompanies the intuitive grasp of an unknown entity already possessed but not yet intelligible, an entity that will not take definite shape except by the action of a constantly vigilant technique.

This appetite that is aroused in me at the mere thought of putting in order musical elements that have attracted my attention is not at all a fortuitous thing like inspiration, but as habitual and periodic, if not as constant, as a natural need.

·   ·   ·   ·   ·

Let us understand each other in regard to [the] word fantasy. We are not using the word in the sense in which it is connected with a definite musical form, but in the acceptation which presupposes an abandonment of one's self to the caprices of imagination. And this presupposes that the composer's will is voluntarily paralyzed. For imagination is not only the mother of caprice but the servant and handmaiden of the creative will as well.

The creator's function is to sift the elements he receives from her, for human activity must impose limits upon itself. The more art is controlled, limited, worked over, the more it is free.

As for myself, I experience a sort of terror when, at the moment of setting to work and finding myself before the infinitude of possibilities that present themselves, I have the feeling that everything is permissible to me. If every- thing is permissible to me, the best and the worst; if nothing offers me any resistance, then any effort is inconceivable, and I cannot use anything as a basis, and consequently every undertaking becomes futile.

Will I then have to lose myself in this abyss of freedom? To what shall I cling in order to escape the dizziness that seizes me before the virtuality of this infinitude? However, I shall not succumb. I shall overcome my terror and shall be reassured by the thought that I have the seven notes of the scale and its chromatic intervals at my disposal, that strong and weak accents are within my reach, and that in all of these I possess solid and concrete elements which offer me a field of experience just as vast as the upsetting and dizzy infinitude that had just frightened me. It is into this field that I shall sink my roots, fully convinced that combinations which have at their disposal twelve sounds in each octave and all possible rhythmic varieties promise me riches that all the activity of human genius will never exhaust.

What delivers me from the anguish into which an unrestricted freedom plunges me is the fact that I am always able to turn immediately to the concrete things that are here in question. I have no use for a theoretic freedom. Let me have something finite, definite—matter that can lend itself to my operation only insofar as it is commensurate with my possibilities. And such matter presents itself to me together with its limitations. I must in turn impose mine upon it. So here we are, whether we like it or not, in the realm of necessity. And yet which of us has ever heard talk of art as other than a realm of freedom? This sort of heresy is uniformly widespread because it is imagined that art is outside the bounds of ordinary activity. Well, in art as in everything else, one can build only upon a resisting foundation: whatever constantly gives way to pressure, constantly renders movement impossible.

My freedom thus consists in my moving about within the narrow frame that I have assigned myself for each one of my undertakings.

I shall go even further: my freedom will be so much the greater and more meaningful the more narrowly I limit my field of action and the more I surround myself with obstacles. Whatever diminishes constraint, diminishes strength. The more constraints one imposes, the more one frees one's self of the chains that shackle the spirit.

To the voice that commands me to create I first respond with fright; then I reassure myself by taking up as weapons those things participating in creation but as yet outside of it; and the arbitrariness of the constraint serves only to obtain precision of execution.

From all this we shall conclude the necessity of dogmatizing on pain of missing our goal. If these words annoy us and seem harsh, we can abstain from pronouncing them. For all that, they nonetheless contain the secret of salvation: "It is evident," writes Baudelaire, "that rhetorics and prosodies are not arbitrarily invented tyrannies, but a collection of rules demanded by the very organization of the spiritual being, and never have prosodies and rhetorics kept originality from fully manifesting itself. The contrary, that is to say, that they have aided the flowering of originality, would be infinitely more true."

4 John Cage

The American composer John Cage (1912–1993) was not only the most controversial composer of the latter part of the twentieth century but arguably the most influential. This essay, written as a lecture in 1957, represents his position after he fully adopted indeterminacy in his work during the early 1950s. He discusses several ideas essential to his work: his belief that sounds are to be enjoyed for their own sake and, to the extent possible, should be left to "be themselves," unaltered by human intervention; the importance of the tape recorder, not so much to allow sounds to be stored but to encourage an entirely new way of thinking about compositional material; his conviction that sound forms an unbroken continuum, encompassing complete silence at one extreme; and his refusal to acknowledge that there are sounds that do not belong to music.

Experimental Music
(1957)

Formerly, whenever anyone said the music I presented was experimental, I objected. It seemed to me that composers knew what they were doing, and that the experiments that had been made had taken place prior to the finished works, just as sketches are made before paintings and rehearsals precede performances. But, giving the matter further thought, I realized that there is ordinarily an essential difference between making a piece of music and hearing one. A composer knows his work as a woodsman knows a path he has traced and retraced, while a listener is confronted by the same work as one is in the woods by a plant he has never seen before.

Now, on the other hand, times have changed; music has changed; and I no longer object to the word "experimental." I use it in fact to describe all the music that especially interests me and to which I am devoted, whether someone else wrote it or I myself did. What has happened is that I have become a listener and the music has become something to hear. Many people, of course, have given up saying "experimental" about this new music. Instead, they either move to a halfway point and say "controversial" or depart to a greater distance and question whether this "music" is music at all.

For in this new music nothing takes place but sounds: those that are notated and those that are not. Those that are not notated appear in the written music as silences, opening the doors of the music to the sounds that happen to be in the environment. This openness exists in the fields of modern sculpture and architecture. The glass houses of Mies van der Rohe reflect their environment, presenting to the eye images of clouds, trees, or grass, according to the situation. And while looking at the constructions in wire of the sculptor Richard Lippold, it is inevitable that one will see other things, and people too, if they happen to be there at the same time, through the network of wires. There is no such thing as an empty space or an empty time. There is always something to see, something to hear. In fact, try as we may to make a silence, we cannot. For certain engineering purposes, it is desirable to have as silent a situation as possible. Such a room is called an anechoic chamber, its six walls made of

TEXT: *Silence* (Middletown: Wesleyan University Press, 1973), pp. 7–12. Reprinted by permission of University Press of New England.

special material, a room without echoes. I entered one at Harvard University several years ago and heard two sounds, one high and one low. When I described them to the engineer in charge, he informed me that the high one was my nervous system in operation, the low one my blood in circulation. Until I die there will be sounds. And they will continue following my death. One need not fear about the future of music.

But this fearlessness only follows if, at the parting of the ways, where it is realized that sounds occur whether intended or not, one turns in the direction of those he does not intend. This turning is psychological and seems at first to be a giving up of everything that belongs to humanity—for a musician, the giving up of music. This psychological turning leads to the world of nature, where, gradually or suddenly, one sees that humanity and nature, not separate, are in this world together; that nothing was lost when everything was given away. In fact, everything is gained. In musical terms, any sounds may occur in any combination and in any continuity.

And it is a striking coincidence that just now the technical means to produce such a free-ranging music are available. When the Allies entered Germany towards the end of World War II, it was discovered that improvements had been made in recording sounds magnetically such that tape had become suitable for the high-fidelity recording of music. First in France with the work of Pierre Schaeffer, later here, in Germany, in Italy, in Japan, and perhaps, without my knowing it, in other places, magnetic tape was used not simply to record performances of music but to make a new music that was possible only because of it. Given a minimum of two tape recorders and a disk recorder, the following processes are possible: 1) a single recording of any sound may be made; 2) a rerecording may be made, in the course of which, by means of filters and circuits, any or all of the physical characteristics of a given recorded sound may be altered; 3) electronic mixing (combining on a third machine sounds issuing from two others) permits the presentation of any number of sounds in combination; 4) ordinary splicing permits the juxtaposition of any sounds, and when it includes unconventional cuts, it, like rerecording, brings about alterations of any or all of the original physical characteristics. The situation made available by these means is essentially a total sound-space, the limits of which are ear-determined only, the position of a particular sound in this space being the result of five determinants: frequency or pitch, amplitude or loudness, overtone structure or timbre, duration, and morphology (how the sound begins, goes on, and dies away). By the alteration of any one of these determinants, the position of the sound in sound-space changes. Any sound at any point in this total sound-space can move to become a sound at any other point. But advantage can be taken of these possibilities only if one is willing to change one's musical habits radically. That is, one may take advantage of the appearance of images without visible transition in distant places, which is a way of saying "television," if one is willing to stay at home instead of going to a theatre. Or one may fly if one is willing to give up walking.

Musical habits include scales, modes, theories of counterpoint and harmony, and the study of the timbres, singly and in combination of a limited number of sound-producing mechanisms. In mathematical terms these all concern discrete steps. They resemble walking—in the case of pitches, on steppingstones twelve in number. This cautious stepping is not characteristic of the possibilities of magnetic tape, which is revealing to us that musical action or existence can occur at any point or along any line or curve or what have you in total sound-space; that we are, in fact, technically equipped to transform our contemporary awareness of nature's manner of operation into art.

Again there is a parting of the ways. One has a choice. If he does not wish to give up his attempts to control sound, he may complicate his musical technique towards an approximation of the new possibilities and awareness. (I use the word "approximation" because a measuring mind can never finally measure nature.) Or, as before, one may give up the desire to control sound, clear his mind of music, and set about discovering means to let sounds be themselves rather than vehicles for man-made theories or expressions of human sentiments.

This project will seem fearsome to many, but on examination it gives no cause for alarm. Hearing sounds which are just sounds immediately sets the theorizing mind to theorizing, and the emotions of human beings are continually aroused by encounters with nature. Does not a mountain unintentionally evoke in us a sense of wonder? otters along a stream a sense of mirth? night in the woods a sense of fear? Do not rain falling and mists rising up suggest the love binding heaven and earth? Is not decaying flesh loathsome? Does not the death of someone we love bring sorrow? And is there a greater hero than the least plant that grows? What is more angry than the flash of lightning and the sound of thunder? These responses to nature are mine and will not necessarily correspond with another's. Emotion takes place in the person who has it. And sounds, when allowed to be themselves, do not require that those who hear them do so unfeelingly. The opposite is what is meant by response ability.

New music: new listening. Not an attempt to understand something that is being said, for, if something were being said, the sounds would be given the shapes of words. Just an attention to the activity of sounds.

Those involved with the composition of experimental music find ways and means to remove themselves from the activities of the sounds they make. Some employ chance operations, derived from sources as ancient as the Chinese *Book of Changes*, or as modern as the tables of random numbers used also by physicists in research. Or, analogous to the Rorschach tests of psychology, the interpretation of imperfections in the paper upon which one is writing may provide a music free from one's memory and imagination. Geometrical means employing spatial superimpositions at variance with the ultimate performance in time may be used. The total field of possibilities may be roughly divided and the actual sounds within these divisions may be indicated as to number but left to the performer or to the splicer to choose. In this latter case, the composer resembles the maker of a camera who allows someone else to take the picture.

Whether one uses tape or writes for conventional instruments, the present musical situation has changed from what it was before tape came into being. This also need not arouse alarm, for the coming into being of something new does not by that fact deprive what was of its proper place. Each thing has its own place, never takes the place of something else; and the more things there are, as is said, the merrier.

But several effects of tape on experimental music may be mentioned. Since so many inches of tape equal so many seconds of time, it has become more and more usual that notation is in space rather than in symbols of quarter, half, and sixteenth notes and so on. Thus where on a page a note appears will correspond to when in time it is to occur. A stop watch is used to facilitate a performance; and a rhythm results which is a far cry from horse's hoofs and other regular beats.

Also it has been impossible with the playing of several separate tapes at once to achieve perfect synchronization. This fact has led some towards the manufacture of multiple-tracked tapes and machines with a corresponding number of heads; while others—those who have accepted the sounds they do not intend—now realize that the score, the requiring that many parts be played in a particular togetherness, is not an accurate representation of how things are. These now compose parts but not scores, and the parts may be combined in any unthought ways. This means that each performance of such a piece of music is unique, as interesting to its composer as to others listening. It is easy to see again the parallel with nature, for even with leaves of the same tree, no two are exactly alike. The parallel in art is the sculpture with moving parts, the mobile.

It goes without saying that dissonances and noises are welcome in this new music. But so is the dominant seventh chord if it happens to put in an appearance.

Rehearsals have shown that this new music, whether for tape or for instruments, is more clearly heard when the several loud-speakers or performers are separated in space rather than grouped closely together. For this music is not concerned with harmoniousness as generally understood, where the quality of harmony results from a blending of several elements. Here we are concerned with the coexistence of dissimilars, and the central points where fusion occurs are many: the ears of the listeners wherever they are. This disharmony, to paraphrase Bergson's statement about disorder, is simply a harmony to which many are unaccustomed.

Where do we go from here? Towards theatre. That art more than music resembles nature. We have eyes as well as ears, and it is our business while we are alive to use them.

And what is the purpose of writing music? One is, of course, not dealing with purposes but dealing with sounds. Or the answer must take the form of paradox: a purposeful purposelessness or a purposeless play. This play, how-

ever, is an affirmation of life—not an attempt to bring order out of chaos nor
to suggest improvements in creation, but simply a way of waking up to the very
life we're living, which is so excellent once one gets one's mind and one's
desires out of its way and lets it act of its own accord.

5 Milton Babbitt

Milton Babbitt (b. 1916) represents the kind of rational, intellectually oriented,
and technologically sophisticated musician that typified the first generation of
composers to reach artistic maturity following World War II. This much-cited
1958 article first appeared in a journal for record enthusiasts, whose editor,
discarding Babbitt's original title "The Composer as Specialist," gave it the considerably more inflammatory "Who Cares if You Listen?" by which it subsequently became known. Acknowledging the "musical and societal isolation" of
contemporary music as an inevitable consequence of its increasing complexity,
Babbitt recommends that composers simply accept this condition as a fact and
act accordingly. This leads him to view serious music as an art that is necessarily
conceived for a small and elite public and that, like a pure science, requires
institutional support in order to flourish.

Who Cares if You Listen?
(1958)

This article might have been entitled "The Composer as Specialist" or, alter-
natively, and perhaps less contentiously, "The Composer as Anachronism." For
I am concerned with stating an attitude towards the indisputable facts of the
status and condition of the composer of what we will, for the moment, desig-
nate as "serious," "advanced," contemporary music. This composer expends an
enormous amount of time and energy—and, usually, considerable money—on
the creation of a commodity which has little, no, or negative commodity value.
He is, in essence, a "vanity" composer. The general public is largely unaware
of and uninterested in his music. The majority of performers shun it and resent
it. Consequently, the music is little performed, and then primarily at poorly
attended concerts before an audience consisting in the main of fellow professionals. At best, the music would appear to be for, of, and by specialists.

TEXT: "Who Cares if You Listen?" *High Fidelity*, vol. 8, no. 2 (February, 1958), pp. 38–40. Copyright © Hachette Filipacchi Magazines, Inc. All rights reserved. Reprinted with permission.

Towards this condition of musical and societal "isolation," a variety of attitudes has been expressed, usually with the purpose of assigning blame, often to the music itself, occasionally to critics or performers, and very occasionally to the public. But to assign blame is to imply that this isolation is unnecessary and undesirable. It is my contention that, on the contrary, this condition is not only inevitable, but potentially advantageous for the composer and his music. From my point of view, the composer would do well to consider means of realizing, consolidating, and extending the advantages.

The unprecedented divergence between contemporary serious music and its listeners, on the one hand, and traditional music and its following, on the other, is not accidental and—most probably—not transitory. Rather, it is a result of a half-century of revolution in musical thought, a revolution whose nature and consequences can be compared only with, and in many respects are closely analogous to, those of the mid-nineteenth-century revolution in theoretical physics. The immediate and profound effect has been the necessity for the informed musician to reexamine and probe the very foundations of his art. He has been obliged to recognize the possibility, and actuality, of alternatives to what were once regarded as musical absolutes. He lives no longer in a unitary musical universe of "common practice," but in a variety of universes of diverse practice.

This fall from musical innocence is, understandably, as disquieting to some as it is challenging to others, but in any event the process is irreversible; and the music that reflects the full impact of this revolution is, in many significant respects, a truly "new" music. Apart from the often highly sophisticated and complex constructive methods of any one composition, or group of compositions, the very minimal properties characterizing this body of music are the sources of its "difficulty," "unintelligibility," and—isolation. In indicating the most general of these properties, I shall make reference to no specific works, since I wish to avoid the independent issue of evaluation. The reader is at liberty to supply his own instances; if he cannot (and, granted the condition under discussion, this is a very real possibility), let him be assured that such music does exist.

First. This music employs a tonal vocabulary which is more "efficient" than that of the music of the past, or its derivatives. This is not necessarily a virtue in itself, but it does make possible a greatly increased number of pitch simultaneities, successions, and relationships. This increase in efficiency necessarily reduces the "redundancy" of the language, and as a result the intelligible communication of the work demands increased accuracy from the transmitter (the performer) and activity from the receiver (the listener). Incidentally, it is this circumstance, among many others, that has created the need for purely electronic media of "performance." More importantly for us, it makes ever heavier demands upon the training of the listener's perceptual capacities.

Second. Along with this increase of meaningful pitch materials, the number of functions associated with each component of the musical event also has been multiplied. In the simplest possible terms, each such "atomic" event is located in a five-dimensional musical space determined by pitch-class, register, dynamic, duration, and timbre. These five components not only together define the single event, but, in the course of a work, the successive values of each component create an individually coherent structure, frequently in parallel with the corresponding structures created by each of the other components. Inability to perceive and remember precisely the values of any of these components results in a dislocation of the event in the work's musical space, an alternation of its relation to all other events in the work, and—thus—a falsification of the composition's total structure. For example, an incorrectly performed or perceived dynamic value results in destruction of the work's dynamic pattern, but also in false identification of other components of the event (of which this dynamic value is a part) with corresponding components of other events, so creating incorrect pitch, registral, timbral, and durational associations. It is this high degree of "determinancy" that most strikingly differentiates such music from, for example, a popular song. A popular song is only very partially determined, since it would appear to retain its germane characteristics under considerable alteration of register, rhythmic texture, dynamics, harmonic structure, timbre, and other qualities.

The preliminary differentiation of musical categories by means of this reasonable and usable criterion of "degree of determinacy" offends those who take it to be a definition of qualitative categories, which—of course—it need not always be. Curiously, their demurrers usually take the familiar form of some such "democratic" counterdefinition as: "There is no such thing as 'serious' and 'popular' music. There is only 'good' and 'bad' music." As a public service, let me offer those who still patiently await the revelation of the criteria of Absolute Good an alternative criterion which possesses, at least, the virtue of immediate and irrefutable applicability: "There is no such thing as 'serious' and 'popular' music. There is only music whose title begins with the letter 'X,' and music whose title does not."

Third. Musical compositions of the kind under discussion possess a high degree of contextuality and autonomy. That is, the structural characteristics of a given work are less representative of a general class of characteristics than they are unique to the individual work itself. Particularly, principles of relatedness, upon which depends immediate coherence of continuity, are more likely to evolve in the course of the work than to be derived from generalized assumptions. Here again greater and new demands are made upon the perceptual and conceptual abilities of the listener.

Fourth, and finally. Although in many fundamental respects this music is "new," it often also represents a vast extension of the methods of other musics, derived from a considered and extensive knowledge of their dynamic principles. For, concomitant with the "revolution in music," perhaps even an integral aspect thereof, has been the development of analytical theory, concerned with the systematic formulation of such principles to the end of greater efficiency, economy, and understanding. Compositions so rooted necessarily ask compara- ble knowledge and experience from the listener. Like all communication, this music presupposes a suitably equipped receptor. I am aware that "tradition" has it that the lay listener, by virtue of some undefined, transcendental faculty, always is able to arrive at a musical judgment absolute in its wisdom if not always permanent in its validity. I regret my inability to accord this declaration of faith the respect due its advanced age.

Deviation from this tradition is bound to dismiss the contemporary music of which I have been talking into "isolation." Nor do I see how or why the situa- tion should be otherwise. Why should the layman be other than bored and puzzled by what he is unable to understand, music or anything else? It is only the translation of this boredom and puzzlement into resentment and denuncia- tion that seems to me indefensible. After all, the public does have its own music, its ubiquitous music: music to eat by, to read by, to dance by, and to be impressed by. Why refuse to recognize the possibility that contemporary music has reached a stage long since attained by other forms of activity? The time has passed when the normally well-educated man without special preparation could understand the most advanced work in, for example, mathematics, phi- losophy, and physics. Advanced music, to the extent that it reflects the knowl- edge and originality of the informed composer, scarcely can be expected to appear more intelligible than these arts and sciences to the person whose musi- cal education usually has been even less extensive than his background in other fields. But to this, a double standard is invoked, with the words "music is music," implying also that "music is *just* music." Why not, then, equate the activities of the radio repairman with those of the theoretical physicist, on the basis of the dictum that "physics is physics"? It is not difficult to find statements like the following, from the *New York Times* of September 8, 1957: "The scien- tific level of the conference is so high ... that there are in the world only 120 mathematicians specializing in the field who could contribute." Specialized music on the other hand, far from signifying "height" of musical level, has been charged with "decadence," even as evidence of an insidious "conspiracy."

It often has been remarked that only in politics and the "arts" does the lay- man regard himself as an expert, with the right to have his opinion heard. In the realm of politics he knows that this right, in the form of a vote, is guaran- teed by fiat. Comparably, in the realm of public music, the concertgoer is secure in the knowledge that the amenities of concert going protect his firmly stated "I didn't like it" from further scrutiny. Imagine, if you can, a layman chancing upon a lecture on "Pointwise Periodic Homeomorphisms." At the conclusion, he announces: "I didn't like it." Social conventions being what they are in such circles, someone might dare inquire: "Why not?" Under duress, our layman discloses precise reasons for his failure to enjoy himself; he found the hall chilly, the lecturer's voice unpleasant, and he was suffering the diges- tive aftermath of a poor dinner. His interlocutor understandably disqualifies these reasons as irrelevant to the content and value of the lecture, and the development of mathematics is left undisturbed. If the concertgoer is at all versed in the ways of musical lifesmanship, he also will offer reasons for his "I didn't like it"—in the form of assertions that the work in question is "inexpressive," "undramatic," "lacking in poetry," etc., etc., tapping that store of vacuous equivalents hallowed by time for: "I don't like it, and I cannot or will not state why." The concertgoer's critical authority is established beyond the possibility of further inquiry. Certainly he is not responsible for the circumstance that musical discourse is a never-never land of semantic confusion, the last resting place of all those verbal and formal fallacies, those hoary dualisms that have been banished from rational discourse. Perhaps he has read, in a widely consulted and respected book on the history of music, the following: "to call him (Tchaikovsky) the 'modern Russian Beethoven' is footless, Beethoven being patently neither modern nor Russian. . . ." Or, the following, by an eminent "nonanalytic" philosopher: "The music of Lourié is an ontological music. . . . It is born in the singular roots of being, the nearest possible juncture of the soul and the spirit. . . ." How unexceptionable the verbal peccadilloes of the average concertgoer appear beside these masterful models. Or, perhaps, in search of "real" authority, he has acquired his critical vocabulary from the pronouncements of officially "eminent" composers, whose eminence, in turn, is founded largely upon just such assertions as the concertgoer has learned to regurgitate. This cycle is of slight moment in a world where circularity is one of the norms of criticism. Composers (and performers), wittingly or unwittingly assuming the character of "talented children" and "inspired idiots" generally ascribed to them, are singularly adept at the conversion of personal tastes into general principles. Music they do not like is "not music," composers whose music they do not like are "not composers."

In search of what to think and how to say it, the layman may turn to newspapers and magazines. Here he finds conclusive evidence for the proposition that "music is music." The science editor of such publications contents himself with straightforward reporting, usually news of the "factual" sciences; books and articles not intended for popular consumption are not reviewed. Whatever the reason, such matters are left to professional journals. The music critic admits no comparable differentiation. He may feel, with some justice, that music which presents itself in the market place of the concert hall automatically offers itself to public approval or disapproval. He may feel, again with some justice, that to omit the expected criticism of the "advanced" work would be to do the composer an injustice in his assumed quest for, if nothing else, public notice and "professional recognition." The critic, at least to this extent, is himself a victim of the leveling of categories.

Here, then, are some of the factors determining the climate of the public world of music. Perhaps we should not have overlooked those pockets of "power" where prizes, awards, and commissions are dispensed, where music is adjudged guilty, not only without the right to be confronted by its accuser, but without the right to be confronted by the accusations. Or those well-meaning souls who exhort the public "just to *listen* to more contemporary music," apparently on the theory that familiarity breeds passive acceptance. Or those, often the same well-meaning souls, who remind the composer of his "obligation to the public," while the public's obligation to the composer is fulfilled, manifestly, by mere physical presence in the concert hall or before a loudspeaker or—more authoritatively—by committing to memory the numbers of phonograph records and amplifier models. Or the intricate social world within this musical world, where the salon becomes bazaar, and music itself becomes an ingredient of verbal canapés for cocktail conversation.

I say all this not to present a picture of a virtuous music in a sinful world, but to point up the problems of a special music in an alien and inapposite world. And so, I dare suggest that the composer would do himself and his music an immediate and eventual service by total, resolute, and voluntary withdrawal from this public world to one of private performance and electronic media, with its very real possibility of complete elimination of the public and social aspects of musical composition. By so doing, the separation between the domains would be defined beyond any possibility of confusion of categories, and the composer would be free to pursue a private life of professional achievement, as opposed to a public life of unprofessional compromise and exhibitionism.

But how, it may be asked, will this serve to secure the means of survival for the composer and his music? One answer is that after all such a private life is what the university provides the scholar and the scientist. It is only proper that the university, which—significantly—has provided so many contemporary composers with their professional training and general education, should provide a home for the "complex," "difficult," and "problematical" in music. Indeed, the process has begun; and if it appears to proceed too slowly, I take consolation in the knowledge that in this respect, too, music seems to be in historically retarded parallel with now sacrosanct fields of endeavor. In E. T. Bell's *Men of Mathematics*, we read: "In the eighteenth century the universities were not the principal centers of research in Europe. They might have become such sooner than they did but for the classical tradition and its understandable hostility to science. Mathematics was close enough to antiquity to be respectable, but physics, being more recent, was suspect. Further, a mathematician in a university of the time would have been expected to put much of his effort on elementary teaching; his research, if any, would have been an unprofitable luxury. . . ." A simple substitution of "musical composition" for "research," of "academic" for "classical," of "music" for "physics," and of "composer" for "mathematician," provides a strikingly accurate picture of the current situation. And as long as the confusion I have described continues to exist, how can the university and its community assume other than that the composer welcomes and courts public competition with the historically certified products of the past, and the commercially certified products of the present?

Perhaps for the same reason, the various institutes of advanced research and the large majority of foundations have disregarded this music's need for means of survival. I do not wish to appear to obscure the obvious differences between musical composition and scholarly research, although it can be contended that these differences are no more fundamental than the differences among the various fields of study. I do question whether these differences, by their nature, justify the denial to music's development of assistance granted these other fields. Immediate "practical" applicability (which may be said to have its musical analogue in "immediate extensibility of a compositional technique") is certainly not a necessary condition for the support of scientific research. And if it be contended that such research is so supported because in the past it has yielded eventual applications, one can counter with, for example, the music of Anton Webern, which during the composer's lifetime was regarded (to the very limited extent that it was regarded at all) as the ultimate in hermetic, specialized, and idiosyncratic composition; today, some dozen years after the composer's death, his complete works have been recorded by a major record company, primarily—I suspect—as a result of the enormous influence this music has had on the postwar, nonpopular, musical world. I doubt that scientific research is any more secure against predictions of ultimate significance than is musical composition. Finally, if it be contended that research, even in its least "practical" phases, contributes to the sum of knowledge in the particular realm, what possibly can contribute more to our knowledge of music than a genuinely original composition?

Granting to music the position accorded other arts and sciences promises the sole substantial means of survival for the music I have been describing. Admittedly, if this music is not supported, the whistling repertory of the man in the street will be little affected, the concert-going activity of the conspicuous consumer of musical culture will be little disturbed. But music will cease to evolve, and, in that important sense, will cease to live.

6 Evan Ziporyn

Evan Ziporyn (b. 1959) is an American composer who has been influenced by a wide variety of music, including both non-Western (especially Balinese) art music and Western popular and vernacular musics. This 1991 article, whose title plays upon "Who Cares if You Listen?," the title assigned by an editor to the previous essay by Milton Babbitt, argues for a more open conception of musical composition consistent with contemporary cultural pluralism. Noting the power of digital technology to "refashion everything under the sun," Ziporyn questions whether the individual compositional voice still has any validity and whether compositions can represent personal "property." This line of thinking leads him to envision a breaking down of old boundaries through creative interactions among previously unrelated musical traditions, spawned by composers who are "rootless cosmopolitans . . . , endlessly wandering in search of a community, an aesthetic, a musical life."

Who Listens if You Care?
(1991)

In 1977, Chris Maher, composer and massage artist, articulated his vision of what he termed "Marxist music." His idea was simple: no musical material could be owned—all music makers should be able to take whatever they want from whomever they want and use it as they see fit. "Material" could range from a melody, a sound, a formal principle, to an entire piece of music (as in Maher's "New Improved Morton Feldman," in which Feldman's spare sonic world is "enhanced" through the use of digital delay). Maher contended that only in this way could music—rather than an individual's musical career—grow and develop freely. By invading and destroying the notion of musical "property," the scope of musical possibilities would be infinitely expanded. An individual's "piece" would still exist and could still be valued, in any and every sense, but, more importantly, his or her ideas—or, more precisely, any real or imagined musical ideas that could be construed from his or her piece—could be built upon, taken in unexpected directions, used by all.

We were young then, and despite the well-known historical precedents for this position—famous borrowers such as Handel (melodies), Barry Manilow (chord progressions), and Webern (formal principles)—I remember that we found the idea somewhat scandalous and terrifying. This was tied into the seeming impossibility of making careers for ourselves as composers: the task seemed to be "finding a voice" or coming up with some kind of original or innovative structural idea. This daunting task was achieved through "the work" one put into one's music—not simply time or deep thought but some ineffable blend of the two, of quantity and quality. This work was what ultimately mattered: our pieces—the product—would be perfect reflections of it, and, in the course of time, this work—if we but had the strength to persevere tirelessly—would be recognized, lauded, rewarded. Our dedication would magically be transformed into stunning, creative work, and from there glory and achievement would be ours. There was a hidden, mystical equation: talent ("quality") times work ("quantity") divided by fate would equal good fortune, fame, success.

The inevitable disillusionment from our naive faith did not result from any

TEXT: *New Observations,* no. 86 (November / December, 1991), pp. 25–28.

inherent failing in this equation. Most of us ultimately were able to do what we wanted to a greater or lesser degree, and the fact that various bozos managed to get famous on a gimmick didn't seem very irksome once we got used to it (none of us lost much sleep over the Milli Vanilli thing, for example).[1] What caused the destruction of this Calvinistic world-view was rather that Maher's dream became reality, in a far more encompassing way than even he could have imagined. For, as we now all know, the need for new products to market and sell has combined with the digital ability to refashion everything under the sun, and this very un-Marxist combination of consumerism and technology has led to the fulfillment of Chris's dream.

In a deeper way than ever before, all music is available to all people, all the time. In the West, this simple and delightful fact has been patently obvious since Karlheinz Stockhausen's 1966 *Telemusik*, a musique concrète piece for which the source material is traditional music from dozens of cultures, all of whom, the composer asserts, "wanted to participate in *Telemusik* . . . not 'my' music, but a music of the whole world, of all countries and all races." But this early harbinger of things to come, like Brian Eno and David Byrne's 1980 *My Life in the Bush of Ghosts*, a pop version of the same thing, has turned out to be a relatively primitive form of musical imperialism compared to the present state of musical multi-nationalism. Across the globe musicians are begging, borrowing, and stealing from each other at a rapacious pace. Brazilian muzenza ensembles are singing praise songs to Bob Marley, Gambian koro players are rushing to finish commissions for the Kronos Quartet, and hordes of rock icons are scurrying around searching for newer, hipper even more undiscovered grooves.

In the West, this process has involved the merging of every concept of musical "otherness": exotica has been annexed, declared null and void. Up until now, the maintenance of any mainstream—be it the standard concert repertoire, top-40 radio, swing, academic modernism, etc.—included a notion of its opposite, the "out there." This is what allowed Cab Calloway to describe bebop as "Chinese music," or Pierre Boulez to pronounce that "the non-serialist composer is useless." Such statements help define a genre, to alert people to accept no substitutes.

The boundaries of any particular mainstream are by nature always in flux, shifting and indeterminate. Even so, such defining gestures—this is music, that is not—are possible and necessary. Territory can expand, but a line has to be drawn somewhere: language must be employed to corral, tame, and ultimately include or exclude the new sound under scrutiny. One can appeal to nature (as does Rameau in justifying his use of chromaticism in "L'Enharmonique"), to

1. The pop-rap group Milli Vanilli, consisting of Robert Pilatus and Fabrice Morvan, won the 1990 Grammy award for best new artist. Rumors soon surfaced that the group's debut album was actually the work of three backup singers and that the duo had not sung a single note. Upon confirmation, the National Academy of Recording Arts and Sciences requested for the first time in its 33-year history that the Grammy be returned.

morals (saying, for example, that certain types of music are "corrupting" or "degenerate"), to common sense ("My 3-year-old could do better than that"), or to taste and sheer willfulness ("I don't know much about music, but I know what I like").

Nowadays such posturing is less viable, because the very notion of "otherness" has become a marketable commodity, incorporated into the aesthetic. Before, depending on who you were and where you stood, the "other" could be a lot of things: non-Western music, early music, computer music, etc. Now all these things have merged, and a typical "new age" recording might use synthesizers imitating Shona mbiras, Balinese genggong imitating synthesizers, all in the service of evoking a fictional Druidic ritual. As critic Joshua Kosman points out, the "authentic performance" movement has caught on partially because it can be recorded digitally and marketed as the "latest thing." People don't give a shit where the music they like comes from, when it was written, for what purpose, by whom, or how it's played. It's the end of history, in a way Francis Fukuyama could never have anticipated. A sampled mbira is as good as a real one—we know what it's trying to sound like, so what possible difference could it make. There's no point in asking if it's live or Memorex anymore. "Otherness" in Western music is now nothing more than a quality of sound to be lifted and used as quickly as possible.

This point is brought home by the obvious irrelevance of today's copyright laws. The musical material most likely to be borrowed is clearly not protectable—a quality of sound, a rhythm, an inflected phrase. If worse comes to worst, give your music away (just keep the nude, transsexual pictures of rock stars off your CD cover and the industry will probably never even notice).

Whether one's motivation is fun or profit, the end result is the same: an imperialistic groove, under which any and every form of music past or present can be subsumed. "The groove" can be defined in a number of ways—as a steady 4/4 disco beat, suitable for DJ mix-and-matching, as a new age wash of sound, suitable for the inducement of bliss and calm, or anything else that feels good. Music thus becomes a service industry, providing listeners with a pleasurable, regulated, and non-threatening surface wash of sound. This results in another Marxian quandary: the byproduct of Maherian/Marxist music is that the listener is now completely cut off from the "means of production," and basically couldn't care less—if I hear the Harmonic Choir on the radio, it is at this point completely irrelevant to me whether David Hykes does it acoustically, electronically or whether it's him doing it at all. And why should I care—such issues are of anecdotal value only, useful in building a reputation, adding to a resume, writing a feature article in *Ear* Magazine.

The traditional boundaries of genre, intended audience, "culture," have been so thoroughly crossed that even when you try it's impossible to take a cohesive stance toward any particular piece of music. One can only applaud when Public Enemy's Chuck D. says that his group's goal is to be a "musician's nightmare," but how is one to respond to David Byrne's use of Cuban rhythms and musicians to sing a song about rent control? Is it exploitative and neo-colonial? Who the hell knows—the beat is good, the words are compelling, and you can dance to it. These are important things. It's catchy, it seems to have vision and imagination. But how does that feeling come about? How much of the power of the music is derived from evocations of other things, from Eddie Palmieri to Ricky Ricardo? (Again, these confusions cut across cultural borders: in 1988 Indonesia's biggest pop star was named Ricki Ricardo, and the biggest hit single was a rock song using traditional gamelan instruments called "Bring Back the Old Bali"). Even if we wanted to, how could we determine what taboos are left to break, what boundaries left to cross?

This situation has had a number of extremely positive effects. Even fifteen years ago, the lack of respect accorded non-Western music (and other "others") seemed somehow unjust. The availability of every form of music to anyone with a record player or a college radio station in the vicinity was an accomplished fact, and yet most college music departments continued to pretend that you could teach "music" as if the term meant something that had existed only in Europe, subsisting until the birth of Bach, flowering until the beginning of this century, and currently experiencing ongoing and agonizing death throes. It seemed important to argue for opening things up, recognizing other vital traditions, talking about musical hybridization, etc.

Now fortunately everything has been turned on its head: cultural critics crawl all over themselves to explain the influence of talking drums on hip-hop; Greg Sandow, composer and critic, once an ardent defender of David Del Tredici and Charles Wuorinen (two ideological enemies currently to be found side by side in the same rubbish heap of history, the "New Music" bin at Tower Records), can now boldly state that "most [!] heavy metal guitarists are influenced by Bach solo violin suites"; Peter Gabriel, a platinum-selling rock star, releases a hit album of "source material" sampled for use in his own work. And even within the academy, the College Music Society issues urgent calls to teach non-Western music, and—luckily—conservative academic trendsetters like Allan Bloom and E. D. Hirsch either don't know enough about music or care enough to target it.

In other words, I'm not complaining: how can I in an era when Boulez' neo-fascist post-war pronouncements seem like medieval schisms, or oracles from another planet? Non-western music doesn't have to fight for respect anymore, and that's an amazing turn of events.

It is also of course true that, here and around the globe, there are still lots of traditional musical uses and users, not just your average Balinese villager (who may have a Michael Jackson poster on his wall), but the classical music lover (for whom Schoenberg is noise), or the academic computer musician (for whom all 19th-century music sounds alike), etc. I am merely asserting that there now exists a large number of us for whom musical boundaries have lost their former meanings. I am talking about people for whom an average day's listening might include the Monroe Brothers, Japanese muzak, Bugandan horns, Sibelius symphonies, and any and everything else, a list more resembling a Borgesian encyclopedia than a radio playlist or concert program. We are the rootless cosmopolitans of music, endlessly wandering in search of a community, an aesthetic, a musical life.

It is difficult for us, faced with this onslaught, to know how to proceed, either pragmatically or philosophically. If we are composers, what instruments to write for? If we teach, what subjects? What set of musical values, technical and aesthetic, are we to subscribe to? Why are we doing it anyway? Even attention and money aren't sufficient motivators, for as Robert Moore puts it, "You can now do whatever you want, because no one will care in any case." What then are we to do?

The answer, I believe, can be found by re-examining the troublesome analogy between music and language. Is music a language at all? Is it a "universal" one? For people who are still able to divide music into traditions, genres, etc., music is like language in that humans do it for other humans (presumably) to hear it, and they do it following spoken or unspoken structural rules that are shared and make sense to various groups of people. Particular musics are associated with particular cultures—your average Balinese, for example, can distinguish between "Balinese music" and everything else in the world. As long as music is defined in this way, as a cultural byproduct or sign system, it's easy to keep our bearings. Music is a code, by definition comprehensible to people within a cultural group. Unfortunately, this also means that any particular music is by definition misunderstood by everyone else in the world, no matter how carefully they listen. In other words, any Ghanaian's subjective hearing of Ghanaian drumming is automatically valid, "authentic"; any non-Ghanaian's invalid, albeit useful, enjoyable, etc. When things are couched in these terms, it becomes clear how inappropriate such distinctions have become, how ridiculous it is to assert the relative validity of anybody's response to any music.

One solution to this is to redefine music as "organized sound," as any collection of noise that is deemed "music" by anybody. Viewed in this light, music is still a sign system, a language, but it's one in which any ordering of "phonemes" is automatically intelligible. (A "musical phoneme" can be defined as any subjectively discerned unit of sound, or as the equivalent of a "syllable" in language.) "Organized sound" might as well mean "sound," since the listener does the organizing—this means everything we hear and don't hear, any combination of sound and silence, and . . . my God! What does sound have to do with music!!!

Phonemically transferable music (music as organized sound) is thus both inherently "universal" and inherently incomprehensible, a sign system in which everyone in the world has their own code book, a language in which no two of us speak a mutually intelligible dialect. We are faced then with an awful choice: a Babel of conflicting tongues or an endless outpouring of gibberish. Either way we're in trouble—either way communication seems impossible.

If music is sound and sound only, then nothing we can do can be more or less understood than anything else. If, on the other hand, music consists of myriad discrete languages, a native speaker confronted with "the other" in any form can do a number of things, among them: 1) ignore it and stick to the purity of the mother tongue (this can be done either as a Boulezian progressive or as a Rochbergian reactionary); 2) exploit it by subsuming it into your own, grander music (*My Life in the Bush of Ghosts, Telemusik*); 3) learn to speak the other like a native (Lou Harrison, Joseph Conrad); 4) respect it and come to terms with it, either by creating self-conscious hybrids (*Finnegans Wake*, Harry Partch), or ones which are designed to have mutually exclusive meanings for different listeners (these are the hardest examples to find—but this was the intention of my own collaboration with Balinese composer Nyoman Windha in *Kekembangan,* a piece for gamelan and saxophone quartet. Malinowski's inclusion of uninterpreted myths in *Argonauts of the Western Pacific* can also be viewed in this way).

Acting linguistically, speaking and writing, all of the above stances can be taken with a clear attitude toward comprehensibility. To be understood, one must subscribe to the hierarchical relationship between languages; in other words, speak one of them at a time. Creating artificial languages—hybrid or synthetic—is possible, but by definition produces incomprehension. But the mere possibility of "phonemic transference," which renders every cultural distinction potentially relative and ephemeral, makes it impossible to honestly assert that this same structure, this same test of understandability, applies to music. Please understand me: it is not our ability to articulate a definition of music as organized sound that creates this relativity, but rather that the experience of "useful misunderstanding," of a meaningful "inauthentic hearing," forces us to consider such a definition. As soon as we have heard the music from another culture in "the wrong way"—listened to West African drumming in 3/4 instead of 12/8, misconstrued the emotional meaning of a praise song, etc.—then we understand how pointless it is to insist that music operates as cultural language only. Despite the rigidity of the language/sound dichotomy, we seem to know that we can make sense of music without thinking of it as a system of signs or sounds. We don't need it to be a symbol of anything at all. And our problems have nothing to do with music, but only with our need to talk about it, to explain music in any way whatsoever.

Our lost youthful vision, that mystical combination of work, integrity, etc., long abandoned, was essentially a Platonic one. We wanted to dig deep within ourselves, to excavate beneath our petty experiences, ideas, etc. in search of the cool and the weird. Making good music meant simply stumbling across that nameless quality that we prayed was in there somewhere. (Our response was, in retrospect, the only reasonable one available to us as products of a system that glorifies individualism. For even if each person is now a society unto himself, with a personal background, interests—and this is the implicit goal of the individualistic project—then the only values can be individual ones, and the search for quality can only be an internal one.)

Plato would have banned music altogether, it being too unwieldy and uncap-turable to be controlled by a rational state. And Plato was right, because to talk about music, to categorize it, define it, explain it, is to attach linguistic con-structs, rational states, to phenomena that only resemble linear thought in the sense that they move uni-directionally through time. The only way to get around this, outside of banning music, is to separate music from linguistic thought, to stop searching for so much meaning. I'm not suggesting that we stop talking about music, stop trying to figure it out, but simply that we get rid of the notion that the value of music is in this incessant chatter, rather than in the music itself. Viewed in this way, what Maher's Marxist music seeks to dis-pense with is not "musical property," but the ability to even articulate the phrase. Once we stop believing that our descriptions and analyses enhance, encapsulate and embody the music in any intrinsic way, then issues of musical ownership will become irrelevant and will simply wither away.

We must begin to listen only to our inner voices, whatever their source, to insist that the Platonic ideal doesn't need a name, a language, a category. We must rid ourselves of the notion that a piece of music can or cannot be politi-cally correct, exploitative, collaborative, traditional, iconoclastic, whatever. We must stop trying to explain music, stop caring whether it's a sign system, a random or deliberate collection of sounds, or a symbol of anything other than itself. We must—we must—oh, shut up and listen, will you?

II

EXPANDED SONIC RESOURCES

7 Ferruccio Busoni

Ferruccio Busoni (1866–1924) was one of the most prominent musicians of the early twentieth century, widely recognized as a composer, pianist, and conductor. His *Sketch of a New Esthetic of Music,* first published in 1907, is the earliest general statement by a major figure to express fully the belief that twentieth-century composers must move beyond the traditional materials of Western music in search of previously untapped compositional possibilities. Though still expressing himself largely within the esthetic categories of Romanticism, emphasizing freedom, individuality, and originality, Busoni argues for the liberation of music from the limited rhythmic and formal structures and tone systems of "hallowed tradition" and from the rules imposed by self-appointed "lawgivers." He exhorts modern composers to embrace novel compositional materials such as "artificial" scales, microtonal divisions, and electro-mechanical instruments, as well as new systems of musical notation.

FROM *Sketch of a New Esthetic of Music*
(1907)

Music as an art, our so-called Western music, is barely four hundred years old. It is in a condition of development, perhaps in the earliest stage of a yet unforeseeable development. Yet we speak of classics and holy traditions.[1] Someone like Cherubini already speaks in his counterpoint textbook of "the ancients."

We have formulated rules, set out principles, and prescribed laws—we apply the maxims of adults to a child who does not yet understand responsibility!

As young as this child is, it already has one radiant characteristic that sets it off from all its older comrades. The lawgivers refuse to recognize this wonderful attribute, for their laws would then be rejected. This child—it floats on air! It does not touch the ground, is not subject to gravity. It is almost incorporeal, its material transparent. It is sonorous air. It is almost nature herself. It is free.

But freedom is something that humans have never fully understood, never completely experienced. They neither recognize it nor acknowledge it.

They deny the destiny of this child and enchain it. This soaring creature is required to walk properly, to conform to the rules of correct behavior, as if it were an ordinary being. It is barely permitted to leap, though it would like to follow the curve of the rainbow and, with the clouds, break apart the rays of the sun.

TEXT: *Entwurf einer neuen Ästhetik der Tonkunst,* 2nd ed. (Leipzig: Insel Verlag, 1916), pp. 7–11, 31, 33, 36–46. Translation by Robert P. Morgan.

1. Tradition is a plaster mask taken from life that, in passing through the course of many years and through the hands of many laborers, retains little resemblance to the original. [Au.]

The art of music was born free and its destiny is to win again its freedom. It will be the most complete of all nature's manifestations, thanks to the limitlessness of its immateriality. Even the poetic word lags behind it in incorporeality. Music can gather into itself and flow outward, can be a motionless calm or a tempestuous storm. It provides the most extreme heights perceptible to humans—what other art does that?—and its perception touches the human breast with an intensity independent of "concepts."

It reproduces an emotion without describing it, through the movement of the soul and the liveliness of continuous moments. The painter or sculptor, on the other hand, presents only one facet, one moment, a "situation"; and the poet must communicate an emotion and its stirrings laboriously, through successive words.

Hence representation and description do not constitute the essence of music. We thus reject program music and move on to consider the goals of music.

Absolute music! What the lawgivers mean thereby is perhaps furthest removed from the true absolute in music. "Absolute music" is a play of forms without a poetic program, the form fulfilling the most important role. True absolute music, however, stands precisely in opposition to form. It has the God-given attribute of floating on air and being free of all material conditions. In a picture, the representation of a sunset ends with the frame. A rectangular boundary is imposed upon the unbounded natural phenomenon; the fixed depiction of a cloud remains forever unchanging. Music can grow brighter, darker, shift position, and finally fade away like the glow of the sunset itself. Instinct leads the creative musician to use just those tones that press the same key, and awaken the same response, in the human heart as does the natural event.

Absolute music, on the other hand, is something quite sober, bringing to mind carefully ordered music stands, relationships of tonic to dominant, or developments to codas.

Now I hear the second violinist laboriously imitate the more adept first violinist a fourth lower; I hear an unnecessary battle being waged so that one can start again at the beginning. Such music should be called architectonic music, or symmetrical music, or sectional music, the result of the way certain composers poured their spirit and emotion into this type of form because it was most natural to them or their time. The lawgivers then identified spirit, emotion, the individuality of those composers, and the character of their time with symmetrical music; and when finally composers could no longer bring forth the spirit or the emotion, nor reproduce the character of that time, the lawgivers retained the form as a symbol, elevating it to a sort of sign, or article of faith. The older composers explored this form and found in it the most suitable means for communicating their thoughts. When they passed on, the lawgivers discovered the garments they left behind on earth and preserved them. . . .

Is it not strange that one demands originality of composers in all things, yet forbids it in matters of form? No wonder that one complains of formlessness when composers become truly original. Mozart! We marvel at and honor the seeker, the discoverer, the great man with a childish heart; not his tonics and dominants, his developments and codas.

Beethoven, the Romantic revolutionary, so longed for freedom that he succeeded in bringing music one small step back toward its higher nature—a small step in the overall task, a large one in his own individual development. Though he failed to achieve fully absolute music, he came close in certain moments, such as the introduction to the fugue of the *Hammerklavier* Sonata. In general, composers have approached nearest the true nature of music in preparatory and intermediary passages (preludes and transitions), where they felt they could ignore symmetrical proportions and, as if unconsciously, breathe more freely. Even a lesser talent like Schumann grasps in such passages something of the boundlessness of this pan-art—one thinks of the transition to the last movement of the D-minor Symphony. And one could say the same of Brahms in the introduction to the finale of his First Symphony.

But as soon as they cross the threshold to the principal subject, composers become stiff and conventional, like someone who has stepped into a business office.

· · · · ·

Creators should not accept on blind faith any rule that has been handed down to them, forcing them from the outset to consider their own creation as an exception thereto. They must seek and find their own appropriate rule for their own particular case and, after applying it successfully, reject it again in order not to repeat themselves in their next work.

The task of the creator should be to set up rules, not to follow rules. Whoever follows prescribed rules ceases to be a creator.

The power of creation is more easily recognized the more it is able to make itself independent of tradition. But deliberateness in the treatment of rules cannot simulate the power of creation, much less produce it.

True creators strive only for perfection. And by bringing this perfection into harmony with their own individuality, a new rule results quite unintentionally.

· · · · ·

Our tonal range has become so narrow, its form of expression so stereotypical, that there is now no known motive which cannot be joined with another known motive so that the two can be played simultaneously. In order not to lose myself in games,[2] I will refrain from offering examples.

2. I played such a game once with a friend in order to determine how many of the best-known compositions were constructed according to the formal scheme of the second theme of the Adagio of the Ninth Symphony. In a few moments we had collected some fifteen samples from the most varied genres, including some of a quite primitive sort. And they included Beethoven himself. Is the theme from the Finale of the Fifth Symphony different from the theme that

• • • • •

What comes closest to the true nature of the art in today's music is the rest and the fermata. Great performing artists, improvisors, know how to give this means of expression its full value. The suspenseful silence between two passages, which is itself also music in this context, provokes us more to presentiment than the more definite, but thus less malleable, sound.

What we today call our "tone system" is nothing but a system of "signs," an ingenious aid in holding fast something of that eternal harmony, a poor pocket edition of that encyclopedic work. Artificial light instead of the sun. Have you noticed how people open their mouths in wonder at the brilliant lighting of a concert hall? They never do so for the midday sunshine, a million times stronger.

And in music too, signs have become more important than what they are supposed to mean, but can only suggest.

How important, after all, are the "third," the "fifth," the "octave"? How strictly do we distinguish "consonances" from "dissonances"—and in a context where there actually can be no dissonances?

We have divided the octave in twelve steps equally separated from one another, because we must somehow make things easier for ourselves. And we have so constructed our instruments that we can never go above, below, or between them. In particular keyboard instruments have thoroughly trained our ears so that we are no longer capable of hearing anything [outside the chromatic octave] except as impurity. And nature created an infinite gradation—infinite! who realizes it today?[3]

And within this twelve-partitioned octave we have marked off yet another succession of particular distances, seven in number, and have constructed our entire tonal art thereon. Did I say one succession? There are two, the major and minor scales. If we construct the same succession of distances starting on one of the other twelve degrees, then there is a new key, and moreover a foreign one. One can read in the rule books what a profoundly limited system this has created:[4] we do not want to repeat it here.

---

begins the Allegro of the Second? Or from the main theme of the Third Piano Concerto, only in minor? [Au.]

3. "Twelve-tone equal temperament, already mentioned theoretically by c. 1500 but not fully formulated until shortly before 1700 (by Andreas Werkmeister), divides the octave into twelve equal divisions (semitones: hence the "twelve-semitone system") and thus produces only average values, enabling no interval to be purely intoned but all to become reasonably serviceable." (Riemann, *Musiklexikon.*) [Au.]

And thus thanks to Andreas Werkmeister, this master workman of art, we have attained the "twelve-semitone system" with many impure yet reasonably serviceable intervals. But what is pure and what impure? Our ear hears as impure an "out-of-tune" piano on which, perhaps, "pure and serviceable" intervals can be heard. The diplomatic twelve-semitone system is an aid born of necessity; yet we take great pains to preserve its imperfections. [Au.]

4. It is called the "theory of harmony." [Au.]

We teach twenty-four keys, twelve each for both types of seven-note scales; yet in fact we make use of only two: the major key and the minor key. The others are simply transpositions. One says that the individual transpositions produce different characters: but that is an illusion. In England, where high voices predominate, the most well-known works are performed a half tone higher than notated, without altering the effect. Singers transpose their arias to suit themselves, yet leave untransposed what precedes and follows them.

Composers of songs often publish their work in three different ranges; the pieces remain in all three entirely the same.

When a familiar face is seen through a window, it is the same whether it looks out from the second or fourth story.

If one could raise or lower a landscape by one hundred meters, as far as the eye could see, it would neither lose nor gain in appearance.

We have created our entire tonal art out of the two seven-note scales, the major and the minor—one limitation requires the other.

We have attributed to each of them a particular character, have taught and learned to hear them as opposite; and they have gradually acquired a symbolic meaning—major and minor, *maggiore e minore,* satisfaction and dissatisfaction, joy and sadness, light and shade. Harmonic symbolism has fenced off musical expression from Bach to Wagner and on to the present day. Minor is used for the same purpose and has the same effect as it had two hundred years ago. Today one can no longer "compose" a funeral march, for it is already eternally at hand. Even the most uneducated amateur knows what is in store as soon as a funeral march—whichever one!—is about to begin. Even the amateur senses in advance the difference between a major and a minor symphony.

It is strange that one experiences major and minor as opposites. They both have the same face, at times lighter and at times more serious; and a small stroke of the pen is sufficient to transform one into the other. The transition from one to the other occurs imperceptibly and without difficulty—and if it occurs quickly enough, the two seem to flow unnoticeably in and out of one another. But if we acknowledge that major and minor form a whole with double meaning, and that the "twenty-four keys" represent merely an elevenfold transposition of the first pair, we recognize immediately the unity of our key system. The notions of related and foreign dissolve—and with them the whole evolved theory of scale degrees and scale relationships. We have a single key, but it is of a very meager sort.

"Unity of key."

—"Perhaps you mean that "key" represents the sunshine while "keys" represent its dispersal into colors?"

No, I do not mean that. For in the heaven of "eternal harmony" our entire key and key system in its totality is but a small fraction of that dispersed radiance of the sun we call "music."

However deeply humankind is tied to habit and inactivity, energy and opposition to the existing order are characteristics of all life. "Nature has her devices" and wins over those who are against progress and change. She moves continuously forward and changes ceaselessly, but in such an unbroken and imperceptible motion that humans can see only stasis. Only when they look back from a more distant perspective are they surprised to discover that they have been deceived.

Reformers thus irritate people of all epochs, because their changes are too unmediated and, above all, too perceptible. Reformers are—in comparison with nature—undiplomatic. And their changes thus become accepted only when the abrupt leaps are imperceptibly blended back into time's advance. Yet in some instances the reformer moves in step with time, while all others fall behind. And then one must forcefully whip these others to leap across the intervening gap. I believe that the major and minor key system with its transpositions, those of the "twelve-semitone system," now constitutes such a lagging behind.

One already finds in certain passages in Liszt and in advanced contemporary music clear examples of such things as different orderings (gradations) of the seven-tone scale. These give expression to a definite urge and desire, to a gifted instinct. But it seems to me that one has yet to form a conscious and systematic conception of such heightened means of expression.

I have made an attempt to find all the possibilities of arranging the seven-tone scale and have succeeded, by lowering and raising the intervals, in producing 113 different scales. These 113 scales (within the octave C–C) not only comprise the greater part of our familiar "twenty-four keys" but also a series of new keys of unusual character. And this does not exhaust the possibilities, as transposition of each of these 113 keys is also possible; and also the inter-mixture of two such keys (and why not still more?) in the harmony and melody.

The scale C–D♭–E♭–F♭–G♭–A♭–B♭–C sounds quite different from the D♭-minor scale if one takes C as its first scale degree. And if one adds a C-major triad as harmony beneath it, a new harmonic effect results. But if one hears the same scale supported by alternating A-minor, E♭-major, and C-major triads, one cannot resist the most pleasant surprise over this strange yet good sound.

And how would a lawgiver classify the scales C–D♭–E♭–F♭–G–A–B–C, C–D♭–E♭–F–G♭–A–B–C, C–D–E♭–F♭–G♭–A–B–C, C–D♭–E–F–G♭–A–B♭–C, or even C–D–E♭–F♭–G–A♯–B–C, C–D–E♭–F♭–G♯–A–B–C, C–D♭–E♭–F♯–G♯–A–B♭–C?

What riches of harmonic and melodic expression this will make available to our ears is not easily foreseen. But one knows without a doubt, and at a glance, that there are a very large number of new possibilities.

With this discussion the unity of all keys should be considered definitively articulated and grounded. A kaleidoscopic shaking up and mixing of all twelve semitones in the three-mirrored chamber of taste, invention and intention: that is the essence of today's harmony.

But only today's harmony, and not for much longer: for everything suggests there will be a revolution, a further step in the direction of "eternal harmony." Let us recall again that in the eternal harmony the division of the octave is infinite, and then try to approach a bit nearer to infinity. The third tone has already been knocking at our door for some time, yet we have failed to answer it. Whoever experiments, as I have done, however modestly, by inserting two equally distant intervals between a whole tone—whether with the voice or with a violin—and trains the ear and practices their technique, will realize that third tones are completely independent intervals of distinct character, not to be confused with out-of-tune half tones. This offers a more refined chromaticism, which for the moment appears to be based on the whole-tone scale. But if we introduce third tones without mediation, we will lose the half tone, the "minor third," and "perfect fifth"; and that loss would be felt to be greater than the relative gain of an "eighteen-tone third-tone system."

But there is no reason why one must give up half tones because of this new system. If we retain within every whole tone a half tone, then we acquire a second succession of whole tones a half step higher than the first. And if we divide this second succession of whole tones into third tones, then every third tone in the lower succession would have a corresponding third tone in the upper one.

A sixth-tone system is actually created thereby; and we may be assured that at some point there will actually be talk of sixth tones. But the tone system that I have sketched should first train the ear to hear third tones, without giving up half tones.

To sum up: Either we construct two successions of third tones a half tone apart, or three successions of the normal half-tone scale, a third tone apart.

Let us take C as the first tone, in order to distinguish it in some way, and C♯ and D♭ as the two next third tones, (small) c as the first half tone, and (small) c♯ and d♭ as the subsequent third divisions. The following table gives the overall result:

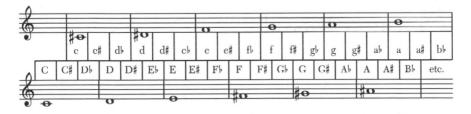

The question of notation seems secondary to me. The question of how the tones are to be produced, on the other hand, is important and pressing. As a happy coincidence, while working on this essay I received an authentic item of news direct from America, which solves the problem in a simple manner. It reports of an invention by Dr. Thaddeus Cahill.[5] This man has constructed a

5. Ray Stannard Baker, "New Music for an Old World. Dr. Thaddeus Cahill's Dynamaphone, an Extraordinary Electrical Invention for Producing Scientifically Perfect Music." *McClure's Magazine*, vol. 28, no. 3 (July, 1906). [Au.]

sizable apparatus which enables one to transform an electrical current into a precisely determined, fixed number of vibrations. Since pitch depends upon the number of vibrations, and the apparatus can be "adjusted" to any desired number, the infinite division of the octave becomes simply the work of a lever, corresponding to the pointer of a quadrant.

Only long and careful experimentation and progressive education of the ear will render this unfamiliar material useful for the coming generation, and for art.

What wonderful hopes and fantastic ideas will become available! Who has not at some time "floated" in a dream, and believed firmly that the dream was real? Let us undertake to return music to its original essence. Let us free it from architectonic, acoustic, and aesthetic dogmas. Let us allow it to be pure invention and experience in harmonies, forms, and tone colors (since invention and experience are not exclusively the provenance of melody). Let us allow it to follow the curve of the rainbow and compete with the clouds in breaking up the rays of the sun. Music is nothing other than nature mirrored in and reflected back by the human soul. It is sounding air, reaching out beyond the air; and it resides just as universally and fully in humanity itself as in all creation. For it can gather into itself and flow outward without losing intensity.

8 Luigi Russolo

Luigi Russolo (1885–1947) was a prominent painter in the early years of the Italian Futurist movement, who gave up painting for music in 1913 when he issued this manifesto. His vision of a new kind of music responsive to modern technology, based on noise rather than pitched sound, far outstripped the recommendations of his Futurist forerunner and dedicatee Balilla Pratella (himself author of two previous manifestos on music), or of Ferruccio Busoni (see the previous entry). Though the noises used were to be produced by specially designed instruments, allowing them to be manipulated and controlled, Russolo argued that they would bring music closer to life itself, a view that placed him in direct opposition to the Romantic ideal of music as "a world apart." Though compositions written by Russolo for noise instruments appeared within a year of this essay, they had little impact on contemporary musical developments. His manifesto nevertheless offers a striking indication of the radical, virtually instantaneous redrawing of musical boundaries that followed the abandonment of traditional tonality in the early years of the century.

The Art of Noises
Futurist Manifesto
(1913)

MY DEAR BALILLA PRATELLA, GREAT FUTURIST COMPOSER:

In the crowded Costanzi Theater, in Rome, while I was listening with my futurist friends Marinetti, Boccioni, and Balla to the orchestral performance of your overwhelming MUSICA FUTURISTA, there came to my mind the idea of a new art: the Art of Noises, a logical consequence of your marvelous innovations.

Life in ancient times was silent. In the nineteenth century, with the invention of machines, Noise was born. Today Noise is triumphant, and reigns supreme over the senses of men. For many centuries life evolved in silence, or, at the most, with but a muted sound. The loudest noises that interrupted this silence were neither violent nor prolonged nor varied, since—if we overlook such exceptional phenomena as hurricanes, tempests, avalanches, waterfalls—nature is silent.

Noises being so scarce, the first *musical sounds* which man succeeded in drawing from a hollow reed or from a stretched string were a new, astonishing, miraculous discovery. By primitive peoples musical sound was ascribed to the gods, regarded as holy, and entrusted to the sole care of the priests, who made use of it to enrich their rites with mystery. Thus was born the conception of musical sound as a thing having an independent existence, a thing different from life and unconnected with it. From this conception resulted an idea of music as a world of fantasy superimposed upon reality, a world inviolate and sacred. It will be readily understood how this idea of music must inevitably have impeded its progress, as compared with that of the other arts. The Greeks themselves—with their theory of music (systematized mathematically by Pythagoras) which permitted the use of a few consonant intervals only—greatly limited music's scope and excluded all possibility of harmony, of which they knew nothing.

The Middle Ages, with their modifications of the Greek tetrachord system, with their Gregorian chants and their folk songs, enriched the art of music. Yet they continued to regard music from the point of view of *linear development in time*—a narrow view of the art which lasted several centuries and which persists in the more complicated polyphony of the Flemish contrapuntists. The *chord* did not exist: the flow of the individual parts was never subordinated to the agreeable effect produced at any given moment by the ensemble of those parts. In a word, the medieval conception of music was horizontal, not vertical.

TEXT: Nicholas Slonimsky, *Music Since 1900*, 4th ed. (New York: Charles Scribner's Sons, 1971), pp. 1298–1302. Translation by Stephen Somervell. Reprinted with permission of Schirmer Books, an imprint of Macmillan Publishing Company.

An interest in the simultaneous union of different sounds, that is, in the chord as a complex sound, developed gradually, passing from the perfect consonance, with a few passing dissonances, to the complicated and persistent dissonances which characterize the music of today.

The art of music at first sought and achieved purity and sweetness of sound; later, it blended diverse sounds, but always with intent to caress the ear with suave harmonics. Today, growing ever more complicated, it seeks those combinations of sounds that fall most dissonantly, strangely, and harshly upon the ear. We thus approach nearer and nearer to the *music of noise.*

This musical evolution parallels the growing multiplicity of machines, which everywhere are assisting mankind. Not only amid the clamor of great cities but even in the countryside, which until yesterday was ordinarily quiet, the machine today has created so many varieties and combinations of noise that pure musical sound—with its poverty and its monotony—no longer awakens any emotion in the hearer.

To excite and exalt our senses, music continued to develop toward the most complex polyphony and the greatest variety of orchestral timbres, or colors, devising the most complicated successions of dissonant chords and preparing in a general way for the creation of MUSICAL NOISE. This evolution toward noise was hitherto impossible. An eighteenth-century ear could not have endured the dissonant intensity of certain chords produced by our modern orchestras—triple the size of the orchestras of that day. But our own ears— trained as they are by the modern world, so rich in variegated noises—not only enjoy these dissonances but demand more and more violent acoustic emotions.

Moreover, musical sound is too limited in qualitative variety of timbre. The most complicated of orchestras reduce themselves to four or five classes of instruments differing in timbre: instruments played with the bow, plucked instruments, brass winds, wood winds, and percussion instruments. So that modern music, in its attempts to produce new kinds of timbre, struggles vainly within this little circle.

We must break out of this narrow circle of pure musical sounds, and conquer the infinite variety of noise-sounds.

Everyone will recognize that every musical sound carries with it an incrustation of familiar and stale sense associations, which predispose the hearer to boredom, despite all the efforts of innovating musicians. We futurists have all deeply loved the music of the great composers. Beethoven and Wagner for many years wrung our hearts. But now we are satiated with them and derive much greater pleasure from ideally combining the noises of street-cars, internal-combustion engines, automobiles, and busy crowds than from re-hearing, for example, the "Eroica" or the "Pastorale."

We cannot see the immense apparatus of the modern orchestra without being profoundly disappointed by its feeble acoustic achievements. Is there anything more absurd than to see twenty men breaking their necks to multiply the meowling of a violin? All this will naturally infuriate the musicomaniacs and perhaps disturb the somnolent atmosphere of our concert halls. Let us enter, as futurists, into one of these institutions for musical anemia. The first measure assails your ear with the boredom of the already-heard and causes you to anticipate the boredom of the measure to come. Thus we sip, from measure to measure, two or three different sorts of boredom, while we await an unusual emotion that never arrives. Meanwhile we are revolted by the monotony of the sensations experienced, combined with the idiotic religious excitement of the listeners, Buddhistically intoxicated by the thousandth repetition of their hypocritical and artificial ecstasy. Away! Let us be gone, since we shall not much longer succeed in restraining a desire to create a new musical realism by a generous distribution of sonorous blows and slaps, leaping nimbly over violins, pianofortes, contrabasses, and groaning organs. Away!

The objection cannot be raised that all noise is loud and disagreeable. I need scarcely enumerate all the small and delicate noises which are pleasing to the ear. To be convinced of their surprising variety one need only think of the rumbling of thunder, the howling of the wind, the roar of a waterfall, the gurgling of a brook, the rustling of leaves, the receding clatter of a horse's hoofs, the bumping of a wagon over cobblestones, and the deep, solemn breathing of a city at night, all the noises made by wild and domesticated animals, and all those that the human mouth can produce, apart from speaking or singing.

Let us wander through a great modern city with our ears more attentive than our eyes, and distinguish the sounds of water, air, or gas in metal pipes, the purring of motors (which breathe and pulsate with an indubitable animalism), the throbbing of valves, the pounding of pistons, the screeching of gears, the clatter of streetcars on their rails, the cracking of whips, the flapping of awnings and flags. We shall amuse ourselves by orchestrating in our minds the noise of the metal shutters of store windows, the slamming of doors, the bustle and shuffle of crowds, the multitudinous uproar of railroad stations, forges, mills, printing presses, power stations, and underground railways.

Nor should the new noises of modern warfare be forgotten. Recently the poet Marinetti, in a letter from the trenches of Adrianopolis, described to me in admirably unfettered language the orchestra of a great battle:

"every 5 seconds siege guns splitting the belly of space with a TZANG-TUMB-TUUUMB *chord revolt of 500 echos to tear it to shreds and scatter it to infinity In the center of these* TZANG-TUMB-TUUUMB *spied out breadth 50 square kilometers leap reports knife-thrusts rapid-fire batteries Violence ferocity regularity this deep bass ascending the strange agitated insane high-pitched notes of battle Fury panting breath eyes ears nostrils open! watching! straining! what joy to see hear smell everything everything taratatata of the machine guns frantically screaming amid bites blows traak-traak whipcracks pic-pac pum-tumb strange goings-on leaps height 200 meters of the infantry Down down at the bottom of the orchestra stirring up pools oxen buffaloes goads wagons pluff plaff rearing of horses flic flac tzing tzing shaak hilarious neighing iiiiiii stamping clanking 3 Bulgarian battalions on the march*

croooc-craaac (lento) *Shumi Maritza or Karvavena* TZANG-TUMB-TUUUMB *toc-toctoctoc* (rapidissimo) *crooc-craac* (lento) *officers' yells resounding like sheets of brass bang here crack there* BOOM *ching chak* (presto) *chacha-cha-cha-chak up down back forth all around above look out for your head chak good shot! Flames flames flames flames flames collapse of the forts over behind the smoke Shukri Pasha talks to 27 forts over the telephone in Turkish in German Hallo! Ibrahim!! Rudolf! Hallo! Hallo, actors playlists echos prompters scenarios of smoke forests applause smell of hay mud dung my feet are frozen numb smell of saltpeter smell of putrefaction Timpani flutes clarinets everywhere low high birds chirping beatitudes shade cheep-cheep-cheep breezes verdure herds dong-dang-dong-ding-baaaa the lunatics are assaulting the musicians of the orchestra the latter soundly thrashed play on Great uproar don't cancel the concert more precision dividing into smaller more minute sounds fragments of echos in the theater area 300 square kilometers Rivers Maritza Tundja stretch out Rudopi Mountains standing up erect boxes balconies 2000 shrapnel spraying exploding snow-white handkerchiefs full of gold* srrrrrrr-TUMB-TUMB *2000 hand-grenades hurled shearing off black-haired heads with their splinters* TZANG-srrrrrr-TUMB-TZANG-TUMB-TUUUMB *the orchestra of the noises of war swells beneath a long-held note of silence in high heaven gilded spherical balloon which surveys the shooting , , ."*

We must fix the pitch and regulate the harmonies and rhythms of these extraordinarily varied sounds. To fix the pitch of noises does not mean to take away from them all the irregularity of tempo and intensity that characterizes their vibrations, but rather to give definite gradation or pitch to the stronger and more predominant of these vibrations. Indeed, noise is differentiated from musical sound merely in that the vibrations that produce it are confused and irregular, both in tempo and in intensity. Every noise has a note—sometimes even a chord—that predominates in the ensemble of its irregular vibrations. Because of this characteristic note it becomes possible to fix the pitch of a given noise, that is, to give it not a single pitch but a variety of pitches, without losing its characteristic quality—its distinguishing timbre. Thus certain noises produced by rotary motion may offer a complete ascending or descending chromatic scale by merely increasing or decreasing the speed of the motion.

Every manifestation of life is accompanied by noise. Noise is therefore familiar to our ears and has the power to remind us immediately of life itself. Musical sound, a thing extraneous to life and independent of it, an occasional and unnecessary adjunct, has become for our ears what a too familiar face is to our eyes. Noise, on the other hand, which comes to us confused and irregular as life itself, never reveals itself wholly but reserves for us innumerable surprises. We are convinced, therefore, that by selecting, co-ordinating, and controlling noises we shall enrich mankind with a new and unsuspected source of pleasure. Despite the fact that it is characteristic of sound to remind us brutally of life, the Art of Noises must not limit itself to reproductive imitation. It will reach its greatest emotional power through the purely acoustic enjoyment which the inspiration of the artist will contrive to evoke from combinations of noises.

These are the futurist orchestra's six families of noises, which we shall soon produce mechanically:

1	2	3	4	5	6
Booms	Whistles	Whispers	Screams	Noises	Voices of
Thunder-	Hisses	Murmurs	Screeches	obtained	animals
claps	Snorts	Mutter-	Rustlings	by per-	and
Explo-		ings	Buzzes	cussion	men:
sions		Bustling	Cracklings	on	Shouts
Crashes		noises	Sounds ob-	metals,	Shrieks
Splashes		Gurgles	tained by	wood,	Groans
Roars			friction	stone,	Howls
				terra-	Laughs
				cotta,	Wheezes
				etc.	Sobs

In this list we have included the most characteristic fundamental noises; the others are but combinations of these.

The rhythmic movements within a single noise are of infinite variety. There is always, as in a musical note, a predominant rhythm, but around this may be perceived numerous secondary rhythms.

CONCLUSIONS

1.—Futurist musicians must constantly broaden and enrich the field of sound. This is a need of our senses. Indeed, we note in present-day composers of genius a tendency toward the most complex dissonances. Moving further and further away from pure musical sound, they have almost reached the *noise sound*. This need and this tendency can only be satisfied *by the supplementary use of noise and its substitution for musical sounds.*

2.—Futurist musicians must substitute for the limited variety of timbres of the orchestral instruments of the day the infinite variety of the timbres of noises, reproduced by suitable mechanisms.

3.—The musician's sensibility, liberating itself from facile, traditional rhythm, must find in noises the way to amplify and renew itself, since each noise offers a union of the most diverse rhythms, in addition to the predominant rhythm.

4.—Since every noise has in its irregular vibrations a general, predominating tone, it will be easy to obtain, in constructing the instruments which imitate it, a sufficiently wide variety of tones, semitones, and quarter-tones. This variety of tones will not deprive any single noise of its characteristic timbre but will merely increase its tessitura, or extension.

5.—The practical difficulties in the construction of these instruments are not serious. Once the mechanical principle producing a given noise is found, one may vary its pitch by applying the general laws of acoustics. For example, in instruments employing rotary motion the speed of rotation will be increased or diminished; in others, the size or tension of the sounding parts will be varied.

6.—Not by means of a succession of noises imitating those of real life, but through a fanciful blending of these varied timbres and rhythms, will the new orchestra obtain the most complex and novel sound effects. Hence every instrument must be capable of varying its pitch and must have a fairly extensive range.

7.—There is an infinite variety of noises. If, today, with perhaps a thousand different kinds of machines, we can distinguish a thousand different noises, tomorrow, as the number of new machines is multiplied, we shall be able to distinguish ten, twenty, or thirty thousand different noises, not merely to be imitated but to be combined as our fancy dictates.

8.—Let us therefore invite young musicians of genius and audacity to listen attentively to all noises, so that they may understand the varied rhythms of which they are composed, their principal tone, and their secondary tones. Then, comparing the varied timbres of noises with those of musical tones, they will be convinced how much more numerous are the former than the latter. Out of this will come not merely an understanding of noises, but even a taste and an enthusiasm for them. Our increased perceptivity, which has already acquired futurist eyes, will then have futurist ears. Thus the motors and machines of our industrial cities may some day be intelligently pitched, so as to make of every factory an intoxicating orchestra of noises.

I submit these statements, my dear Pratella, to your futuristic genius, and invite you to discuss them with me. I am not a professional musician; I have therefore no acoustic prejudices and no works to defend. I am a futurist painter projecting into an art he loves and has studied his desire to renovate all things. Being therefore more audacious than a professional musician could be, caring nought for my seeming incompetence, and convinced that audacity makes all things lawful and all things possible, I have imagined a great renovation of music through the Art of Noises.

Milan, March 11, 1913

9 Charles Ives

Though Charles Ives (1874–1954) was the earliest American composer to acquire widespread international recognition, his fame did not come until after his death. During the first half of the century Ives was almost totally unknown, earning his living outside music as a very successful insurance executive. Yet this professional independence undoubtedly helped foster Ives's remarkable musical daring, allowing him to fuse a style out of apparent contradictions: complexity and simplicity, innovation and conservatism, radical experimentation along with quotation of popular tunes and hymns. This essay was originally conceived as a long footnote to the second movement of Ives's Fourth Symphony, written for its first publication in 1929. The movement features multi-orchestral textures made up of dense strands of contrasting materials combining different keys and tempos in an extraordinarily rich tapestry. Addressing problems raised by the work, Ives discusses spatial separation as an aid for the ear in sorting out simultaneous musical layers. He also considers the effect of distance on sound and the importance of active listening for the comprehension of new music. Above all, Ives advocates exploring possibilities rather than setting down fixed principles: the future of music, in his view, lies "in the way it encourages and extends, rather than limits."

Music and Its Future
(1929)

To give the various instrumental parts of the orchestra in their intended relations is, at times, as conductors and players know, more difficult than it may seem to the casual listener. After a certain point it is a matter which seems to pass beyond the control of any conductor or player into the field of acoustics. In this connection, a distribution of instruments or group of instruments or an arrangement of them at varying distances from the audience is a matter of some interest; as is also the consideration as to the extent it may be advisable and practicable to devise plans in any combination of over two players so that the distance sounds shall travel from the sounding body to the listener's ear may be a favorable element in interpretation. It is difficult to reproduce the sounds and feeling that distance gives to sound wholly by reducing or increasing the number of instruments or by varying their intensities. A brass band playing *pianissimo* across the street is a different-sounding thing from the same band, playing the same piece *forte,* a block or so away. Experiments, even on a limited scale, as when a conductor separates a chorus from the orchestra or places a choir off the stage or in a remote part of the hall, seem to indicate that there are possibilities in this matter that may benefit the presentation of music, not only from the standpoint of clarifying the harmonic, rhythmic, thematic material, etc., but of bringing the inner content to a deeper realization (assuming, for argument's sake, that there is an inner content). Thoreau found a deeper import even in the symphonies of the Concord church bell when its sounds were rarefied through the distant air. "A melody, as it were, imported into the wilderness. . . . at a distance over the woods the sound acquires a cer-

TEXT: *American Composers on American Music,* ed. by Henry Cowell (Palo Alto: Stanford University Press, 1933), pp. 191–98. Copyright renewed 1961 by Henry Cowell. Reprinted with permission of the publishers.

tain vibratory hum as if the pine needles in the horizon were the strings of a harp which it swept. . . . a vibration of the universal lyre, just as the intervening atmosphere makes a distant ridge of earth interesting to the eye by the azure tint it imparts."

A horn over a lake gives a quality of sound and feeling that it is hard to produce in any other way. It has been asked if the radio might not help in this matter. But it functions in a different way. It has little of the ethereal quality. It is but a photographing process which seems only to hand over the fore-ground or parts of it in a clump.

The writer remembers hearing, when a boy, the music of a band in which the players were arranged in two or three groups around the town square. The main group in the bandstand at the center usually played the main themes, while the others, from the neighboring roofs and verandas, played the varia-tions, refrains, and so forth. The piece remembered was a kind of paraphrase of "Jerusalem the Golden," a rather elaborate tone-poem for those days. The bandmaster told of a man who, living nearer the variations, insisted that they were the real music and it was more beautiful to hear the hymn come sifting through them than the other way around. Others, walking around the square, were surprised at the different and interesting effects they got as they changed position. It was said also that many thought the music lost in effect when the piece was played by the band all together, though, I think, the town vote was about even. The writer remembers, as a deep impression, the echo parts from the roofs played by a chorus of violins and voices.

Somewhat similar effects may be obtained indoors by partially inclosing the sounding body. For instance, in a piece of music which is based, on its rhythmic side, principally on a primary and wider rhythmic phrase and a secondary one of shorter span, played mostly simultaneously—the first by a grand piano in a larger room which opens into a smaller one in which there is an upright piano playing the secondary part—if the listener stands in the larger room about equidistant from both pianos but not in a direct line between them (the door between the rooms being partially closed), the contrasting rhythms will be more readily felt by the listener than if the pianos are in the same room. The foregoing suggests something in the way of listening that may have a bearing on the interpretation of certain kinds of music.

In the illustration described above, the listener may choose which of these two rhythms he wishes to hold in his mind as primal. If it is the shorter-spaced one and it is played after the longer has had prominence, and the listener stands in the room with the piano playing this, the music may react in a differ-ent way, not enough to change its character, but enough to show possibilities in this way of listening. As the eye, in looking at a view, may focus on the sky, clouds, or distant outlines, yet sense the color and form of the foreground, and then, by observing the foreground, may sense the distant outlines and color, so, in some similar way, the listener can choose to arrange in his mind the relation of the rhythmic, harmonic, and other material. In other words, in music the ear may play a rôle similar to the eye in the foregoing instance.

Some method similar to that of the inclosed parts of a pipe organ played by the choir or swell manuals might be adopted in some way for an orchestra. That similar plans, as suggested, have been tried by conductors and musicians is quite certain, but the writer knows only of the ways mentioned in the instances above.

When one tries to use an analogy between the arts as an illustration, especially of some technical matter, he is liable to get it wrong. But the general aim of the plans under discussion is to bring various parts of the music to the ear in their relation to each other, as the perspective of a picture brings each object to the eye. The distant hills, in a landscape, range upon range, merge at length into the horizon; and there may be something corresponding to this in the presentation of music. Music seems too often all foreground, even if played by a master of dynamics.

Among the physical difficulties to be encountered are those of retarded sounds that may affect the rhythmic plan unfavorably and of sounds that are canceled as far as some of the players are concerned, though the audience in general may better hear the various groups in their intended relationships. Another difficulty, probably less serious, is suggested by the occasional impression, in hearing sounds from a distance, that the pitch is changed to some extent. That pitch is not changed by the distance a sound travels unless the sounding body is moving at a high velocity is an axiom of acoustics; that is, the number of the vibrations of the fundamental is constant, but the effect does not always sound so—at least to the writer—perhaps because, as the overtones become less acute, the pitch seems to sag a little. There are also difficulties transcending those of acoustics. The cost of trial rehearsals, of duplicate players, and of locations or halls suitably arranged and acoustically favorable is very high nowadays.

The matter of placement is only one of the many things which, if properly examined, might strengthen the means and functions of interpretation, and so forth. The means to examine seem more lacking than the will to examine. Money may travel faster than sound in some directions, but not in the direction of musical experimentation or extension. If only one one-hundredth part of the funds that are expended in this country for the elaborate production of opera, spectacular or otherwise, or of the money invested in soft-headed movies with their music resultants, or in the manufacture of artless substitutes for the soul of man, putting many a true artist in straitened circumstances—if only a small part of these funds could be directed to more of the unsensational but important fields of musical activity, music in general would be the gainer.

Most of the research and other work of extending and distributing new premises, either by the presentation of new works or other means, has been done by societies and individuals against trying obstacles. Organizations like the Pro-Musica Society, with its chapters throughout this and foreign countries, the League of Composers, the Friends of Music (in its work of uncovering neglected premises of the past), and similar societies in the cities of this and other countries, are working with little or no aid from the larger institutions and foundations which could well afford to help them in their cause. The same may be said of individual workers—writers, lecturers, and artists who take upon themselves unremunerative subjects and unremunerative programs for the cause, or, at least, for one of the causes they believe in; the pianist and teacher who, failing to interest any of the larger piano companies in building a quarter-tone piano for the sake of further study in that field, after a hard day's work in the conservatory, takes off his coat and builds the piano with his own hands; the self-effacing singing teacher who, by her genius, character, and unconscious influence, puts a new note of radiance into the life of a shop-girl; the open-minded editor of musical literature and the courageous and unselfish editor of new music quarterlies who choose their subject-matter with the commercial eye closed.

Individual creative work is probably more harmed than helped by artificial stimulants, such as contests, prizes, commissions, and subsidies; but some material aid in better organizing the medium through which the work is done and through which it is interpreted will be of some benefit to music as a whole.

In closing, and to go still farther afield, it may be suggested that in any music based to some extent on more than one or two rhythmic, melodic, harmonic schemes, the hearer has a rather active part to play. Conductors, players, and composers (as a rule or at least some) do the best they can and for that reason get more out of music and, incidentally, more out of life, though, perhaps, not more in their pockets. Many hearers do the same. But there is a type of auditor who will not meet the performers halfway by projecting himself, as it were, into the premises as best he can, and who will furnish nothing more than a ticket and a receptive inertia which may be induced by predilections or static ear habits, a condition perhaps accounting for the fact that some who consider themselves unmusical will get the "gist of" and sometimes get "all set up" by many modern pieces, which those who call themselves musical (this is not saying they're not)—probably because of long acquaintance solely with certain consonances, single tonalities, monorhythms, formal progressions, and struc-ture—do not like. Some hearers of the latter type seem to require pretty con-stantly something, desirable at times, which may be called a kind of ear-easing, and under a limited prescription; if they get it, they put the music down as beautiful; if they don't get it, they put it down and out—to them it is bad, ugly, or "awful from beginning to end." It may or may not be all of this; but whatever its shortcomings, they are not those given by the man who does not listen to what he hears.

"Nature cannot be so easily disposed of," says Emerson. "All of the virtues are not final"—neither are the vices.

The hope of all music—of the future, of the past, to say nothing of the present—will not lie with the partialist who raves about an ultra-modern opera (if there is such a thing) but despises Schubert, or with the party man who viciously maintains the opposite assumption. Nor will it lie in any cult or any idiom or in any artist or any composer. "All things in their variety are of one essence and are limited only by themselves."

The future of music may not lie entirely with music itself, but rather in the way it encourages and extends, rather than limits, the aspirations and ideals of the people, in the way it makes itself a part with the finer things that humanity does and dreams of. Or to put it the other way around, what music is and is to be may lie somewhere in the belief of an unknown philosopher of half a century ago who said: "How can there be any bad music? All music is from heaven. If there is anything bad in it, I put it there—by my implications and limitations. Nature builds the mountains and meadows and man puts in the fences and labels." He may have been nearer right than we think.

10 Edgard Varèse

The French-born composer Edgard Varèse (1883–1965) lived primarily in the United States after 1915, eventually acquiring American citizenship. Epitomizing a new type of twentieth-century composer, Varèse was deeply influenced by his scientific background and committed to exploiting new technology for compositional purposes. The following excerpts were taken from three lectures—the first two dating from the late 1930s, the third from 1959—that were assembled for publication by Varèse's former student Chou Wen-chung. They reflect his belief in the need for artists and scientists to collaborate in expanding the realm of musical sound, his recognition of the close links between creativity and experimentation, his fascination with sound-producing machines, and his new conception of musical form as the interaction of "attractive and repulsive forces."

The Liberation of Sound

I dream of instruments obedient to my thought and which with their contribution of a whole new world of unsuspected sounds, will lend themselves to the exigencies of my inner rhythm.[1]

TEXT: *Contemporary Composers on Contemporary Music*, ed. by Elliott Schwartz and Barney Childs (New York: Holt, Rinehart and Winston, 1967), pp. 196–204. The Varèse entry was compiled and edited by Chou Wen-chung; the first part is from a lecture given at Mary Austin House, Santa Fe, in 1936, the second from a lecture given at the University of Southern California in 1939, and the third from a lecture given at Princeton University in 1959.

1. From *391* (periodical), no. 5 (June, 1917); trans. from the French by Louise Varèse.

NEW INSTRUMENTS AND NEW MUSIC
(1936)

At a time when the very newness of the mechanism of life is forcing our activities and our forms of human association to break with the traditions and the methods of the past in the effort to adapt themselves to circumstances, the urgent choices which we have to make are concerned not with the past but with the future. We cannot, even if we would, live much longer by tradition. The world is changing, and we change with it. The more we allow our minds the romantic luxury of treasuring the past in memory, the less able we become to face the future and to determine the new values which can be created in it.

Art's function is not to prove a formula or an esthetic dogma. Our academic rules were taken out of the living works of former masters. As Debussy has said, *works of art make rules but rules do not make works of art*. Art exists only as a medium of expression.

The emotional impulse that moves a composer to write his scores contains the same element of poetry that incites the scientist to his discoveries. There is solidarity between scientific development and the progress of music. Throwing new light on nature, science permits music to progress—or rather to grow and change with changing times—by revealing to our senses harmonies and sensations before unfelt. On the threshold of beauty science and art collaborate. John Redfield voices the opinion of many when he says: "There should be at least one laboratory in the world where the fundamental facts of music could be investigated under conditions reasonably conducive to success. The interest in music is so widespread and intense, its appeal so intimate and poignant, and its significance for mankind so potent and profound, that it becomes unwise not to devote some portion of the enormous outlay for music to research in its fundamental questions."[2]

When new instruments will allow me to write music as I conceive it, the movement of sound-masses, of shifting planes, will be clearly perceived in my work, taking the place of the linear counterpoint. When these sound-masses collide, the phenomena of penetration or repulsion will seem to occur. Certain transmutations taking place on certain planes will seem to be projected onto other planes, moving at different speeds and at different angles. There will no longer be the old conception of melody or interplay of melodies. The entire work will be a melodic totality. The entire work will flow as a river flows.

We have actually three dimensions in music: horizontal, vertical, and dynamic swelling or decreasing. I shall add a fourth, sound projection—that feeling that sound is leaving us with no hope of being reflected back, a feeling akin to that aroused by beams of light sent forth by a powerful searchlight—for the ear as for the eye, that sense of projection, of a journey into space.

Today with the technical means that exist and are easily adaptable, the differentiation of the various masses and different planes as well as these beams of

2. John Redfield, *Music, a Science and an Art* (New York, 1928). [Chou]

sound, could be made discernible to the listener by means of certain acoustical arrangements. Moreover, such an acoustical arrangement would permit the delimitation of what I call "zones of intensities." These zones would be differentiated by various timbres or colors and different loudnesses. Through such a physical process these zones would appear of different colors and of different magnitude, in different perspectives for our perception. The role of color or timbre would be completely changed from being incidental, anecdotal, sensual or picturesque; it would become an agent of delineation, like the different colors on a map separating different areas, and an integral part of form. These zones would be felt as isolated, and the hitherto unobtainable non-blending (or at least the sensation of non-blending) would become possible.

In the moving masses you would be conscious of their transmutations when they pass over different layers, when they penetrate certain opacities, or are dilated in certain rarefactions. Moreover, the new musical apparatus I envisage, able to emit sounds of any number of frequencies, will extend the limits of the lowest and highest registers, hence new organizations of the vertical resultants: chords, their arrangements, their spacings—that is, their oxygenation. Not only will the harmonic possibilities of the overtones be revealed in all their splendor, but the use of certain interferences created by the partials will represent an appreciable contribution. The never-before-thought-of use of the inferior resultants and of the differential and additional sounds may also be expected. An entirely new magic of sound!

I am sure that the time will come when the composer, after he has graphically realized his score, will see this score automatically put on a machine that will faithfully transmit the musical content to the listener. As frequencies and new rhythms will have to be indicated on the score, our actual notation will be inadequate. The new notation will probably be seismographic. And here it is curious to note that at the beginning of two eras, the Mediaeval primitive and our own primitive era (for we are at a new primitive stage in music today), we are faced with an identical problem: the problem of finding graphic symbols for the transposition of the composer's thought into sound. At a distance of more than a thousand years we have this analogy: our still primitive electrical instruments find it necessary to abandon staff notation and to use a kind of seismographic writing much like the early ideographic writing originally used for the voice before the development of staff notation. Formerly the curves of the musical line indicated the melodic fluctuations of the voice; today the machine-instrument requires precise design indications.

MUSIC AS AN ART-SCIENCE
(1939)

The philosophers of the Middle Ages separated the liberal arts into two branches: the *trivium,* or the Arts of Reason as applied to language—grammar, rhetoric and dialectic—and the *quadrivium,* or the Arts of Pure Reason, which today we would call the Sciences, and among which music has its place in the company of mathematics, geometry and astronomy.

Today, music is more apt to be rated with the arts of the *trivium*. At least, it seems to me that too much emphasis is placed on what might be called the grammar of music.

At different times and in different places music has been considered either as an Art or as a Science. In reality music partakes of both. Hoëne Wronsky and Camille Durutte,[3] in their treatise on harmony in the middle of the last century, were obliged to coin new words when they assigned music its place as an "Art-Science," and defined it as "the corporealization of the intelligence that is in sounds." Most people rather think of music solely as an art. But when you listen to music do you ever stop to realize that you are being subjected to a physical phenomenon? Not until the air between the listener's ear and the instrument has been disturbed does music occur. Do you realize that every time a printed score is brought to life it has to be re-created through the different sound machines, called musical instruments, that make up our orchestras [and] are subject to the same laws of physics as any other machine? In order to anticipate the result, a composer must understand the mechanics of the instruments and must know just as much as possible about acoustics. Music must live in sound. On the other hand, the possession of a perfectly pitched ear is only of a relative importance to a composer. What a composer must have, must have been born with, is what I call the "inner ear," the ear of imagination. The inner ear is the composer's Pole Star! Let us look at music as it is more popularly considered—as an Art—and inquire: what is composition?

Brahms has said that composition is the *organizing of disparate elements*. But what is the situation of the would-be creator today, shaken by the powerful impulses and rhythms of this age? How is he to accomplish this "organizing" in order to express himself and his epoch? Where is he to find those "disparate elements"? Are they to be found in the books he studies in his various courses in harmony, composition, and orchestration? Are they in the great works of the great masters that he pores over with love and admiration and, with all his might, means to emulate? Unfortunately too many composers have been led to believe that these elements can be found as easily as that.[4]

Eric Temple Bell, in a book called *The Search for Truth*, says: "Reverence for the past no doubt is a virtue that has had its uses, but if we are to go forward the reverent approach to old difficulties is the wrong one!" I should say that in music the "reverent approach" has done a great deal of harm: it has kept would-

3. Hoëne Wronsky (1778–1853), also known as Joseph Marie Wronsky, was a Polish philosopher and mathematician, known for his system of *Messianism*. Camille Durutte (1803–1881), in his *Technie Harmonique* (1876), a treatise on "musical mathematics," quoted extensively from the writings of Wronsky. [Chou]

4. This, Varèse said in the same lecture, "undoubtedly accounts for one of the most deplorable trends of music today—the impotent return to the formulas of the past that has been called neo-Classicism." [Chou]

be appreciators from really appreciating! And it has created the music critic! The very basis of creative work is irreverence! The very basis of creative work is experimentation—bold experimentation. You have only to turn to the revered past for the corroboration of my contention. The links in the chain of tradition are formed by men who have all been revolutionists! To the student of music I should say that the great examples of the past should serve as spring-boards from which he may leap free, into his own future.

In every domain of art, a work that corresponds to the need of its day carries a message of social and cultural value. Preceding ages show us that changes in art occur because societies and artists have new needs. New aspirations ema-nate from every epoch. The artist, being always of his own time, is influenced by it and, in turn, is an influence. It is the artist who crystallizes his age—who fixes his age in history. Contrary to general notion, the artist is never ahead of his own time, but is simply the only one who is not way behind.

Now let me come back to the subject of music as an Art-Science. The raw material of music is sound. That is what the "reverent approach" has made most people forget—even composers. Today, when science is equipped to help the composer realize what was never before possible—all that Beethoven dreamed, all that Berlioz gropingly imagined possible—the composer contin-ues to be obsessed by the traditions that are nothing but the limitations of his predecessors. Composers, like everyone else today, are delighted to use the many gadgets continually put on the market for our daily comfort. But when they hear sounds that no violins, no woodwind or percussion instruments of the orchestra can produce, it does not occur to them to demand those sounds of science. Yet science is even now equipped to give them everything they may require.

Personally, for my conceptions, I need an entirely new medium of expres-sion: a sound-*producing* machine (not a sound-*reproducing* one). Today it is possible to build such a machine with only a certain amount of added research.

If you are curious to know what such a machine could do that the orchestra with its man-powered instruments cannot do, I shall try briefly to tell you: whatever I write, whatever my message, it will reach the listener unadulterated by "interpretation." It will work something like this: after a composer has set down his score on paper by means of a new graphic notation, he will then, with the collaboration of a sound engineer, transfer the score directly to this electric machine. After that, anyone will be able to press a button to release the music exactly as the composer wrote it—exactly like opening a book.

And here are the advantages I anticipate from such a machine: liberation from the arbitrary, paralyzing tempered system; the possibility of obtaining any number of cycles or, if still desired, subdivisions of the octave, and conse-quently the formation of any desired scale; unsuspected range in low and high registers; new harmonic splendors obtainable from the use of sub-harmonic combinations now impossible; the possibility of obtaining any differentiation of timbre, of sound-combinations; new dynamics far beyond the present human-powered orchestra; a sense of sound-projection in space by means of the emission of sound in any part or in many parts of the hall, as may be required by the score; cross-rhythms unrelated to each other, treated simultaneously, or, to use the old word, "contrapuntally," since the machine would be able to beat any number of desired notes, any subdivision of them, omission or fraction of them—all these in a given unit of measure or time that is humanly impossible to attain.

In conclusion, let me read to you something that Romain Rolland said in his *Jean Christophe* and which remains pertinent today. Jean Christophe, the hero of his novel, was a prototype of the modern composer and was modeled on different composers whom Romain Rolland knew—among others, myself.

> The difficulty began when he tried to cast his ideas in the ordinary musical forms: he made the discovery that none of the ancient molds were suited to them; if he wished to fix his visions with fidelity he had to begin by forgetting all the music he had heard, all that he had written, to make a clean slate of all the formalism he had learned, of traditional technique, to throw away those crutches of impotency, that bed, all prepared for the laziness of those who, fleeing the fatigue of thinking for themselves, lie down in other men's thoughts.[5]

RHYTHM, FORM AND CONTENT
(1959)

Because for so many years I crusaded for new instruments[6] with what may have seemed fanatical zeal, I have been accused of desiring nothing less than the destruction of all musical instruments and even of all performers. This is, to say the least, an exaggeration. Our new liberating medium—the electronic—is not meant to replace the old musical instruments, which composers, including myself, will continue to use. Electronics is an additive, not a destructive, factor in the art and science of music. It is because new instruments have been constantly added to the old ones that Western music has such a rich and varied patrimony.

Grateful as we must be for the new medium, we should not expect miracles from machines. The machine can give out only what we put into it. The musical principles remain the same whether a composer writes for orchestra or tape. Rhythm and form are still his most important problems and the two elements in music most generally misunderstood.

Rhythm is too often confused with metrics. Cadence or the regular succes-

5. Romain Rolland (1866–1944), *Jean Christophe* (1904–12); published in English as *John Christopher* (G. Cannan, 1910–13). [Chou]
6. As early as 1916, Varèse was quoted in the New York *Morning Telegraph* as saying: "Our musical alphabet must be enriched. We also need new instruments very badly. . . . In my own works I have always felt the need of new mediums of expression . . . which can lend themselves to every expression of thought and can keep up with thought." And in the *Christian Science Monitor,* in 1922: "The composer and the electrician will have to labor together to get it." [Chou]

sion of beats and accents has little to do with the rhythm of a composition. Rhythm is the element in music that gives life to the work and holds it together. It is the element of stability, the generator of form. In my own works, for instance, rhythm derives from the simultaneous interplay of unrelated elements that intervene at calculated, but not regular, time-lapses. This corresponds more nearly to the definition of rhythm in physics and philosophy as "a succession of alternate and opposite or correlative states."

As for form, Busoni once wrote: "Is it not singular to demand of a composer originality in all things and to forbid it as regards form? No wonder that once he becomes original, he is accused of formlessness."[7]

The misunderstanding has come from thinking of form as a point of departure, a pattern to be followed, a mold to be filled. Form is a result—the result of a process. Each of my works discovers its own form. I could never have fitted them into any of the historical containers. If you want to fill a rigid box of a definite shape, you must have something to put into it that is the same shape and size or that is elastic or soft enough to be made to fit in. But if you try to force into it something of a different shape and harder substance, even if its volume and size are the same, it will break the box. My music cannot be made to fit into any of the traditional music boxes.

Conceiving musical form as a *resultant*—the result of a process—I was struck by what seemed to me an analogy between the formation of my compositions and the phenomenon of crystallization. Let me quote the crystallographic description given me by Nathaniel Arbiter, professor of mineralogy at Columbia University:

> The crystal is characterized by both a definite external form and a definite internal structure. The internal structure is based on the unit of crystal which is the smallest grouping of the atoms that has the order and composition of the substance. The extension of the unit into space forms the whole crystal. But in spite of the relatively limited variety of internal structures, the external forms of crystals are limitless.

Then Mr. Arbiter added in his own words:

> Crystal form itself is a *resultant* [the very word I have always used in reference to musical form] rather than a primary attribute. Crystal form is the consequence of the interaction of attractive and repulsive forces and the ordered packing of the atom.

This, I believe, suggests, better than any explanation I could give, the way my works are formed. There is an idea, the basis of an internal structure, expanded and split into different shapes or groups of sound constantly changing in shape, direction, and speed, attracted and repulsed by various forces. The form of the work is the consequence of this interaction. Possible musical forms are as limitless as the exterior forms of crystals.

Connected with this contentious subject of form in music is the really futile

7. Ferruccio Busoni, *Sketch of a New Esthetic of Music,* trans. by Dr. Theodore Baker (New York, 1911), reprinted in *Three Classics in the Aesthetics of Music* (New York, Dover Publications, 1962), p. 79. [Chou] See also this collection, pp. 52–53.

question of the difference between form and content. There is no difference. Form and content are one. Take away form, and there is no content, and if there is no content, there is only a rearrangement of musical patterns, but no form. Some people go so far as to suppose that the content of what is called program music is the subject described. This subject is only the ostensible motive I have spoken of, which in program music the composer chooses to reveal. The content is still only music. The same senseless bickering goes on over style and content in poetry. We could very well transfer to the question of music what Samuel Beckett has said of Proust: "For Proust the quality of language is more important than any system of ethics or esthetics. Indeed he makes no attempt to dissociate form from content. The one is the concretion of the other—the revelation of a world."[8] To reveal a new world is the function of creation in all the arts, but the act of creation defies analysis. A composer knows about as little as anyone else about where the substance of his work comes from.

As an epigraph to his book,[9] Busoni uses this verse from a poem by the Danish poet Oelenschläger:

> What seek you? Say! And what do you expect?
> I know not what; the Unknown I would have!
> What's known to me is endless; I would go
> Beyond the known: The last word still is wanting.
>
> (*Der mächtige Zauberer*)

And so it is for any artist.

8. Samuel Beckett, *Proust* (1957).
9. Busoni, *Sketch*, p. 75.

11 Pierre Boulez

As both composer and conductor, Pierre Boulez (b. 1926) has occupied an important position in music of the second half of the twentieth century. In this essay, published in 1957 but based on material dating to the early 1950s, Boulez echoes ideas voiced by Edgard Varèse in the previous essay, but they are now delivered within the context of a rapidly emerging new technology that seems to make the possibilities for future sonic development virtually unlimited. Boulez interprets earlier twentieth-century music in essentially negative terms, as destroying an old language and thus providing the necessary groundwork for the creation of a new and less restricted one. The music of his own day, on the other hand, he sees as poised on "the brink of an undreamt-of sound world," which he feels can be fully realized only through serial control and electro-acoustical extensions. These ideas would assume more concrete form in 1976 when Boulez founded the Institute for Research and Electro-acoustical Coordination (IRCAM) in Paris, dedicated to bringing together scientists and musicians in joint creative enterprises.

Tendencies in Recent Music
(1957)

When one considers what has happened to the language of music, it is obvious that we are at present in a period of stocktaking and reorganization, which has been preceded by a period of destructive experiment in which tonality and regular metre have been abolished. There has also come about a curious phenomenon of dissociation in the evolution of music.

On the one hand, Stravinsky developed rhythm on entirely new structural principles, based on the dissymmetry, independence, and development of rhythmic cells, but remaining trapped, linguistically, in what one could call an impasse (since we know it ended up as one) but which I prefer to call a survival, and even a reinforced survival where the processes of aggregation round very elementary poles give the vocabulary unaccustomed force.

On the other hand, in Vienna at the same time a new language was being formulated, patiently and by stages; first, the dissolution of tonal attraction—the opposite step to the one taken by Stravinsky—then functional ultra-thematicization, which was to lead to the discovery of serialism, a method used in quite different ways by Schoenberg, Berg, and Webern. The only one, in truth, who was conscious of a new dimension in sound, of the abolition of the horizontal–vertical opposition in favour of a view of the series as simply a way of giving structure, or *texture*, to musical space, was Webern, who arrived at this position, when all is said and done, by specious means which in some transitional works I find disturbing; by trying, on the basis of regular canonic forms, to use the series as a contrapuntal device with harmonic controls. Later on, he adopted a functional distribution of intervals which, in my opinion, marks a crucial moment in the history of the language. On the other hand, the rhythmic element has no connection at all with the serial technique.

It should perhaps be pointed out that this phenomenon of dissociation applied to both aspects of the language. For his rhythmic discoveries, Stravinsky needed a simpler and more malleable material with which to experiment. In the same way, Webern could only concentrate on a proper morphology by, to a considerable extent, ignoring rhythmic structure.

Admittedly this is a little too schematic to be completely accurate. Which is why, to test it, I should like to follow a less well-worn path and start by playing truant with the music of Varèse, that lone ranger whose conception of music has happily never fitted into any orthodoxy. This music, it has to be recognized,

TEXT: *Stocktakings from an Apprenticeship*, ed. by Paule Thévenin, trans. by Stephen Walsh (Oxford: Clarendon Press, 1991), pp. 173–79.

is essentially concerned with the physical phenomenon of sound itself; I imagine Varèse preoccupied constantly with the effect of chords as objects; chord function no longer has anything to do with traditional harmony, but becomes a property of the whole body of sound, calculated as a function of natural harmonics, inferior resonances, and the various tensions necessary to the vitality of such a body. Hence the remarkable dynamic qualities so often observed in the music of Varèse. One may notice the flat rejection of anything that could be called expressive nuance, in the pejorative sense (a constraint inherited from certain aspects of *fin-de-siècle* romanticism); dynamics here play the role of tensor, an essential factor for the optimum rendering of a note-aggregate, and a far more highly evolved role than usual, since, instead of remaining at the purely affective level, they participate in the actual harmonic structure, from which they cannot be detached without completely destroying the equilibrium of the music thus composed. These two points—the abolition of the traditional function of chords in favour of their intrinsic quality as sound, and the incorporation of dynamics as an element of structure—can be combined into a single overriding preoccupation of Varèse: acoustics.

Taking acoustics as the basis of all sound relationships, Varèse set himself to discover in what way they could control a musical construction. This led him—as an isolated experiment—to write for percussion alone *(Ionisation)*.

We should finally note of Varèse—for the moment only in passing—his profound rejection of equal temperament, which he called 'the octave's cheese-wire'.[1] It is well known that equal temperament is the most artificial thing possible, and that it was adopted in the eighteenth century merely as a convenience. If it was temperament that enabled the full flowering of western music—which it is hardly possible to forget—it must be admitted that it remains a purely western phenomenon, and that in other musical civilizations there has never been any question of temperament, just as there has never been any question of disallowing any unit interval other than the semitone. For Varèse, with his acoustical attitude to musical structure, temperament was obviously pure nonsense. Recently he has even spoken of non-octave-based scales, which reproduce on a *spiral* principle or, to put it more clearly, a principle by which the transposition of pitch scales no longer works in octaves, but according to different intervallic functions.

In the next generation an American musician, John Cage, came to believe that, if it was such an effort to avoid the clichés of tonal music, this was largely the fault of our instruments, which were specifically designed to meet the needs of tonality. He thus turned, like Varèse, to percussion, with its world of unpitched sounds, in which rhythm is the only architectonic element of sufficient power to allow a valid non-improvised structure—apart, obviously, from the timbre and acoustical relations which exist between the different categories of such instruments (skin, wood, or metal).

1. Orig. "le fil à couper l'octave." [Tr.]

At the opposite pole to this music which deliberately does not concern itself with pitch or registral relations, stands the work of Webern, whose main preoccupation was, on the contrary, to find a new way of structuring pitch. Certainly the most important figure of our time, and the threshold to contemporary music, in the sense that he rethought the whole notion of polyphonic music in serial terms (terms which he himself established through his own music by assigning an increasingly primary role to interval as such, and even to the sound in isolation): such is Webern. Throughout his work one senses an urge to reduce the articulation of the discourse as far as possible to pure serial functions. In his view, the purity and rigour of the experiment had to be preserved at all costs. Increasingly he enlarged his field of musical possibilities, without thereby losing any of his fanatical intransigence. And from this moment there irrupt into the acquired sensibility the first rudiments of a musical mentality that cannot be reduced to the basic schemas of previous sound-worlds. Here it really seems a question of an upheaval comparable to what the passage from monody to polyphony may have been, that is a radically new conception of the available sound-space. But, while melody remained the fundamental element at the heart of polyphony, one can say that in the serial method as conceived by Webern it is polyphony itself which becomes the basic element: and that is how his way of thinking comes to transcend the notions of vertical and horizontal. So the significance of Webern's work, its historical *raison d'être*—quite apart from its indisputable intrinsic value—is to have introduced a new mode of musical being.

This mode lacks, however, the rigour necessary to its complete fulfilment. While Webern concentrated on pitch structure—eminently a western problem—matters of rhythm interested him much less, as did dynamics, even though dynamics do play a certain structural role in his music.

Recently, Olivier Messiaen has crystallized these scattered preoccupations of valid contemporary music in his *Mode de valeurs et d'intensités,* in which the idea of global—in this case modal—organization is applied not only to register, but equally to duration (that is to say, the rhythmic organization of music time), dynamics (that is, the amplitude of the sound) and attack (or the initial profile of the sound). With Varèse, remember, dynamics played a structural role by virtue of his preoccupation with acoustics; here, in Messiaen, dynamics, like duration and pitch, are organized as an actual compositional function, which is to say that, over and above acoustics as such, there is a concern to integrate all sound elements into a study of form.

The one area still needing to be explored is the world of non-tempered sound. Why indeed should one regard as inviolate a decision which has rendered immense service but has no further *raison d'être,* since the tonal organization which required such standardization is now practically destroyed? Admittedly the question of instruments is a by no means negligible obstacle to the development of a musical thought based on non-tempered intervals and concerned with such things as complex tones and sound-complexes. All the acoustical approximations which have gradually accumulated in the course of western musical evolution ought to disappear, since they are no longer needed; but how, for the moment, do we get round the problem of sound-production?

•   •   •

The prepared piano of John Cage provides an artisan solution, embryonic, but none the less plausible. At least the prepared piano has the great virtue of making already tangible a sound universe which we would have for the time being to renounce, given its difficulty of realization. The piano thus becomes an instrument capable, by means of an artisan tablature, of yielding complex frequency patterns: artisan tablature since, to prepare the piano, objects of various materials such as metal, wood, or rubber are inserted between the strings at certain critical points along their length, materials which modify the four characteristics of the sound produced by a vibrating string: duration, amplitude, frequency, and timbre. If we bear in mind that, for much of the piano, any given key has three corresponding strings, and if we then imagine these various modifying materials at critical points on these three strings, we can get an idea of the variety and complexity of the sounds produced by such means. The route is marked out from here towards a future evolution of music in which, with the help of increasingly perfected tablatures, instruments will be able to assist in the creation of a new sound-world which needs and demands them.

If now, after this excursion into a region where Webern never ventured, we return to his work, we will find in it an extraordinary preoccupation with timbre and with new ways of using it. The musical evidence, of which I spoke earlier, is by no means neglected at this level. Orchestration no longer has a purely decorative value, but participates in the actual structure, providing a particularly effective way of relating and synthesizing pitch, duration and dynamics. To such an extent that, with Webern, we are no longer talking about the historical orchestra, but must seek out new and essential orchestral functions.

•   •   •

We can now see how urgent it is to gather up our various investigations, generalize our discoveries, and expand the resources of this now known technique, which, having hitherto been largely an instrument of destruction—and hence bound up with what it wanted to destroy—has now to be given its autonomy, by linking rhythmic to serial structures through a common organization which embraces not only duration, but also timbre and dynamics. It is easy to imagine the bewildering range of discoveries waiting to be made through constructive research. The development of musical thought is called upon to fling itself powerfully in Webern's wake, since it is possible to justify an entire musical organization in terms of the serial principle, from the tiniest component up to the complete structure.

Such serial thinking can at last escape the number twelve, in which it has been imprisoned for so long and with such good reason, since it was precisely the twelve notes, that is the chromatic scale, which allowed the transition from the increasingly feeble structure of tonality to that of serialism. But in the end it is not the twelve notes that are paramount, so much as the serial idea itself, the idea, that is, of a sound universe, specific to each work, derived from a phenomenon that is undifferentiated until the moment the series is chosen, at which point it becomes unique and essential. The permutations thereby defined on the basis of the original permutation can be generalized into whatever sound-space is given as material, which is why we should speak of series of non-tempered intervals, even of frequency characteristics, and with no predetermined number, leading eventually to defining intervals other than the octave. (And this brings us back to Varèse.) There is then no longer anything incompatible between micro-intervals, non-tempered intervals, and the familiar twelve semitones.

Similarly with rhythm, one can envisage not only rational divisions of the unit, but also irrational fractions which would mainly be used within the basic unit. If we want to break the unit down into fractions—a necessity we face, for example, when superimposing series of units and series of durations, which makes performance virtually impossible and notation unrealizable except by recourse to a scale of the unit and its fractions—if, then, we want to introduce a concept of total rhythmic freedom, what can we do except turn to the machine?

We are here on the brink of an undreamt-of sound-world, rich in possibilities and still practically unexplored, whose implications we are only now beginning to perceive. We may notice one happy coincidence in the present state of musical thinking (but perhaps it is not mere chance: certainly we should not be surprised that the musicians in different countries who take most interest in these developments are the ones who unite a certain body of opinion): this coincidence lies in the need for certain means of realization having arisen at the very moment when electro-acoustic techniques are in a position to supply them. In effect, there are two ways of producing a sound: either with a natural sounding body or through artificial production by electronics. Or, in between the two, the electro-acoustical transformation of a sound produced by a natural sounding body. In the two extreme cases, the procedure envisaged is radically different; the sounding body produces sounds whose essential definition is timbre, duration, register, and the limits of its dynamic range; if we make use of a natural sounding body, we must first take account of the possibilities it offers, since the only possible modifications are in dynamics and variations in attack and decay: we therefore need an ensemble of sounding bodies each with a different set of characteristics. These characteristics exist in a virtual state in the sounding body, within precise and well-understood limits. But if we think of the domain of electronics, it is pretty obvious that we are dealing initially with a non-limitation of possibilities, whether of timbre, of register, of dynamics, or of duration; we thus create the characteristics of each sound, characteristics which depend on the overall structure; the sound is reciprocally linked to the work as the work is linked to the sound. The far end of the serial perspective which was already proposing a universe peculiar to each work, but solely from the point of view of serialized frequencies, thus brings us into the domain of sound itself, and the actual interior of the sound.

Rarely, in the whole history of music, could we have assisted at a more radical development, or one which confronts the musician with a more unfamiliar requirement: the choice of sound material, not merely for decorative effect or for the musical evidence—a banal version of the problem of orchestration or instrumentation—but the real choice of material for its intrinsic structural properties. The composer becomes performer, in a field where performance and realization have an enhanced importance, and like a painter he acts directly on the quality of the realization.

Moreover, questions of tempered or non-tempered, vertical or horizontal, no longer have any meaning: we arrive instead at the "sound-figure," which is the most general object that presents itself to the composer's imagination: sound-figure, or even, with the new techniques, sound-object. If in fact we extend the notion of series to the way the basic temporal unfolding acts upon the organizational differences between these objects—if, that is, we expand it to include the modifications that can be made to such objects—we shall have established a category of works free at last from all constraint outside what is specific to themselves. Quite an abrupt transformation, when one considers that previously music was a collection of codified possibilities applicable to any work indifferently.

These observations are nevertheless still premature; we are merely on the road to such a music. The crucial research into the intrinsic qualities of sound has yet to be undertaken; the perfected and manageable equipment necessary to the composition of such works has yet to be built. All the same, the ideas are not so utopian that we can ignore them; it is even probable that the growing interest aroused by the epiphany of this unfamiliar and undreamt-of sound-world will only hasten their solution. We may modestly hope to be the first practitioners.

III

COMPOSITIONAL APPROACHES

12 Arnold Schoenberg

Mirroring the general esthetic transformations in Western music following the First World War, Arnold Schoenberg moved away from the extreme "intuitive" approach he favored in the prewar years (compare pp. 13–21, passim). In this excerpt from a lecture dating from 1934 (that achieved final form in 1941), Schoenberg retains his earlier belief in creation as "inspiration and perfection" but now stresses clarity, communication, and the hard work required to bring a compositional vision to realization. And looking back on the music he composed during the early years of the century, written as he was breaking away from traditional tonality, he finds limitations stemming from the absence of the constructive force of traditional tonality: either the pieces were short or they required texts to provide large-scale coherence. Schoenberg justifies his twelve-tone system, developed in the early postwar years, as having been a necessary response to the need for "conscious control" over the new chromatic material, providing post-tonal music with a resource "comparable to the regularity and logic of the earlier harmony."

FROM Composition with Twelve Tones
(1941)

I

To understand the very nature of creation one must acknowledge that there was no light before the Lord said: "Let there be Light." And since there was not yet light, the Lord's omniscience embraced a vision of it which only His omnipotence could call forth.

We poor human beings, when we refer to one of the better minds among us as a creator, should never forget what a creator is in reality.

A creator has a vision of something which has not existed before this vision.

And a creator has the power to bring his vision to life, the power to realize it.

In fact, the concept of creator and creation should be formed in harmony with the Divine Model; inspiration and perfection, wish and fulfilment, will and accomplishment coincide spontaneously and simultaneously. In Divine Creation there were no details to be carried out later; 'There was Light' at once and in its ultimate perfection.

Alas, human creators, if they be granted a vision, must travel the long path between vision and accomplishment; a hard road where, driven out of Paradise, even geniuses must reap their harvest in the sweat of their brows.

TEXT: *Style and Idea*, ed. by Leonard Stein, trans. by Leo Black (Berkeley: University of California Press, 1975), pp. 214–26.

Alas, it is one thing to envision in a creative instant of inspiration and it is another thing to materialize one's vision by painstakingly connecting details until they fuse into a kind of organism.

Alas, suppose it becomes an organism, a homunculus or a robot, and possesses some of the spontaneity of a vision; it remains yet another thing to organize this form so that it becomes a comprehensible message "to whom it may concern."

II

Form in the arts, and especially in music, aims primarily at comprehensibility. The relaxation which a satisfied listener experiences when he can follow an idea, its development, and the reasons for such development is closely related, psychologically speaking, to a feeling of beauty. Thus, artistic value demands comprehensibility, not only for intellectual, but also for emotional satisfaction. However, the creator's *idea* has to be presented, whatever the *mood* he is impelled to evoke.

Composition with twelve tones has no other aim than comprehensibility. In view of certain events in recent musical history, this might seem astonishing, for works written in this style have failed to gain understanding in spite of the new medium of organization. Thus, should one forget that contemporaries are not final judges, but are generally overruled by history, one might consider this method doomed. But, though it seems to increase the listener's difficulties, it compensates for this deficiency by penalizing the composer. For composing thus does not become easier, but rather ten times more difficult. Only the better-prepared composer can compose for the better-prepared music lover.

III

The method of composing with twelve tones grew out of a necessity.

In the last hundred years, the concept of harmony has changed tremendously through the development of chromaticism. The idea that one basic tone, the root, dominated the construction of chords and regulated their succession—the concept of *tonality*—had to develop first into the concept of *extended tonality*. Very soon it became doubtful whether such a root still remained the center to which every harmony and harmonic succession must be referred. Furthermore, it became doubtful whether a tonic appearing at the beginning, at the end, or at any other point really had a constructive meaning. Richard Wagner's harmony had promoted a change in the logic and constructive power of harmony. One of its consequences was the so-called impressionistic use of harmonies, especially practised by Debussy. His harmonies, without constructive meaning, often served the coloristic purpose of expressing moods and pictures. Moods and pictures, though extra-musical, thus became constructive elements, incorporated in the musical functions; they produced a sort of emotional comprehensibility. In this way, tonality was already dethroned in practice, if not in theory. This alone would perhaps not have caused a radical change in compositional technique. However, such a change became necessary when there occurred simultaneously a development which ended in what I call the *emancipation of the dissonance.*

The ear had gradually become acquainted with a great number of dissonances, and so had lost the fear of their "sense-interrupting" effect. One no longer expected preparations of Wagner's dissonances or resolutions of Strauss's discords; one was not disturbed by Debussy's non-functional harmonies, or by the harsh counterpoint of later composers. This state of affairs led to a freer use of dissonances comparable to classic composers' treatment of diminished seventh chords, which could precede and follow any other harmony, consonant or dissonant, as if there were no dissonance at all.

What distinguishes dissonances from consonances is not a greater or lesser degree of beauty, but a greater or lesser degree of *comprehensibility.* In my *Harmonielehre* I presented the theory that dissonant tones appear later among the overtones, for which reason the ear is less intimately acquainted with them. This phenomenon does not justify such sharply contradictory terms as concord and discord. Closer acquaintance with the more remote consonances—the dissonances, that is—gradually eliminated the difficulty of comprehension and finally admitted not only the emancipation of dominant and other seventh chords, diminished sevenths and augmented triads, but also the emancipation of Wagner's, Strauss's, Moussorgsky's, Debussy's, Mahler's, Puccini's, and Reger's more remote dissonances.

The term *emancipation of the dissonance* refers to its comprehensibility, which is considered equivalent to the consonance's comprehensibility. A style based on this premise treats dissonances like consonances and renounces a tonal centre. By avoiding the establishment of a key modulation is excluded, since modulation means leaving an established tonality and establishing *another* tonality.

The first compositions in this new style were written by me around 1908 and, soon afterwards, by my pupils, Anton von Webern and Alban Berg. From the very beginning such compositions differed from all preceding music, not only harmonically but also melodically, thematically, and motivically. But the foremost characteristics of these pieces *in statu nascendi* were their extreme expressiveness and their extraordinary brevity. At that time, neither I nor my pupils were conscious of the reasons for these features. Later I discovered that our sense of form was right when it forced us to counterbalance extreme emotionality with extraordinary shortness. Thus, subconsciously, consequences were drawn from an innovation which, like every innovation, destroys while it produces. New colourful harmony was offered; but much was lost.

Formerly the harmony had served not only as a source of beauty, but, more important, as a means of distinguishing the features of the form. For instance, only a consonance was considered suitable for an ending. Establishing functions demanded different successions of harmonies than roving functions; a bridge, a transition, demanded other successions than a codetta; harmonic variation could be executed intelligently and logically only with due consideration of the fundamental meaning of the harmonies. Fulfilment of all these functions—comparable to the effect of punctuation in the construction of sentences, of subdivision into paragraphs, and of fusion into chapters—could scarcely be assured with chords whose constructive values had not as yet been explored. Hence, it seemed at first impossible to compose pieces of complicated organization or of great length.

A little later I discovered how to construct larger forms by following a text or a poem. The differences in size and shape of its parts and the change in character and mood were mirrored in the shape and size of the composition, in its dynamics and tempo, figuration and accentuation, instrumentation and orchestration. Thus the parts were differentiated as clearly as they had formerly been by the tonal and structural functions of harmony.

IV

Formerly the use of the fundamental harmony had been theoretically regulated through recognition of the effects of root progressions. This practice had grown into a subconsciously functioning *sense of form* which gave a real composer an almost somnambulistic sense of security in creating, with utmost precision, the most delicate distinctions of formal elements.

Whether one calls oneself conservative or revolutionary, whether one composes in a conventional or progressive manner, whether one tries to imitate old styles or is destined to express new ideas—whether one is a good composer or not—one must be convinced of the infallibility of one's own fantasy and one must believe in one's own inspiration. Nevertheless, the desire for a conscious control of the new means and forms will arise in every artist's mind; and he will wish to know *consciously* the laws and rules which govern the forms which he has conceived "as in a dream." Strongly convincing as this dream may have been, the conviction that these new sounds obey the laws of nature and of our manner of thinking—the conviction that order, logic, comprehensibility and form cannot be present without obedience to such laws—forces the composer along the road of exploration. He must find, if not laws or rules, at least ways to justify the dissonant character of these harmonies and their successions.

V

After many unsuccessful attempts during a period of approximately twelve years, I laid the foundations for a new procedure in musical construction which seemed fitted to replace those structural differentiations provided formerly by tonal harmonies.

I called this procedure *Method of Composing with Twelve Tones Which are Related Only with One Another.*

This method consists primarily of the constant and exclusive use of a set of twelve different tones. This means, of course, that no tone is repeated within the series and that it uses all twelve tones of the chromatic scale, though in a different order. It is in no way identical with the chromatic scale.[1]

Ex. 1

Example 1 shows that such a basic set (BS) consists of various intervals. It should never be called a scale, although it is invented to substitute for some of the unifying and formative advantages of scale and tonality. The scale is the source of many figurations, parts of melodies and melodies themselves, ascending and descending passages, and even broken chords. In approximately the same manner the tones of the basic set produce similar elements. Of course, cadences produced by the distinction between principal and subsidiary harmonies will scarcely be derived from the basic set. But something different and more important is derived from it with a regularity comparable to the regularity and logic of the earlier harmony; the association of tones into harmonies and their successions is regulated (as will be shown later) by the order of these tones. The basic set functions in the manner of a motive. This explains why such a basic set has to be invented anew for every piece. It has to be the first creative thought. It does not make much difference whether or not the set appears in the composition at once like a theme or a melody, whether or not it is characterized as such by features of rhythm, phrasing, construction, character, etc.

Why such a set should consist of twelve different tones, why none of these tones should be repeated too soon, why, accordingly, only one set should be used in one composition—the answers to all these questions came to me gradually.

1. Curiously and wrongly, most people speak of the "system" of the chromatic scale. Mine is no system but only a method, which means a *modus* of applying regularly a preconceived formula. *A method can, but need not,* be one of the consequences of a system. I am also not the inventor of the chromatic scale; somebody else must have occupied himself with this task long ago. [Au.]

Discussing such problems in my *Harmonielehre* (1911), I recommended the avoidance of octave doublings.[2] To double is to emphasize, and an emphasized tone could be interpreted as a root, or even as a tonic; the consequences of such an interpretation must be avoided. Even a slight reminiscence of the former tonal harmony would be disturbing, because it would create false expectations of consequences and continuations. The use of a tonic is deceiving if it is not based on *all* the relationships of tonality.

The use of more than one set was excluded because in every following set one or more tones would have been repeated too soon. Again there would arise the danger of interpreting the repeated tone as a tonic. Besides, the effect of unity would be lessened.

Justified already by historical development, the method of composing with twelve tones is also not without esthetic and theoretical support. On the contrary, it is just this support which advances it from a mere technical device to the rank and importance of a scientific theory.

Music is not merely another kind of amusement, but a musical poet's, a musical thinker's representation of musical ideas; these musical ideas must correspond to the laws of human logic; they are a part of what man can apperceive, reason and express. Proceeding from these assumptions, I arrived at the following conclusions:

THE TWO-OR-MORE-DIMENSIONAL SPACE IN WHICH MUSICAL IDEAS ARE PRESENTED IS A UNIT. Though the elements of these ideas appear separate and independent to the eye and the ear, they reveal their true meaning only through their co-operation, even as no single word alone can express a thought without relation to other words. All that happens at any point of this musical space has more than a local effect. It functions not only in its own plane, but also in all other directions and planes, and is not without influence even at remote points. For instance, the effect of progressive rhythmical subdivision, through what I call "the tendency of the shortest notes" to multiply themselves, can be observed in every classic composition.

A musical idea, accordingly, though consisting of melody, rhythm, and harmony, is neither the one nor the other alone, but all three together. The elements of a musical idea are partly incorporated in the horizontal plane as successive sounds, and partly in the vertical plane as simultaneous sounds. The mutual relation of tones regulates the succession of intervals as well as their association into harmonies; the rhythm regulates the succession of tones as well as the succession of harmonies and organizes phrasing. And this explains why, as will be shown later, a basic set of twelve tones (BS) can be used in either dimension, as a whole or in parts.

The basic set is used in diverse mirror forms. The composers of the last century had not employed such mirror forms as much as the masters of contrapuntal times; at least, they seldom did so consciously. Nevertheless, there exist

2. Still sometimes occurring in my first compositions in this style. [Au.]

examples, of which I want to mention only one from Beethoven's last String Quartet, Op. 135, in F major:

Ex. 2: BEETHOVEN, STRING QUARTET, OP. 135, 4TH MOVEMENT, INTRODUCTION

The original form, *a,* "Muss es sein," appears in *b* inverted and in the major; *c* shows the retrograde form of this inversion, which, now reinverted in *d* and filled out with passing notes in *e,* results in the second phrase of the main theme.

Whether or not this device was used consciously by Beethoven does not matter at all. From my own experience I know that it can also be a subconsciously received gift from the Supreme Commander.

Ex. 3: KAMMERSYMPHONIE, OP. 9, E MAJOR

The two principal themes of my *Kammersymphonie* (Chamber Symphony) can be seen in Example 3 under *a* and *b.* After I had completed the work I worried very much about the apparent absence of any relationship between the two themes. Directed only by my sense of form and the stream of ideas, I had not asked such questions while composing; but, as usual with me, doubts arose as soon as I had finished. They went so far that I had already raised the sword for the kill, taken the red pencil of the censor to cross out the theme *b.* Fortunately, I stood by my inspiration and ignored these mental tortures. About twenty years later I saw the true relationship. It is of such a complicated nature that I doubt whether any composer would have cared deliberately to construct a theme in this way; but our subconscious does it involuntarily. In *c* the true principal tones of the theme are marked, and *d* shows that all the intervals ascend. Their correct inversion *e* produces the first phrase *f* of the theme *b.*

It should be mentioned that the last century considered such a procedure cerebral, and thus inconsistent with the dignity of genius. The very fact that there exist classical examples proves the foolishness of such an opinion. But the validity of this form of thinking is also demonstrated by the previously stated law of the unity of musical space, best formulated as follows: *the unity of musical space demands an absolute and unitary perception.* In this space, as in Swedenborg's heaven (described in Balzac's *Seraphita*) there is no absolute down, no right or left, forward or backward. Every musical configuration, every movement of tones has to be comprehended primarily as a mutual relation of sounds, of oscillatory vibrations, appearing at different places and times. To the imaginative and creative faculty, relations in the material sphere are as independent from directions or planes as material objects are, in their sphere, to our perceptive faculties. Just as our mind always recognizes, for instance, a knife, a bottle or a watch, regardless of its position, and can reproduce it in the imagination in every possible position, even so a musical creator's mind can operate subconsciously with a row of tones, regardless of their direction, regardless of the way in which a mirror might show the mutual relations, which remain a given quality.

VI

The introduction of my method of composing with twelve tones does not facilitate composing; on the contrary, it makes it more difficult. Modernistically-minded beginners often think they should try it before having acquired the necessary technical equipment. This is a great mistake. The restrictions imposed on a composer by the obligation to use only one set in a composition are so severe that they can only be overcome by an imagination which has survived a tremendous number of adventures. Nothing is given by this method; but much is taken away.

It has been mentioned that for every new composition a special set of twelve tones has to be invented. Sometimes a set will not fit every condition an experienced composer can foresee, especially in those ideal cases where the set appears at once in the form, character, and phrasing of a theme. Rectifications in the order of tones may then become necessary.

In the first works in which I employed this method, I was not yet convinced that the exclusive use of one set would not result in monotony. Would it allow the creation of a sufficient number of characteristically differentiated themes, phrases, motives, sentences, and other forms? At this time, I used complicated devices to assure variety. But soon I discovered that my fear was unfounded; I could even base a whole opera, *Moses and Aron,* solely on one set; and I found that, on the contrary, the more familiar I became with this set the more easily I could draw themes from it. Thus, the truth of my first prediction had received splendid proof. One has to follow the basic set; but, nevertheless, one composes as freely as before.

VII

It has been mentioned that the basic set is used in mirror forms.

Ex. 4

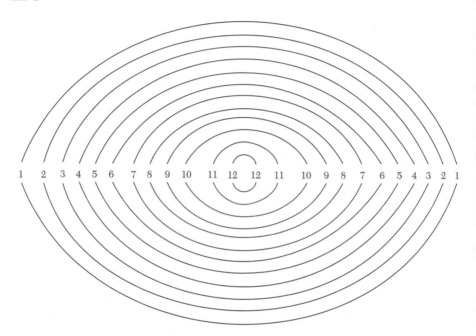

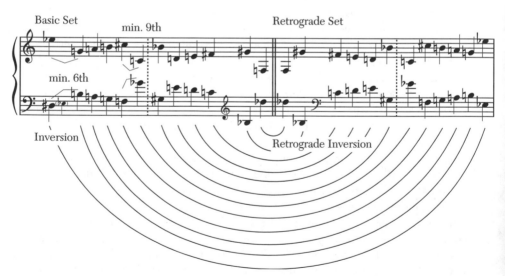

BS means Basic Set; INV means inversion of the Basic Set; INV 8, INV 5, INV 3, INV 6 means inversion at the 8ve, 5th, minor 3rd, or major 6th from the beginning tone.

From the basic set, three additional sets are automatically derived: (1) the inversion; (2) the retrograde; and (3) the retrograde inversion. The employment of these mirror forms corresponds to the principle of *the absolute and unitary perception of musical space*. The set of Example 4 is taken from the Wind Quintet Op. 26, one of my first compositions in this style.

Later, especially in larger works, I changed my original idea, if necessary, to fit the following conditions: the inversion a fifth below of the first six tones, the antecedent, should not produce a repetition of one of these six tones, but should bring forth the hitherto unused six tones of the chromatic scale. Thus, the consequent of the basic set, the tones 7 to 12, comprises the tones of this inversion, but, of course, in a different order.

•   •   •   •   •

VIII

In every composition preceding the method of composing with twelve tones, all the thematic and harmonic material is primarily derived from three sources: the tonality, the *basic motive* which in turn is a derivative of the tonality, and the *rhythm*, which is included in the basic motive. A composer's whole thinking was bound to remain in an intelligible manner around the central root. A composition which failed to obey these demands was considered "amateurish"; but a composition which adhered to it rigorously was never called "cerebral." On the contrary, the capacity to obey the principle instinctively was considered a natural condition of a talent.[3]

The time will come when the ability to draw thematic material from a basic set of twelve tones will be an unconditional prerequisite for obtaining admission into the composition class of a conservatory.

IX

The possibilities of evolving the formal elements of music—melodies, themes, phrases, motives, figures, and chords—out of a basic set are unlimited. In the following pages, a number of examples from my own works will be analysed to reveal some of these possibilities. It will be observed that the succession of the tones according to their order in the set has always been strictly observed. One could perhaps tolerate a slight digression from this order (according to the same principle which allowed a remote variant in former styles)[4] in the later part of a work, when the set had already become familiar to the ear. However, one would not thus digress at the beginning of a piece.

3. There are scores of mathematical geniuses who can square and cube in their minds. There are scores of chess players who play blindfolded, and every chess player has to work out in his mind the possibilities of the next five moves. There must not be many who can exceed ten moves, but only to them should one compare the imaginative capacity of a real musical mind. [Au.]
4. As, for instance, in the fourth of the Diabelli Variations, Beethoven omits, in an inexplicable manner, one measure. [Au.]

The set is often divided into groups; for example, into two groups of six tones, or three groups of four, or four groups of three tones. This grouping serves primarily to provide a regularity in the distribution of the tones. The tones used in the melody are thereby separated from those to be used as accompaniment, as harmonies or as chords and voices demanded by the nature of the instrumentation, by the instrument, or by the character and other circumstances of a piece. The distribution may be varied or developed according to circumstances, in a manner comparable to the changes of what I call the "Motive of the Accompaniment."

•   •   •   •   •

13 Karlheinz Stockhausen

Karlheinz Stockhausen (b. 1926) was a leading figure in the development of "integral serialism," one of the two principal compositional esthetics to emerge in the early years following World War II (the other was indeterminacy). Reacting against the neoclassicism evident in European music since the end of World War I, the serialists aspired to develop a completely integrated structural approach to composition, as independent of traditional conceptions as possible. Ideally, even traditional instruments should be discarded, since they necessarily bring "preformed" material into the compositional mix. This article, written during the early 1960s and drawing upon the advantages of the electronic medium, proposes that the entire sonic structure be understood as a unified phenomenon: that all of its individual components—timbre, pitch, intensity, and duration—represent different manifestations of a single event, "the temporal structure of sound waves," which can thus be placed under the control of a "single principle of ordering."

FROM The Concept of Unity in Electronic Music

(1962)

On several previous occasions, when I have been asked to explain the composition of electronic music, I have described four characteristics that seem

TEXT: *Perspectives of New Music* 1 (Fall 1962): 39–43. Translation by Elaine Barkin.

important to me for electronic composition as distinguished from the composition of instrumental music:

1) the correlation of the coloristic, harmonic-melodic, and metric-rhythmic aspects of composition
2) the composition and de-composition of timbres
3) the characteristic differentiation among degrees of intensity
4) the ordered relationships between sound and noise

Here, I would like to discuss only the correlation of timbre, pitch, intensity, and duration. In the past, it has been customary to regard these correlative properties of sound as mutually independent, as belonging to fundamentally distinct spheres. They have appeared increasingly separate as our acoustical perception developed along such lines.

Similarly, the means employed for the production of sound, as well as the compositional process itself, were consequent upon this conceptual separation. To generate sound-events having single perceptible pitches, we used the so-called sine tone, square-wave, or saw-tooth generators, which produce periodic oscillations. Sound-events of indeterminate pitch, those that are more or less noise-like, were produced by means of noise generators.

We varied such sound- or noise-colors by means of electrical filters, with which one can strengthen, attenuate, or suppress entirely individual partials or whole frequency-bands—the so-called formants, or bands of noise—of the spectra.

Intensity was controlled by regulating, with the aid of a voltmeter, the voltages recorded on tape (whereby the spectrum itself automatically varied with the variations in intensity), whereas duration was determined simply by the length of tape on which a sound was recorded.

Compositionally, in terms of the production and manipulation of sound, these individual sound-properties had to be dealt with separately. But, on the other hand, we perceive a sound-event as a homogeneous phenomenon rather than as a composite of four separate properties. At a relatively early stage of my work in electronic composition, I had already considered the possibility of equating this unity of perception with an analogous unity in composition itself. In the preparatory work for my composition *Kontakte,* I found, for the first time, ways to bring all properties under a single control. I deduced that all differences of acoustic perception can be traced to differences in the temporal structure of sound waves. These temporal relations enable us to distinguish the many different manifestations of pitch, timbre, simultaneity, sound-mixture, and noise: their speed of oscillation, their particular intervals—either equal and regular or more or less irregular—their density, and the frequency with which pulsations reach the ear. It seemed to me that the differences in intensity among sounds ultimately derive from the latter property: when pulsations of equal value follow one another in closer temporal succession, the over-all intensity increases; to effect this, the density would, in fact, have to be so great that the individual pulses were no longer conveyed as a succession of equal perturbations of the atmosphere but rather as mutually interfering sound-waves: the particles of air agitated by the initial pulses would thus be reactivated by further pulses before they have become quiescent and are, so to speak, "shaken up," so that the impression given is of an increase in over-all intensity. The total complex thus appears as a *single* greater wave rather than *several* smaller ones. The faster the succession of pulses, the stronger will be the appearance of the resultant wave.

A periodic sound wave, such as a simple tone, fluctuating regularly in intensity, would thus be the result of a succession of pulses that alternately accelerate and decelerate within each period. The difference between the fastest and slowest rates of speed of the pulses in each period would define the direction of its intensity (its "intensity envelope") and its amplitude. The distance between periodically recurring equal rates of speed would determine the pitch.

Ex. 1

· · · ···· · · · · · ···· · · · · · · ···· · · · · · etc.

If a succession of pulses of this kind were to be accelerated so that between the periodic recurrences of the highest speed there were a time interval of, say, 1/440 sec., one would hear a simple tone with the pitch of A-440.

If the rate of speed of the pulse-succession did not fluctuate regularly (‿‿‿‿) but consisted instead of periods of several unequal parts within each equal time-span (as, for example, ⌒ᴠᴧᴠᴧ᷈⌒), the so-called "color" of a steady sound would vary according to the wave crests. A "period" divided into two parts would be represented as follows:

Ex. 2

In a more or less noiselike sound-event the periods would no longer be regular; i.e. the time intervals between recurrences of equal rates of speed would not remain constant but would vary irregularly between a given fastest and slowest speed. These extremes determine the limits of a frequency band, a so-called "colored noise" band. If the rate of speed of the pulse succession were so widely varied that the smallest interval between pulses were ca. 1/16,000 sec., and the longest ca. 1/20 sec., occurring at regular time-intervals, and everything between these extremes occurred in a highly aperiodic fashion (in a manner that one might term "aleatoric") the result would be "white noise."

For most musicians, these considerations may seem specifically related to acoustics rather than to music. Actually, however, a musical composition is no more than a temporal ordering of sound events, just as each sound event in a composition is a temporal ordering of pulses. It is only a question of the point at which composition begins: in composing for instruments whose sounds are predetermined, a composer need not be concerned with these problems. On the other hand, in electronic music, one can either compose each sound directly in terms of its wave succession, or, finally, each individual sound wave may be determined in terms of its actual vibration, by an ordering of the succession of pulses.

If, in fact, all of the experiential properties of sound could be traced to a single principle of ordering—such temporally composed successions of pulses—compositional thought would have to be radically reoriented. The distinction between the "acoustical prearrangement" *within* the material and "musical ordering" *using* this material would now have to be discarded. The prevailing additive, or "synthetic" compositional procedure, in which the different properties are bound together, would now be expanded through a proto-generative and more unified approach. One would not proceed from sound properties that had already been experienced and then allow these to determine temporal variations; instead, one would compose the temporal arrangements of pulses themselves, and discover their resultant sound properties experimentally.

After my first, relatively simple, attempt at such a procedure, I was able to predict roughly the particular temporal orderings of the pulses. I then proceeded to record fixed successions of pulses on tape within a relatively low speed range (using pulsation intervals of between 1/16 and 16 secs.) and then increased the speed until I arrived at the "field" of frequencies and color that I desired. This was done by means of a pulse generator with which the speed of the pulse succession was regulated by hand. Thus, for example, if I wished to generate a periodic wave—that is, a sound of constant pitch—from a succession of pulses lasting eight seconds whose speed variations are fixed, I would have to accelerate the rhythmized eight-second succession 1,024 times, that is, transpose it ten octaves upwards, reducing its duration from eight to 1/128 sec. In order to sustain this pitch of 128 cps. for 10 sec., I would have to re-record the original succession 128 × 10, or 1,280 times, which can easily be done by means of a tape loop. The "color" of the resulting sound would be determined by the variations of speed among the pulses of the original succession, which are now determined by the periodic duplications and accelerations of the wave form within each time span—i.e. the "intensity envelope."

With such a compositional procedure, then, one must proceed from a basic concept of a *single, unified musical time;* and the different perceptual categories, such as color, harmony and melody, meter and rhythm, dynamics, and "form," must be regarded as corresponding to the different *components* of this unified time, as follows:

1. Harmony and melody correspond to periodic waves (that is, to sound-events of constant pitch) whose individual periods should not be greater than ca. 1/16 or less than ca. 1/6,000 sec. because beyond these limits they are no longer audible as "pitches."

2. The color of harmonic spectra corresponds to the whole number fractions which, as "fundamentals," refer to periods of between ca. 1/13,000 and ca. 1/16 sec.; the color of nonharmonic or noiselike spectra corresponds to more or less aperiodic successions of periods.

3. Between ca. 1/30 and 1/16 sec. our perception of duration gradually changes into perception of meter and rhythm; i.e., *periodic* periods may then be considered as *meters,* and the *internal intervallic relationships* of the distances between pulses within any given meter—that which determines the tone color for periods shorter than ca. 1/16 sec.—may here be considered as "rhythm."

Aperiodic relationships of periods, which are considered *"noises"* in the sphere of color, correspond, when the periods are longer than ca. 1/16 sec. to *aperiodic rhythms* having no recognizable meters—i.e. no recognizable periodicity (just as a deviation from simple periodicity in the sphere of frequency—*"dissonance"*—corresponds, in the sphere of duration, to *syncopation*).

Although many of the new compositions have been criticized for their alleged "lack of rhythm," they may actually be considered to have "pure rhythm" without meter. This objection, moreover, is exactly analogous to that directed against the use of aperiodic sound waves, i.e. against "noises."

4. Meter and rhythm correspond to the time intervals whose order of magnitude is between ca. 1/8 and ca. 8 secs. At about 8 secs. our ability to distinguish durational relationships gradually breaks down. With values of greater length we are no longer able to remember the exact lengths of durations or perceive their proportions as accurately as we can those that lie between ca. 1/8 and ca. 8 secs.

"Form" in a special sense—the time relationships of longer events—corresponds to durations of the order of magnitude of from several seconds to about 15–60 minutes (for "movements" or whole "compositions").

The transitions and overlappings between all the time spheres are quite flexible, but this is especially so with reference to "form," which is most obviously an approximation (in the literature of music, of course, the durations of "movements" or *continuous* works vary from several minutes to ca. one hour).

•   •   •

14 Iannis Xenakis

Like Edgard Varèse, Iannis Xenakis (b. 1925) was trained as a scientist; and even more than his predecessor, he has applied the ideas and methods of mathematics and science to develop a new conception of musical structure and compositional process. Xenakis views both earlier Western music in general and integral serialism in particular as inconsistent with modern scientific views of the nature of reality, since he sees both as based upon assumptions of absolute causality and determinism. During the early 1950s he thus began introducing the concept of indeterminacy into his work—not the absolute indeterminacy of a John Cage, which he finds equally unscientific, but the indeterminacy of probability theory and polyvalent logic, consistent with modern physics. Rejecting the "linear category" characteristic of Western musical thought up to his time, Xenakis proposes that music be reconceived in terms of "mass events," as an interaction of complex multitudes of sound that can be experienced and understood only as totalities. This conception will enable composers to mediate between the unmanageable extremes of complete order on the one hand and complete disorder on the other. Originally published in 1960, the following article provides a nontechnical introduction to this radically new approach.

Free Stochastic Music
(1960)

Art, and above all, music has a fundamental function, which is to catalyze the sublimation that it can bring about through all means of expression. It must aim through fixations which are landmarks to draw towards a total exaltation in which the individual mingles, losing his consciousness in a truth immediate, rare, enormous, and perfect. If a work of art succeeds in this undertaking even for a single moment, it attains its goal. This tremendous truth is not made of objects, emotions, or sensations; it is beyond these, as Beethoven's Seventh Symphony is beyond music. This is why art can lead to realms that religion still occupies for some people.

But this transmutation of every-day artistic material which transforms trivial products into meta-art is a secret. The "possessed" reach it without knowing its "mechanisms." The others struggle in the ideological and technical mainstream of their epoch which constitutes the perishable "climate" and the stylistic fashion. Keeping our eyes fixed on this supreme meta-artistic goal, we shall attempt to define in a more modest manner the paths which can lead to it from our

TEXT: *Formalized Music*, rev. ed. (Stuyvesant, NY: Pendragon Press, 1992); pp. 3–5, 8–10, 264.

point of departure, which is the magma of contradictions in present music.

There exists a historical parallel between European music and the successive attempts to explain the world by reason. The music of antiquity, causal and deterministic, was already strongly influenced by the schools of Pythagoras and Plato. Plato insisted on the principle of causality, "for it is impossible for anything, to come into being without cause" *(Timaeus)*. Strict causality lasted until the nineteenth century when it underwent a brutal and fertile transformation as a result of statistical theories in physics. Since antiquity the concepts of chance *(tyche)*, disorder *(ataxia)*, and disorganization were considered as the opposite and negation of reason *(logos)*, order *(taxis)*, and organization *(systasis)*. It is only recently that knowledge has been able to penetrate chance and has discovered how to separate its degrees—in other words to rationalize it progressively, without, however, succeeding in a definitive and total explanation of the problem of "pure chance."

After a time lag of several decades, atonal music broke up the tonal function and opened up a new path parallel to that of the physical sciences, but at the same time constricted by the virtually absolute determinism of serial music.

It is therefore not surprising that the presence or absence of the principle of causality, first in philosophy and then in the sciences, might influence musical composition. It caused it to follow paths that appeared to be divergent, but which, in fact, coalesced in probability theory and finally in polyvalent logic, which are kinds of generalization and enrichments of the principle of causality. The explanation of the world, and consequently of the sonic phenomena which surround us or which may be created, necessitated and profited from the enlargement of the principle of causality, the basis of which enlargement is formed by the law of large numbers. This law implies an asymptotic evolution towards a stable state, towards a kind of goal, of *stochos*, whence comes the adjective "stochastic."

But everything in pure determinism or in less pure indeterminism is subjected to the fundamental operational laws of logic, which were disentangled by mathematical thought under the title of general algebra. These laws operate on isolated states or on sets of elements with the aid of operations, the most primitive of which are the union, notated $\cup$, the intersection, notated $\cap$, and the negation. Equivalence, implication, and quantifications are elementary relations from which all current science can be constructed.

Music, then, may be defined as an organization of these elementary operations and relations between sonic entities or between functions of sonic entities. We understand the first-rate position which is occupied by set theory, not only for the construction of new works, but also for analysis and better comprehension of the works of the past. In the same way a stochastic construction or an investigation of history with the help of stochastics cannot be carried through without the help of logic—the queen of the sciences, and I would even venture to suggest, of the arts—or its mathematical form algebra. For everything that is said here on the subject is also valid for all forms of art (painting, sculpture, architecture, films, etc.).

From this very general, fundamental point of view, from which we wish to examine and *make* music, primary time appears as a wax or clay on which operations and relations can be inscribed and engraved, first for the purposes of work, and then for communication with a third person. On this level, the asymmetric, noncommutative character of time is used (B after $A \neq A$ after B, i.e., lexicographic order). Commutative, metric time (symmetrical) is subjected to the same logical laws and can therefore also aid organizational speculations. What is remarkable is that these fundamental notions, which are necessary for construction, are found in man from his tenderest age, and it is fascinating to follow their evolution as Jean Piaget[1] has done.

After this short preamble on generalities we shall enter into the details of an approach to musical composition which I have developed over several years. I call it "stochastic," in honor of probability theory, which has served as a logical framework and as a method of resolving the conflicts and knots encountered.

The first task is to construct an abstraction from all inherited conventions and to exercise a fundamental critique of acts of thought and their materialization. What, in fact, does a musical composition offer strictly on the construction level? It offers a collection of sequences which it wishes to be causal. When, for simplification, the major scale implied its hierarchy of tonal functions— tonics, dominants, and subdominants—around which the other notes gravitated, it constructed, in a highly deterministic manner, linear processes, or melodies on the one hand, and simultaneous events, or chords, on the other. Then the serialists of the Vienna school, not having known how to master logically the indeterminism of atonality, returned to an organization which was extremely causal in the strictest sense, more abstract than that of tonality; however, this abstraction was their great contribution. Messiaen generalized this process and took a great step in systematizing the abstraction of all the variables of instrumental music. What is paradoxical is that he did this in the modal field. He created a multimodal music which immediately found imitators in serial music. At the outset Messiaen's abstract systematization found its most justifiable embodiment in a multiserial music. It is from here that the postwar neo-serialists have drawn their inspiration. They could now, following the Vienna school and Messiaen, with some occasional borrowing from Stravinsky and Debussy, walk on with ears shut and proclaim a truth greater than the others. Other movements were growing stronger; chief among them was the systematic exploration of sonic entities, new instruments, and "noises." Varèse was the pioneer in this field, and electromagnetic music has been the beneficiary (electronic music being a branch of instrumental music). However, in electro-

---

1. Jean Piaget, *Le Développement de la notion de temps chez l'enfant* (Paris: Presses Universitaires de France, 1946). [Au.]

magnetic music, problems of construction and of morphology were not faced conscientiously. Multiserial music, a fusion of the multimodality of Messiaen and the Viennese school, remained, nevertheless, at the heart of the fundamental problem of music.

But by 1954 it was already in the process of deflation, for the completely deterministic complexity of the operations of composition and of the works themselves produced an auditory and ideological nonsense. I described the inevitable conclusion in "The Crisis of Serial Music":

> Linear polyphony destroys itself by its very complexity; what one hears is in reality nothing but a mass of notes in various registers. The enormous complexity prevents the audience from following the intertwining of the lines and has as its macroscopic effect an irrational and fortuitous dispersion of sounds over the whole extent of the sonic spectrum. There is consequently a contradiction between the polyphonic linear system and the heard result, which is surface or mass. This contradiction inherent in polyphony will disappear when the independence of sounds is total. In fact, when linear combinations and their polyphonic superpositions no longer operate, what will count will be the statistical mean of isolated states and of transformations of sonic components at a given moment. The macroscopic effect can then be controlled by the mean of the movements of elements which we select. The result is the introduction of the notion of probability, which implies, in this particular case, combinatory calculus. Here, in a few words, is the possible escape route from the "linear category" in musical thought.[2]

This article served as a bridge to my introduction of mathematics in music. For if, thanks to complexity, the strict, deterministic causality which the neo-serialists postulated was lost, then it was necessary to replace it by a more general causality, by a probabilistic logic which would contain strict serial causality as a particular case. This is the function of stochastic science. "Stochastics" studies and formulates the law of large numbers, which has already been mentioned, the laws of rare events, the different aleatory procedures, etc. As a result of the impasse in serial music, as well as other causes, I originated in 1954 a music constructed from the principle of indeterminism; two years later I named it "Stochastic Music." The laws of the calculus of probabilities entered composition through musical necessity.

But other paths also led to the same stochastic crossroads—first of all, natural events such as the collision of hail or rain with hard surfaces, or the song of cicadas in a summer field. These sonic events are made out of thousands of isolated sounds; this multitude of sounds, seen as a totality, is a new sonic event. This mass event is articulated and forms a plastic mold of time, which itself follows aleatory and stochastic laws. If one then wishes to form a large mass of point-notes, such as string pizzicati, one must know these mathematical laws, which, in any case, are no more than a tight and concise expression of a chain of logical reasoning. Everyone has observed the sonic phenomena of a political crowd of dozens or hundreds of thousands of people. The human river shouts a slogan in a uniform rhythm. Then another slogan springs from the head of

2. I. Xenakis, *Gravesaner Blätter*, no. 1 (1955). [Au.]

the demonstration; it spreads towards the tail, replacing the first. A wave of transition thus passes from the head to the tail. The clamor fills the city, and the inhibiting force of voice and rhythm reaches a climax. It is an event of great power and beauty in its ferocity. Then the impact between the demonstrators and the enemy occurs. The perfect rhythm of the last slogan breaks up in a huge cluster of chaotic shouts, which also spreads to the tail. Imagine, in addition, the reports of dozens of machine guns and the whistle of bullets adding their punctuations to this total disorder. The crowd is then rapidly dispersed, and after sonic and visual hell follows a detonating calm, full of despair, dust, and death. The statistical laws of these events, separated from their political or moral context, are the same as those of the cicadas or the rain. They are the laws of the passage from complete order to total disorder in a continuous or explosive manner. They are stochastic laws.

Here we touch on one of the great problems that have haunted human intelligence since antiquity: continuous or discontinuous transformation. The sophisms of movement (e.g., Achilles and the tortoise) or of definition (e.g., baldness), especially the latter, are solved by statistical definition; that is to say, by stochastics. One may produce continuity with either continuous or discontinuous elements. A multitude of short glissandi on strings can give the impression of continuity, and so can a multitude of pizzicati. Passages from a discontinuous state to a continuous state are controllable with the aid of probability theory. For some time now I have been conducting these fascinating experiments in instrumental works; but the mathematical character of this music has frightened musicians and has made the approach especially difficult.

Here is another direction that converges on indeterminism. The study of the variation of rhythm poses the problem of knowing what the limit of total asymmetry is, and of the consequent complete disruption of causality among durations. The sounds of a Geiger counter in the proximity of a radioactive source give an impressive idea of this. Stochastics provides the necessary laws.

Before ending this short inspection tour of events rich in the new logic, which were closed to the understanding until recently, I would like to include a short parenthesis. If glissandi are long and sufficiently interlaced, we obtain sonic spaces of continuous evolution. It is possible to produce ruled surfaces by drawing the glissandi as straight lines. I performed this experiment with *Metastasis* (this work had its premiere in 1955 at Donaueschingen). Several years later, when the architect Le Corbusier, whose collaborator I was, asked me to suggest a design for the architecture of the Philips Pavilion in Brussels, my inspiration was pin-pointed by the experiment with *Metastasis*. Thus I believe that on this occasion music and architecture found an intimate connection.[3]

•   •   •   •   •

3. I. Xenakis, *Revue technique Philips*, vol. 20, no. 1 (1958), and Le Corbusier, *Modulor 2* (Boulogne-Seine: Architecture d'Aujourd'hui, 1955). [Au.]

15 György Ligeti

György Ligeti (b. 1926) left his native Hungary following the 1956 Revolution there and settled in Western Europe, where he became closely associated with Karlheinz Stockhausen and other composers of the integral serialist movement. This article dates from 1960, when the serialists were beginning to move in new directions, bringing them somewhat closer to such composers as Iannis Xenakis and John Cage. Ligeti discusses the emergence of a "general new feeling for musical form," less beholden to determinacy and automatism. He sees this development as following inevitably from the negative effects of serialism itself, such as its tendencies to neutralize musical content, subvert hierarchical connections, undermine metrical regularity, and increase "entropy," thereby lowering the degree of perceptible contrast. Ligeti notes that serial composers are consequently turning away from their earlier obsession with matters of detail to focus more on issues of overall musical structure and perceptible effect. Though strict determinacy is not entirely abandoned, it is applied to "global categories" and general planning, leaving the composers more freedom in working out individual details.

FROM Metamorphoses of Musical Form
(1960)

A general new feeling for musical form seems to be emerging, despite the not inconsiderable idiomatic differences in the works of the various "serial" composers. It is irrelevant to consider whether this is the result of research into the serial ordering of the musical material, or whether the serial manipulations are themselves the consequence of the new idea of form. Technique and imagination influence one another in a constant interchange. Every artistic innovation in the craft of composition ferments the whole spiritual edifice, and every change in this edifice demands constant revision of compositional procedure.

Relations of this sort have always urged us on to metamorphoses in the way we work. The modifications of pitch, once seemingly insignificant, in the modal framework—at first a mere sharpening of individual leading-notes—led to the formation of functional harmony, together with the whole architecture of periodic forms and their specific world of expression. In the craft of com-

TEXT: *Die Reihe*, ed. by Karlheinz Stockhausen and Herbert Eimert, trans. Cornelius Cardew (Bryn Mawr: Theodore Presser, 1965) 7, pp. 5–11. This reference and all others below to *Die Reihe* pertain to the English-language edition. © copyright 1965 by Universal Edition A. G. Wien. © copyright renewed. All Rights Reserved. Used by permission of European American Music Distributors Corporation, Sole U. S. and Canadian agent for Universal Edition A. G. Wien.

position this process led to techniques of modulation and development that undermined and finally ruined the periodic forms themselves, and the leading note—which had spawned the tonal system—then condemned it to extinction by annexing to itself more and more of the harmonic and melodic activity.

But the newly installed chromatic republic stood in need of its own legislation. The which having been supplied by Schönberg's "composition with twelve notes related only to one another," the serial principle—originally set up only for the dimension of pitches—sought to spread itself over the totality of form. This led to the discrete quantification of all parameters, and the music became a product of superpositions of prefabricated arrangements. In this way the musical structure acquired a "pointillistic" character.

Hard on the heels of the serial organization of durations, intensities and timbres, came the expansion of the method to cover more global categories like relationships of register and density, distribution of various types of movement and structure, and also the proportionalization of the whole formal sequence. Considerable adjustments in compositional planning now came into play: as the larger form-categories came under serial control, the serial ordering of the elementary parameters became looser and looser. A strict determination of these took second place in the total composition, and this again put a new complexion on the form: the concept of "pointillism" was extended to embrace "statistical fields."[1]

The serial arrangement of pitches, which had initiated the whole process, was the first thing sacrificed in this shift of emphasis.[2] Disintegration had set in here even before the "statistical" phase of serial technique, in fact during the period of composition with series of fixed elements.

Within this disintegration we can distinguish various "destruction-types," as follows:

1. The individual character of the various serial arrangements fades as a result of the superposition of several horizontal series, in which, wherever possible, common notes occur at the same pitch. Such interweaving obscures the single serial threads (especially when all the parts are played on one instrument), and the resulting intervals have little or nothing to do with the original arrangement. Where such a procedure is coupled with series of durations the composer can hardly even retain an influence over the intervals that are to result, let alone determine them. They follow automatically from the type of procedure. In this way the pitch series loses its last remnant of function, paralysed by the emerging complex. This situation is especially typical for the early

1. Cf. K. Stockhausen ". . . how time passes . . ." *Die Reihe* 3, p. 10. [Au.]
2. Cf. Luciano Berio: "Aspetti di artigianato formale," *Incontri Musicali* 1 (Milan 1956), p. 62. Berio writes expressly of the "superamento della sensazione di serie di altezze focali e di intervallo a favore di una sensazione di qualità sonore e di registro, considerando questi ultimi gli elementi attivi e determinanti della struttura formale." [Au.] The Italian quote reads: "the supression of a sensation of discrete scale degrees and intervals in favor of a sensation of sonic quality and register, these last two being considered the active and determining elements of the formal structure."

stages of integral-serial composition, particularly for the case of composers—
Boulez amongst others—who tend to think in terms of horizontal layers.[3]

Self-propagating automatisms of this kind evince a relation of indeterminacy, and
the structural contexts are of necessity subject to this. For the degree of indeterminacy of the structure increases in proportion to the number of directives that are
issued, and vice versa: in proportion as a composer worries about determining the
result, he finds he can determine less and less about the order and relationships of
the elements. It is essential to recognize this contradiction, if one is not to be entirely
at the mercy of the arbitrary dictates of compositional "craftsmanship," for it has its
roots deep in the peculiar nature of the serial conception of musical material. When
this is recognized, it is of course a personal matter for the composer how he regards
the situation: should he allow the form to follow from pre-stabilized elements and
schemes of organization, fully aware of the risk he runs of virtually allowing the result
to slip through his fingers? Or should he take the other path and progress from a
total vision into particularities, accepting as part of the bargain the fact that he will
have to sacrifice any number of attractive and, in themselves, logically developed
details?

2. The character of pitch-series is weakened by the increasing preference for
homogeneous sequences of intervals, particularly the chromatic scale. Stockhausen in his "Klavierstück 2," for example, instead of a fixed 12-note series,
uses various permutations of the notes of sections of the chromatic scale.[4] The
basis of Nono's "Il canto sospeso" is the series A, B-flat, A-flat, B, G, C, F-
sharp, C-sharp, F, D, E, E-flat. At first glance this poses as an all-interval series,
but it can be seen to consist of an interpolation of two sequences of semitones
in contrary motion.[5] Finally, in his "Cori di Didone," Nono has chosen the
chromatic scale itself for his raw material; this is really no longer a series but
simply a regulator to ensure an even distribution of the 12 notes. The vertical
disposition of this material results in a piling up of neighbouring tones. It is no
longer primarily the intervals that constitute the structure but relations of density, distribution of registers and various displacements in the building up and
breaking down of the vertical complexes. From the point of view of "traditional" 12-note composition, this technique would doubtless be regarded as an
impoverishment. But seen in the light of the requirements of integral-serial
composition, this accusation misses fire. Nono's attention is concentrated
mainly on the construction and dismantling of piles of layers (which represents
in a way a macroscopic projection of attack and decay processes that are not
usually analysable by the human ear), and in this context a pitch-series, however artfully constructed, would have been no use to him at all—it would have
gone astray and succumbed in a network of structures such as these.

3. Cf. G. Ligeti: "Pierre Boulez—Decision and Automatism in Structure Ia," *Die Reihe* 4, p. 36ff.
   [Au.]
4. See L. Nono: "Zur Entwicklung der Serientechnik," *Gravesaner Blätter*, vol . 4 (1956), pp. 17–
   18. [Au.]
5. Cf. U. Unger: "Luigi Nono," *Die Reihe* 4, p. 12. A transposition of the same series serves as the
   basis of the "Varianti." (Cf. R. Kolisch: "Nono's 'Varianti,' " *Melos*, October 1957, p. 292ff.) [Au.]

3. The succession of notes becomes subject to a higher ruling, which has the prerogative of altering—to a greater or lesser degree—the original series of pitches. This state of affairs can be observed in Stockhausen's "Gruppen für drei Orchester." In this composition, the individual groups are characterized in various ways, among others by the specific ambitus of the sounds involved. The limits of the ambitus in each case are determined by a higher order series. The ambitus is a feature of the group as a whole, whereas the succession of pitches is executed discretely with the entry of each note; consequently the requirements of the pitch series are compelled to accommodate themselves to the larger, more comprehensive order. If the ambitus in question covers an octave or some larger span, the 12-note series is of course not threatened, because only the registers of the notes are influenced. But if a group is required to fit into a span of less than an octave, then the series suffers a compression; its elements tend towards identity with each other in proportion as the span is narrower. The original series can, it is true, be retained in its proportions if electronic means of sound-production are employed, or if intervals smaller than a semitone are available (as they are with instruments of the string family). But with even temperament (the division of the octave into twelve equal parts) the original series is inevitably destroyed.

4. The function of the pitch-series is grafted on to other parameters. For example, in Pousseur's Quintet for clarinet, bass clarinet, piano, violin, and cello, the basic 12-note series—borrowed from Webern's Saxophone quartet Op 22 in homage—is shorn of its function simply by filling out each interval chromatically The pitch series has been transformed into a series of densities.[6]

5. Any pre-formation of pitches is completely abandoned in favour of serial depositions of a higher order. Among other things, this step enables us to reassert our sovereignty over intervallic relationships. This can be observed in Koenig's Wind Quintet, for instance. However paradoxical this state of affairs may seem, it is logical: the 12-note method, created for the purpose of allowing a compositional control over the intervals, has to be liquidated in order that the same control can be exercised in the changed situation.

Taken as a whole, this tendency (outlined in the above points) leads to an erosion of any intervallic profile. (The possibility mentioned in point 5 is an exception). Sequences of notes and vertical complexes of notes are for the most part indifferent in respect of the intervals of which they are composed. Concepts of "consonance" and "dissonance" can no longer be applied: tension and relaxation are surrendered to the statistical properties of form, e.g. relationships of register, the density and weave of the structure.[7]

Pousseur documents the growing impediment of the intervallic function by regarding major sevenths and minor ninths not as fixed relationships of pitch

6. See H. Pousseur: "Outline of a Method," *Die Reihe* 3, p. 50ff. [Au.]
7. The tendency towards melodic and harmonic indifference has its roots firmly planted in "traditional" twelve-note composition. See T. W. Adorno: *Philosophie der neuen Musik* (Tübingen, 1949), p. 49ff. [Au.]

but as "impure octaves."[8] Note that the octave is taken as the comparative measure.[9] In the midst of the general erosion this interval seems the least affected. In any case, our sensibility regarding the octave is rather negative; the interval is generally shunned—a well-developed idiosyncrasy even in the days of traditional twelve-note composition.[10] There are several reasons for this: on the one hand, the discrepancy between the melodic breadth and reach of the octave and its high degree of harmonic fusibility—i.e. its lack of harmonic tension—is disturbing, and on the other hand the octave's overt relationship of overtone to fundamental advertises too plainly a tonal and hierarchical connection, and this makes it appear a foreign body in a context that is not tonal.[11]

Sensitiveness on this point leads to the practice of fixing the register of individual recurring tones, and preferring unisons to octaves. Despite its close relationship to the octave, the prime position (unison) has completely different properties: it is free of the contradiction we mentioned between the harmonic and melodic dimension, and is free of tension in both directions; and because in itself the unison presents no overtone-relationships—apart from the spectra necessarily produced by specific instruments—it cannot be suspected of defaulting back into the tonal sphere.

In dense textures we are not so allergic to the octave; progressively less so as the texture becomes more and more difficult to "hear through" (in the sense undergrowth is difficult to "see through"). In a particularly complex pile-up it is hardly possible to distinguish the individual intervals; octaves cannot be recognized as an individual shape, and consequently no longer disturb us. This explains the use of octaves in the denser passages of Stockhausen's "Gruppen," to take a familiar example.

Our decreasing sensitivity to intervals gives rise to a condition which, for want of a better word, we may call "permeability." This means that structures of different textures can run concurrently, penetrate each other and even merge into one another completely, whereby the horizontal and vertical density-relationships are altered, it is true, but it is a matter of indifference which intervals coincide in the thick of the fray.

Permeability has not in the past exerted any great influence on form; nevertheless it was not entirely unknown in earlier musical styles.

Palestrina's music had perhaps the lowest degree of permeability; simultaneous parts had to fit into each other in a manner prescribed by unequivocal laws. The high-degree determination of the various possibilities of combining intervals would not tolerate the slightest confusion in the structure, and as a

8. Cf. Pousseur, loc. cit., p. 54, and G. M. Koenig: "Henri Pousseur," *Die Reihe* 4, p. 23f. [Au.]
9. The octave performs this special role already in Webern's music. H. Eimert points out that "Webern achieves spatial tension by, so to speak, knocking in his acoustic objects right at the edge of the octave-gaps." ("A Change of Focus," *Die Reihe* 2, p. 34.) [Au.]
10. See H. Jelinek: *Anleitung zur Zwölftonkomposition* I (Vienna 1952), p. 47ff. [Au.]
11. Works in which the octave plays an important part in the construction, as in *Nones* by Berio, do not weaken this assertion. The use of octaves is legitimized by overemphasizing their role (Cf. P. Santi: "Luciano Berio," *Die Reihe* 4, p. 99.) [Au.]

consequence of this the handling of consonance and dissonance was most sensitive in that school.[12]

The tonal music following this was also fairly impermeable, although much less than the harmony books intended for school use would have us believe. It is well known that the hierarchy of functional harmony permitted a certain freedom in the treatment of passing notes and suspensions occurring simultaneously since, as a consequence of cadential connexions, the attention was directed more towards the role of these subsidiary notes in relation to the harmony notes. Particularly where simultaneous parts are strongly contrasted in timbre—as voices and instruments, strings and wind, solo instrument and accompaniment—the music can well tolerate small harmonic impurities, and slight delays and anticipations in time. In such cases the intervals relinquish some of their sensitivity about conflicting with each other; the higher order regulator is more important, i.e. the functional progression of the harmony. This permeability increases considerably in more complex structures; there are places in Bach—in the Brandenburgs, notably the first Brandenburg, and in many choral works with instrumental accompaniment that is rich in figuration—where the functional interval-relationships are retained, but where the individuality of many single intervals is lost in the general harmonic field of the complex figurative texture.

This is only one of many historical examples. Similar points could be made with reference to the medieval motet composers, the heterophonic folk music of certain areas, the music of non-European cultures, the music of Debussy, and many other spheres.

Of necessity, serial structures possess a different sort of permeability; the historical state of the material is after all a different one. Statistical-serial regulation is however slightly reminiscent of traditional systems of control, as for instance the system of figured basses.

The high degree of permeability of many serial structures has decisive formal consequences:

1. It makes possible the mobility of individual shapes—this mobility is in direct proportion to the size of the field in question—and this effects a loosening of the temporal flow. For its part, this loosening now permits the simultaneous control of activity in various different tempi, as in Stockhausen's "Zeitmasse" for five wind instruments.

2. The interpenetration of different structures gave rise to those specific forms that are concerned with the superposition of several layers that are different in quality. In electronic compositions such a method of construction is inspired by the technical conditions of the process of realization, i.e. the necessary procedure of producing individual contexts first and later synchronizing them. However, even the instrumental works of almost all serial composers show a tendency towards "layer-composition". The overlapping groups in

12. See K. Jeppesen: *The Style of Palestrina and the Dissonance* (2nd ed., London, 1946). [Au.]

Stockhausen's cited work for three orchestras[13] and many of Pousseur's methods[14] are examples chosen at random from a varied host. Koenig's 'Zwei
Klavierstücke' are an example of the purest layer-composition; the form is completely ruled by this procedure. Separate layers of various different types of
configuration are pressed together into a simultaneous activity, smelted
together as it were by the uniform timbre of the piano. The final form is thus
a product of interferences amongst the originally heterogeneous shapes. This
method of work is related to that of weaving simultaneous series together, as,
for example, in Boulez's "Structures." In this latter case, however, the individual layers were simply single horizontal threads of notes, whereas in the Koenig
piece it is a matter of complex prefabricated textures, folded into each other
according to a higher order plan.

High permeability and insensibility to intervals are even more essential features of the music of Cage and his circle, although this music proceeds from
quite different points of departure. Cage has written pieces which can be
played either on their own or together with other pieces. The separate pieces
of music thus become layers of a larger whole, which, though more dense than
its constituent parts, is yet not different in principle. The indifference of such
structures—which are the result of chance manipulations—is closely related to
the indifference of the automatic products of early serial music.

This indifference shows a tendency to spread beyond interval relationships
to other musical dimensions. Now that hierarchical connections have been
destroyed, regular metrical pulsations dispensed with, and durations, degrees
of loudness, and timbres have been turned over to the tender mercies of serial
distribution, it becomes increasingly difficult to achieve contrast. A flattening-
out process has begun to absorb the whole musical form. The more integral
the preformation of serial connections, the greater the entropy of the resulting
structures; for—in accordance with the relation of indeterminacy mentioned
earlier—the result of knitting together separate chains of connexions falls victim to automatism, in proportion to the degree of predetermination.

Let us take an illuminating analogy: playing with plasticine. The distinct
lumps of the various colors gradually become dispersed the more you knead
the stuff; the result is a conglomeration in which patches of the colors can still
be distinguished, whereas the whole is characterized by lack of contrast. Knead
on, and the little patches of color disappear in their turn, and give place to a
uniform gray. This flattening-out process cannot be reversed. Similar symptoms
can be discerned in elementary serial compositions. The postulation of series
means, here, that each element should be used with equal frequency and
should be given equal importance. This leads irresistably to an increase of
entropy. The finer the network of operations with pre-ordered material, the

13. Cf. Stockhausen, loc. cit., p. 24. [Au.]
14. The reader's attention is drawn to Pousseur's remarks (in the article already quoted) about
    "Polyphonic density" as one of the compositional parameters. His *Quintett* is conceived almost
    entirely in layers. (Cf. loc. cit., p. 52.) [Au.]

higher the degree of levelling-out in the result. Total, consistent application of the serial principle negates, in the end, serialism itself. There is really no basic difference between the results of automatism and the products of chance; total determinacy comes to be identical with total indeterminacy. This is the place to seek the parallelism (mentioned earlier) between integral-serial music and music governed by chance (John Cage). The following is characteristic of both types: pause—event—pause—event—pause, etc.;[15] naturally the events are variously structured and the pauses have different durations but the more differentiated the individual events and caesuras, the more evident becomes the levelling-out process in the result. This is a consequence of the fact that increased differentiation in the separate moments is only possible at the expense of the differentiation of the whole.

At the same time however there are tendencies at work in opposition to the levelling-out process that we have been describing. They result from the dissolution of the elementary serial organizations, which stands in direct and mutual relation to the levelling-out process. The primitive stage to which composition is relegated by automatism will only be supported by musicians who succumb to the fetish of total integration, and debase musical form to a simple arithmetical game, thus preparing the way for an imitative academicism that is certainly no better than the traditional sort. Adorno's negative diagnosis may well apply to such musicians (but not to the élite who pursue their thoughts further).[16]

It is only possible to take adequate measures against the levelling-out process when predetermination and chance are kept within bounds, i.e. when the highest possible degree of order is sought by means of decisions made by the composer in the process of composition. This is the only way in which a composer can work out individual, unconfused characters, and write music that is not content with the cheap function of being a more or less pleasant wallpaper-pattern in sound.

The possibilities of organizing such an order and defining such musical characters are available where the weight of serial composition has been shifted onto the global categories that we mentioned earlier. The total form is serially guided, but the individual moments are, within given limits, left to the composer's discretion.[17] "Musical office-work"[18] is thus thrust back into its proper place, where it fulfils its function in general planning. It ensures a control of the emerging form in its general shape, but raises no claims to being the work

15. However it is perhaps noteworthy that the pauses in Cage's music are generally longer than those in serial structures. [Au.]
16. See Adorno, "Das Altern der Neuen Musik" (The aging of new music), which appeared in the book *Dissonanzen* (Göttingen, 1956), p. 102ff. [Au.]
17. Several composers have given expression to these ideas in their theoretical articles, and despite their differences in orientation, they show remarkable unanimity. See the quoted articles by Stockhausen and Pousseur in *Die Reihe* 3, and also "Alea" by Boulez, which appeared in the *Darmstädter Beiträger zur neuen Musik* (Mainz, 1958), p. 44ff. [Au.]
18. We are indebted to Antoine Goléa for this term. [Au.]

itself. The formal function of this sort of serial "programming"[19] corresponds approximately to the modulations, cadential progressions and connected methods of articulation in tonal music. But here the planning is non-centralized and non-hierarchical (as opposed to the case of tonal music) and the controlling directives enjoy equal rights and even distribution in the determination of the form. The network of serial connections stands in the same relation to the form as do the genes in the chromosomes to the emerging organism.

When such a procedure is adopted, the compositional labor divides into two successive phases:

1. Serial preformation of the global determining factors.
2. Filling out by detailed decisions the network of possibilities that is the result of the first phase.[20] The desired characters can be worked out by postulating or avoiding certain specific constellations.[21]

A form conceived in this way, free of the rigid static quality of automatic products, can be handled with great flexibility, and this makes possible the composition of transitions. An example: in his "Gruppen" Stockhausen was in a position to compose, besides passages of homogeneous instrumentation—passages for strings alone, brass alone, percussion alone—passages of various degrees and mixtures, in which the transition from one dominant timbre to another was never a linear transition but always a transition proceeding by serial dosages. Stockhausen succeeded—with his specific ranges or ambituses, his statistical mobility-resultants and his group-densities—in typically characterizing the individual regions of his composition. These typical characteristics counteracted the otherwise general effect of the pulverization of the durations and thus maintained and articulated the form.

•   •   •   •   •

19. H. Eimert, "The composer's freedom of choice," *Die Reihe* 3, p. 7. [Au.]
20. Cf. Pousseur, loc. cit., p. 67, second paragraph. [Au.]
21. This idea is similar to one developed by Boulez in his article "Alea." However I cannot agree with his intention of making the network of possibilities submit to a method of "guided chance." Any latitude achieved by the loosening of the network should not be thrown open to chance but submitted to further ordered decisions, as I said before, with the aim of reducing the entropy of the structure to a relative minimum. It is a deceptive fallacy that the design of the resulting form can be left to the interpreter in the form of "freedom"—as is the case for example in Stockhausen's "Klavierstück XI" and Boulez's Third Piano Sonata. The interpreter is given a set of more or less finished building blocks and finds himself in a confusing position: he is supposed to be helping with the composition, but cannot escape from the circle of possible permutations that has been circumscribed by the composer. All possible "interpretations" have in fact been envisaged by the composer—and if not, then so much the worse for the overall form. In any case there is no genuine freedom of interpretation, simply a manifold *ossia* form (however much Boulez would like to defend himself against this view in his article). [Au.]

16 Steve Reich

Steve Reich (b. 1934) was a pioneer in the minimalist movement, which began in the 1960s. Minimalism marked a departure not only from the extremes of integral serialism and indeterminacy, but also from the sort of compositional complexities associated with composers such as Iannis Xenakis; and it proved to be greatly influential on subsequent musical developments. In the first of these two articles, which were written in 1968 and 1973, Reich advocates a process-oriented music that proceeds, like serial music, more or less automatically once it is set in motion while limiting itself to processes that transform the materials (in Reich's case, relatively simple diatonic patterns) in easily perceptible ways. The second essay reveals Reich's discomfort with contemporary musical specialization. Reflecting upon his dual status as composer and performer, he discusses the relationship of his work to the small ensemble for which it was then written and in which he himself performed, and to his fellow musicians, who played such a vital role in shaping that music.

FROM *Writings about Music*

MUSIC AS A GRADUAL PROCESS
(1968)

I do not mean the process of composition, but rather pieces of music that are, literally, processes.

The distinctive thing about musical processes is that they determine all the note-to-note (sound-to-sound) details and the over all form simultaneously. (Think of a round or infinite canon.)

I am interested in perceptible processes. I want to be able to hear the process happening throughout the sounding music.

To facilitate closely detailed listening a musical process should happen extremely gradually.

Performing and listening to a gradual musical process resembles:

> pulling back a swing, releasing it, and observing it gradually come to rest;
> turning over an hour glass and watching the sand slowly run through to the bottom;
> placing your feet in the sand by the ocean's edge and watching, feeling, and listening to the waves gradually bury them.

TEXT: *Writings about Music* (New York: New York University Press, 1974), pp. 9–11, 45–48.

Though I may have the pleasure of discovering musical processes and composing the musical material to run through them, once the process is set up and loaded it runs by itself.

Material may suggest what sort of process it should be run through (content suggests form), and processes may suggest what sort of material should be run through them (form suggests content). If the shoe fits, wear it.

As to whether a musical process is realized through live human performance or through some electro-mechanical means is not finally the main issue. One of the most beautiful concerts I ever heard consisted of four composers playing their tapes in a dark hall. (A tape is interesting when it's an interesting tape.)

It is quite natural to think about musical processes if one is frequently working with electro-mechanical sound equipment. All music turns out to be ethnic music.

Musical processes can give one a direct contact with the impersonal and also a kind of complete control, and one doesn't always think of the impersonal and complete control as going together. By "a kind" of complete control I mean that by running this material through this process I completely control all that results, but also that I accept all that results without changes.

John Cage has used processes and has certainly accepted their results, but the processes he used were compositional ones that could not be heard when the piece was performed. The process of using the *I Ching* or imperfections in a sheet of paper to determine musical parameters can't be heard when listening to music composed that way. The compositional processes and the sounding music have no audible connection. Similarly in serial music, the series itself is seldom audible. (This is a basic difference between serial (basically European) music and serial (basically American) art, where the perceived series is usually the focal point of the work.)

What I'm interested in is a compositional process and a sounding music that are one and the same thing.

James Tenney said in conversation, "then the composer isn't privy to anything." I don't know any secrets of structure that you can't hear. We all listen to the process together since it's quite audible, and one of the reasons it's quite audible is, because it's happening extremely gradually.

The use of hidden structural devices in music never appealed to me. Even when all the cards are on the table and everyone hears what is gradually happening in a musical process, there are still enough mysteries to satisfy all. These mysteries are the impersonal, unintended, psycho-acoustic by-products of the intended process. These might include sub-melodies heard within repeated melodic patterns, stereophonic effects due to listener location, slight irregularities in performance, harmonics, difference tones, etc.

Listening to an extremely gradual musical process opens my ears to *it*, but *it* always extends farther than I can hear, and that makes it interesting to listen to that musical process again. That area of every gradual (completely controlled) musical process, where one hears the details of the sound moving out away from intentions, occuring for their own acoustic reasons, is *it*.

I begin to perceive these minute details when I can sustain close attention and a gradual process invites my sustained attention. By "gradual" I mean extremely gradual; a process happening so slowly and gradually that listening to it resembles watching a minute hand on a watch—you can perceive it moving after you stay with it a little while.

Several currently popular modal musics like Indian classical and drug oriented rock and roll may make us aware of minute sound details because in being modal (constant key center, hypnotically droning and repetitious) they naturally focus on these details rather than on key modulation, counterpoint and other peculiarly Western devices. Nevertheless, these modal musics remain more or less strict frameworks for improvisation. They are not processes.

The distinctive thing about musical processes is that they determine all the note-to-note details and the over all form simultaneously. One can't improvise in a musical process—the concepts are mutually exclusive.

While performing and listening to gradual musical processes one can participate in a particular liberating and impersonal kind of ritual. Focusing in on the musical process makes possible that shift of attention away from *he* and *she* and *you* and *me* outwards towards *it*.

NOTES ON THE ENSEMBLE
(1973)

Since late in 1966 I have been rehearsing and performing my music with my own ensemble.

In 1963 I first decided that despite my limitations as a performer I had to play in all my compositions. It seemed clear that a healthy musical situation would only result when the functions of composer and performer were united.

In San Francisco in 1963 I formed my first ensemble which was devoted to free, and sometimes controlled, improvisation. This quintet met at least once a week for about six months, but because we were improvising on nothing but spur of the moment reactions I felt there was not any musical growth except when I brought in what I called *Pitch Charts,* which gave all players the same notes to play at the same time, but with free rhythm. Even with these charts the musical growth was much too limited, and the group was disbanded.

In the fall of 1965 I returned to New York, and by late in 1966 I had formed a group of three musicians; pianist Art Murphy, woodwind player Jon Gibson, and myself playing piano. This ensemble was able to perform *Piano Phase* for two pianos; *Improvisations on a Watermelon* for two pianos (later discarded); *Reed Phase* for soprano saxophone and tape (later discarded), and several tape pieces. This trio remained intact with occasional additions, notably that of composer/pianist James Tenney in 1967 to play a four piano version of *Piano Phase* and other pieces, until 1970 when the composition of *Phase Patterns* for four electric organs, and *Four Organs* for four electric organs and maracas created the need for a quintet adding pianist Steve Chambers and occasionally, composer/performer Phil Glass. In 1971, with the composition of *Drumming,* the ensemble underwent a significant expansion to twelve musicians and singers. At this time I sought out and found a number of fine percussionists, the most outstanding of whom, Russ Hartenberger and James Preiss, continue to play in the present ensemble. Also, and for the first time, I had to find singers who had the sense of time, intonation, and timbre necessary to blend in with the sound of the marimbas in *Drumming.* Joan LaBarbara and Jay Clayton proved to be perfectly suited to this new vocal style. It was in 1971 that the name of the ensemble, *Steve Reich and Musicians,* was first adopted.

I have thus become a composer with a repertory ensemble. Each new composition is added to the repertoire and our concerts present a selection of new and/or older works.

The question often arises as to what contribution the performers make to the music. The answer is that they select the resulting patterns in all compositions that have resulting patterns, and that certain details of the music are worked out by members of the ensemble during rehearsals. Resulting patterns are melodic patterns that result from the combination of two or more identical instruments playing the same repeating melodic pattern one or more beats out of phase with each other. During the selection of resulting patterns to be sung in the second section of *Drumming,* Joan LaBarbara, Jay Clayton, Judy Sherman and I all contributed various patterns we heard resulting from the combination of the three marimbas. These patterns were selected, and an order for singing them worked out, with the help of tape loops of the various marimba combinations played over and over again at my studio during rehearsals held throughout the summer of 1971. Similarly, in the resulting patterns for *Six Pianos,* Steve Chambers, James Preiss and I worked out the resulting patterns and the order in which to play them during rehearsals at the Baldwin Piano store during the fall and winter of 1972–73.

During the summer of 1973 in Seattle I worked with different singers in the marimba section of *Drumming* who heard and sang very different resulting patterns from the singers in New York. When I returned to New York I showed the new resulting patterns to Jay Clayton and Joan LaBarbara who decided to incorporate some of these patterns into their own version. The details of the music changed when the performers changed.

Selecting resulting patterns is not improvising; it is actually filling in the details of the composition itself. It offers the performer the opportunity to listen to minute details and to sing or play the ones he or she finds most musical.

There's a certain idea that's been in the air, particularly since the 1960's, and it's been used by choreographers as well as composers and I think it is an extremely misleading idea. It is that the only pleasure a performer (be it musician or dancer) could get was to improvise, or in some way be free to express his or her momentary state of mind. If anybody gave them a fixed musical score or specific instructions to work with this was equated with political control and it meant the performer was going to be unhappy about it. John Cage has said that a composer is somebody who tells other people what to do, and that it is not a good social situation to do that. But if you know and work with musicians you will see that what gives them joy is playing music they love, or at least find musically interesting, and whether that music is improvised or completely worked out is really not the main issue. The main issue is what's happening *musically;* is this beautiful, is this sending chills up and down my spine, or isn't it?

The musicians play in this ensemble, usually for periods of three to five years or more, because, presumably, they like playing the music, or at least because they find it of some musical interest. They do not make all their income from playing in this ensemble. Some are Doctoral candidates in the study of African, Indonesian and Indian music, some teach percussion, and all perform professionally in a variety of musical ensembles including orchestras, chamber groups, Medieval music ensembles, South Indian, African and Indonesian classical ensembles, free improvisation and jazz groups. It is precisely the sort of musician who starts with a strong Western classical background and then later gravitates towards these other types of music that I find ideally suited for this ensemble.

The presence of musicians who play certain instruments or sing encourages me to write more music for those instruments or voices. The percussionists and singers I began working with in *Drumming* encouraged me to write more percussion and vocal music. *Music for Mallet Instruments, Voices and Organ* is one of the results. Since the keyboard music I write involves up and down movements of the hands exclusively, instead of conventional keyboard technique, percussionists are better suited to play pieces like *Six Pianos* than most pianists are. Most of the musicians in my ensemble are therefore percussionists who double on the keyboard.

These musicians are also my first and most important critics. During early rehearsals when a first version of a new piece is being tried out, the reactions of the players will often tell me whether the new composition really works, or not. Not only direct verbal comments during or after rehearsal, but an appreciative laugh or an embarrassed averted glance may be enough to let me know I am on the right or wrong track. This was particularly the case in the early fall of 1972 when the reactions of James Preiss, Russell Hartenberger and Steve Chambers were enough to make me throw away several attempts at multiple piano pieces that preceded the finished version of *Six Pianos*.

There is also the question of frequency of rehearsals. Most new pieces of about 20 minutes in length will be rehearsed once or twice a week for two or three months. *Drumming*, which lasts about an hour and twenty minutes took almost a year of weekly rehearsals. This amount of rehearsing allows for many small compositional changes while the work is in progress and at the same time builds a kind of ensemble solidity that makes playing together a joy.

IV

MUSIC, SOCIETY, POLITICS

17 Kurt Weill

The changes in musical language that occurred in the early years of the twentieth century also raised basic questions about the social responsibilities of music:
for whom and what purpose was new music to be written? This became particularly evident in the period following the First World War. One of the first "classical" composers who attempted to address a larger and more diverse public
was the German Kurt Weill (1900–1950). In the 1920s he abandoned the more
traditionally modernist approach of his younger years to write theater works of
social commitment that drew heavily upon popular and vernacular traditions.
In this article, written in 1927, he stresses the need for music to assume a social
function, urging composers to address larger audiences and explore outlets
extending beyond the traditional concert hall. Turning from the "individualistic
principle" of previous Western art music, Weill considers modes of artistic collaboration and the possibility of developing an epic form of music better able
to affect public opinion.

Shifts in Musical Production
(1927)

If I am to address the question of the current musical situation from the
point of view of the creative musician, then I must restrict myself to considering that situation as it relates to the state of development in my own production.

The development of music in recent years has chiefly been an aesthetic one.
The emancipation from the 19th century, the opposition to extra-musical
influences (programme music, symbolism, realism), the return to absolute
music, the hard-won acquisition of new expressive means (the enrichment of
harmonic language, the cultivation of a new linearity) or an expansion of the
old means—these were the ideas which claimed musicians' attention. Today
we have come a step further. A clear split is becoming apparent between, on
the one hand, those musicians who, full of disdain for their audience, continue
as it were by shutting out the public sphere to work on the solution to aesthetic
problems and, on the other, those who enter into contact with some sort of
audience, integrating their work into some sort of larger concern, because they
see that above the artistic there is also a common human attitude that springs
from some sense of communal belonging and which has to be the determining
factor behind the genesis of a work of art.

It is clear that this withdrawal from the individualistic principle of art,
observable everywhere, has nowhere emerged with such eruptive force as in

TEXT: *Musik und Theater: Gesammelte Schriften*, ed. by Stephen Hinton and Jürgen Schebera
(Berlin: Hemschelverlag, 1990), pp. 45–47. Translation by Stephen Hinton. Used by permission of
the Kurt Weill Foundation.

Germany, where the foregoing development (the influence of the 19th century and the violent emancipation from it) was much more intense. While the search for a community is, for us, by no means to be confused with any concession to public taste, a large number of musicians from Latin countries are thoroughly attuned to a very cultivated type of *Gebrauchsmusik*. (Rieti, Poulenc, Auric, etc.) The serious musicians in search of new expressive means are apparently much more isolated and receive much less public attention there than in Germany. Yet precisely in Paris, among a budding generation of musicians, a rejuvenation of Catholicism, which originates from literature, seems to be leading to a new sense of community. Moreover, a ritualistic tendency, untypical for French art and finding expression in a preference for themes from antiquity, is characteristic of the current situation. (Stravinsky's *Oedipus Rex*, Milhaud's minute operas.) As far as they are known to us, however, the Russian musicians seem to have little affinity for communal art, although it is from them that one would most expect it. A conspicuous dependence on Scriabin among many Russian musicians would seem to preclude a 'revolutionary' attitude.

In Germany, then, there are the clearest signs that musical production must find a new justification for its existence. Here a restructuring of the public is clearly observable. The arts engendered by established society, originating as they do from another age and another aesthetic, are increasingly losing ground. The new orchestral and chamber music, for which a genuine demand used to exist on the part of the public, nowadays relies almost exclusively on music societies and organizations devoted to the cultivation of new music whose patrons are themselves mainly musicians. That is why music is seeking a rapprochement with the interests of a wider public since only in this way will it retain its viability. It does so, first of all, by utilizing the lightness and musical facility [*Musizierfreudigkeit*] acquired in recent years, in order to create a worthwhile *Gebrauchsmusik*. The whole area of mechanical music and film music should no longer be the sole preserve of a cheap, everyday commodity. Rather, a young generation of musicians has set about cultivating this area of musical life, for which the public at large also displays an interest. It now depends on the resolve of the appropriate 'industry' to lure the most talented young musicians and to provide them with the basis for a new development, which by no means needs to involve trivialization of any kind.

In addition, we find attempts to attract an audience specifically for the appreciation and cultivation of New Music. Of decisively symptomatic significance in this connection is the activity of a number of musicians within the Amateur Musicians' Guild [*Musikantengilde*] (Hindemith, Ludwig Weber), though it remains to be seen whether this youth movement is not too restricted to certain circles really to create the basis for the renewal of our musical culture or even for the creation of a people's art. More important than these endeavours is, for me, the fact that a large number of musicians whose merit is beyond doubt are again considering the possibility of speaking immediately to a wider public. This much is certain: the clarity of language, the precision of expression and the simplicity of emotion, which new music has regained by pursuing a straight line of development, form together the secure aesthetic foundation for a wider dissemination of this art.

The current situation is most clearly evinced in the field of music theatre. For opera today no longer represents a discrete musical genre (as in the 19th century) but has again taken its rightful place (starting, say, with Busoni's *Doktor Faust*) in the whole area of absolute music. It will also represent a most decisive factor in the development whereby music is no longer accorded the role of an art form engendered by established society but rather that of a socially regenerative or promoting force. Hence it cannot restrict itself either to a purely aesthetic renaissance, which allows principles of musical style to be the sole determinants, or to representing matters of merely superficial, topical relevance which are valid only for the briefest period of the work's genesis. I believe, above all, that musicians ought first to overcome their fear of truly equal collaborators. It has proved to be quite possible, working closely with representatives of equal stature in the sister arts, to set about creating the kind of music theatre that can provide an untopical [*unaktuelle*], unique and definitive representation of our age. I am also convinced, thanks to the newly attained inner and outer uncomplicatedness of subject matter and means of expression, that a branch of opera is developing into a new epic form such as I have employed with Brecht in the *Mahagonny* Songspiel.[1] True, this form of music theatre presupposes a basically theatrical type of music. Yet it also makes it possible to give opera a structure that is absolutely musical, even instrumental.

In this and in other areas of contemporary opera it is quite evident that the development of music is receiving new impulses from stage works produced for the cinema [*Theaterfilm*].

1. "Songspiel" is a term coined by Weill that he retained in English.

18 Joseph Goebbels

This is a shortened version of an address Joseph Goebbels, the German Minister of Enlightenment and Propaganda during the Third Reich, delivered in May 1938 at a music festival in Düsseldorf. An exhibition titled "Degenerate Music" was held in connection with this festival, modeled on the much more expansive and widely publicized exhibition of "degenerate visual art" held in Munich the previous summer. The cover of the guide for the music exhibition featured a caricature of a black man playing a saxophone and wearing a Star of David, joining in one image an expression of racial, religious, and musical hatred.

Speech for the Düsseldorf Music Festival
(1938)

The decline of German spiritual and artistic life in the years 1918 to 1933 did not spare music. The great sins of the time were also evident there and produced the most fruitful destruction in the domain of an art that until then had been seen throughout the world as the most German of all. A certain period of transition was thus required to remove the errors, failures, and manifestations of decline through systematic reform and the removal of the causes and symptoms of illness, and through the cultivation of the true artistic strengths of our German music. In a five-year plan of reconstruction we have attempted to overcome the severe crisis and gradually secure a firm new hold.

In the year 1933 German music life was in a truly desperate state. A threatening spiritual and artistic disintegration was imminent. The dissolution of all inner value, something that in Germany's past music had enabled it to achieve predominance throughout the entire world, seemed almost inevitable. The German masters, who with true artistic command had created immortal works of German tonal art, were suppressed by the flagrantly commercial elements of international Jewry. The so-called music that the latter produced and propagated inevitably led in time to the total constriction of public musical life.

It thus seemed like an impossible task to produce change and to direct the creative powers of the time back again to their own roots and to the strength-dispensing foundation of the German People. Here one could not prescribe, decree, or implement through force. The damage that had been produced had to be gradually alleviated through systematic cultivation of all the valuable strengths of German music. And good will alone would not suffice; time was necessary.

National Socialism has produced change. In a great burst it has swept away the pathological products of Jewish musical intellectualism. The power of Jewry is now broken in the realm of German music; German musical life is now cleansed of the last traces of Jewish arrogance and predominance. Our classical masters again appear before the public in pure and untarnished form. They will be brought before the broad masses of the People in large-scale concerts. In place of pure construction and desolate atonal expressionism, artistic intuition will again step forward as the source of musical creation. Perhaps this represents more than merely a work of national reform. Perhaps it is the beginning of the delivery of all Western music from a threatening decline.

TEXT: Joseph Wulf, *Musik im Dritten Reich: eine Dokumentation* (Gütersloh: Sigbert Mohn Verlag, 1963), pp. 416–17. Translation by Robert P. Morgan.

19 *Pravda*

Dmitri Shostakovich's opera *Lady Macbeth of the Mtsensk District* was reviewed in the official Soviet Party newspaper *Pravda* in January 1936. The opera, completed in 1932, had already been performed with considerable critical and public success both within Russia and abroad, but after ninety-seven performances in Moscow, it was chosen as the vehicle for announcing a new official policy of musical and artistic repression, delivered in the form of this review. Though the Soviets had tolerated considerable experimentation and innovation in the arts in the early years following the Revolution, this liberal attitude had been under attack for some time, especially since the full consolidation of Stalin's power in the early 1930s. The *Lady Macbeth* review marked an important milestone, signaling the onset of an extended period of severe artistic repression: never before had a Soviet composer been so ruthlessly and publicly denounced.

Chaos Instead of Music
(1936)

With the general cultural development of our country there grew also the necessity for good music. At no time and in no other place has the composer had a more appreciative audience. The people expect good songs, but also good instrumental works, and good operas.

Certain theaters are presenting to the new culturally mature Soviet public Shostakovich's opera *Lady Macbeth* as an innovation and an achievement. Musical criticism, always ready to serve, has praised the opera to the skies and given it resounding glory. The young composer, instead of hearing serious business-like criticism, which could have helped him in his future work, hears only enthusiastic compliments.

From the first minute, the listener is shocked by deliberate dissonance, by a confused stream of sounds. Snatches of melody, the beginnings of a musical phrase, are drowned, emerge again, and disappear in a grinding and squealing roar. To follow this "music" is most difficult; to remember it, impossible.

Thus it goes practically throughout the entire opera. The singing on the stage is replaced by shrieks. If the composer chances to come on the path of a clear and simple melody, then immediately, as though frightened at this misfortune, he throws himself back into a wilderness of musical chaos—in places becoming cacophony. The expression which the listener demands is supplanted by wild rhythm. Passion is here supposed to be expressed by musical noise. All this is

TEXT: Victor Seroff, *Dimitri Shostakovich: the Life and Background of a Soviet Composer* (New York: Alfred A. Knopf, 1943), pp. 204–7. Reprint permission granted by Ayer Company Publishers.

not due to lack of talent, or to lack of ability to depict simple and strong emotions in music. Here is music turned deliberately inside out in order that nothing will be reminiscent of classical opera, or have anything in common with symphonic music or with simple and popular musical language accessible to all. This music is built on the basis of rejecting opera—the same basis on which leftist[1] art rejects in the theater simplicity, realism, clarity of image, and the unaffected spoken word—which carries into the theater and into music the most negative features of "Meyerholdism"[2] infinitely multiplied. Here we have leftist confusion instead of natural, human music. The power of good music to infect the masses has been sacrificed to a petty-bourgeois, "formalist" attempt to create originality through cheap clowning. It is a game of clever ingenuity that may end very badly.

The danger of this trend to Soviet music is clear. Leftist distortion in opera stems from the same source as the leftist distortion in painting, poetry, teaching, and science. Petty-bourgeois "innovations" lead to a break with real art, real science, and real literature.

The author of *Lady Macbeth* was forced to borrow from jazz its nervous, convulsive, and spasmodic music in order to lend "passion" to his characters. While our music critics swear by the name of socialist realism, the stage serves us, in Shostakovich's creation, the coarsest kind of naturalism. He reveals[3] the merchants and the people monotonously and bestially. The predatory merchant woman who scrambles into possession of wealth through murder is pictured as some kind of "victim" of bourgeois society. The story of Leskov has been given a significance it does not possess.

And all this is coarse, primitive, and vulgar. The music quacks, grunts, and growls, and suffocates itself, in order to express the amatory scenes as naturalistically as possible. And "love" is smeared all over the opera in the most vulgar manner. The merchant's double bed occupies the central position on the stage. On it all "problems" are solved. In the same coarse, naturalistic style is shown the death from poisoning and the flogging—both practically on stage.

The composer apparently never considered the problem of what the Soviet audience expects and looks for in music. As though deliberately, he scribbles down his music, confusing all the sounds in such a way that his music would reach only the effete "formalists" who had lost their wholesome taste. He ignored the demand of Soviet culture that all coarseness and wildness be abolished from every corner of Soviet life. Some critics call this glorification of merchants' lust a satire. But there is no question of satire here. The author has

1. V. I. Lenin occasionally used the word "left" in his writings to characterize negatively the extreme "petty-bourgeois," "semi-anarchist," and "anti-Marxist" branch of the Russian revolutionary movement. See for example his article " 'Left-Wing' Communism—An Infantile Disorder," in Lenin, *Selected Writings* (Moscow: Progress Publishers, 1968), esp. p. 521.
2. Vsevolod Emilievich Meyerhold (1874–1942) was head of theater in the postrevolutionary U.S.S.R.; his progressive theatrical productions came under increasing criticism during the 1930s, ending in his arrest and disappearance in 1939.
3. "Reveals" presumably means "depicts" here—i.e., "depicts the merchants [on the stage]."

tried, with all the musical and dramatic means at his command, to arouse the sympathy of the spectators for the coarse and vulgar leanings and behavior of the merchant woman, Katerina Ismailova.

Lady Macbeth is having great success with bourgeois audiences abroad. Is it not because the opera is absolutely unpolitical and confusing that they praise it? Is it not explained by the fact that it tickles the perverted tastes of the bourgeoisie with its fidgety, screaming, neurotic music?

Our theaters have expended a great deal of labor on giving Shostakovich's opera a thorough presentation. The actors have shown exceptional talent in dominating the noise, the screaming, and the roar of the orchestra. With their dramatic action they tried to reinforce the weakness of melodic content. Unfortunately, this served only to bring out the opera's vulgar features more vividly. The talented acting earns gratitude; the wasted efforts, regrets.

20 Sergey Prokofiev

The relationship between Soviet composers and the official government policy toward the arts was complex and shifting. In order to function professionally, composers had to follow the party line, but just what that was could vary, especially in the earlier years. In its broad outlines, moreover, Soviet artistic policy was not so different from that promulgated by many non-Soviets during the years between the wars, and even the major Russian figures could often agree with it, at least in general. Certainly the following excerpts from writings by Sergey Prokofiev (1891–1953), the first and third dating from the late 1930s, the second from 1951, express views that seem in themselves innocuous enough: that music should appeal to large audiences without "playing down" to them; that it should be "clear" and "straightforward" in construction; and that composers should have a sense of social responsibility. Precisely how these recommendations were to be interpreted, however, or carried through, was another matter; and one is no doubt justified in reading Prokofiev's statements with some misgiving, considering the conditions of artistic repression and censorship that prevailed after the 1930s and the extent to which this composer himself suffered from them.

Three Commentaries

THE MASSES WANT GREAT MUSIC

The time is past when music was written for a handful of esthetes. Today vast crowds of people have come face to face with serious music and are waiting with eager impatience. Composers: take heed of this if you repel these crowds they will turn away from you to jazz or vulgar music. But if you can hold them you will win an audience such as the world has never before seen. But this does not mean that you must pander to this audience. Pandering always has an element of insincerity about it and nothing good ever came of that. The masses want great music, great events, great love, lively dances. They understand far more than some composers think, and they want to deepen their understanding.

I ADHERE TO THE CONVICTION . . .
(1951)

In America and Western Europe much is said about the mission of an artist and the freedom of his creativity. Indeed, can an artist stand aloof from life? Can he lock himself in an ephemeral "tower," circumscribe the circle of his creativity with subjective emotions, or should he be there where he is needed, where his word, his music, his chisel can help the people live a better and more interesting life?

Let us recall the creative paths of Beethoven and Shakespeare, Mozart and Tolstoy, Tchaikovsky and Dickens—those titans of the human intellect. Does not their greatness lie precisely in the fact that they, by their own will, by the call of duty and their souls, gave their mighty talents to the service of mankind? Are not their immortal works noted first and foremost for this trait?

When I was in the United States and in England I often heard people discuss the following questions: whom should music serve, what should a composer write about, and what should direct his creativity? I adhere to the conviction that a composer just as a poet, sculptor or painter is called upon to serve man and his people. He should beautify man's life and defend it. He is obligated, above all, to be a citizen in his art and to glorify man's life and lead man to a bright future. From my point of view, such is the firm code of art.

TEXT: *Materials, Articles, Interviews,* compiled by Vladimir Blok (Moscow: Progress Publishers, 1978), pp. 42, 52. *Autobiography, Articles, Reminiscences,* ed. by S. Shlifstein, trans. by Rose Prokofieva (Moscow, 1960), pp. 101–2. "The Masses Want Great Music" comes from a 1937 notebook, "I Adhere to the Conviction . . ." from the article "Music and Life," *Novosti,* No. 10, 1951, and "Flourishing of Art" from notes probably for the main points of an article or speech.

FLOURISHING OF ART

The search for a musical idiom in keeping with the epoch of socialism is a worthy, but difficult task for the composer. Music in our country has become the heritage of vast masses of people. Their artistic taste and demands are growing with amazing speed. And this is something the Soviet composer must take into account in each new work.

It is something like shooting at a moving target: only by aiming ahead, at tomorrow, will you avoid being left behind at the level of yesterday's needs. That is why I consider it a mistake for a composer to strive for simplification. Any attempt to "play down" to the listener is a subconscious underestimation of his cultural maturity and the development of his tastes; such an attempt has an element of insincerity. And music that is insincere cannot be enduring.

In my own work written in this fruitful year, I have striven for clarity and melodiousness. At the same time I have scrupulously avoided palming off familiar harmonies and tunes.

That is where the difficulty of composing clear, straightforward music lies: the clarity must be new, not old.

My main work this year has been a large cantata dedicated to the 20th anniversary of October. Its principal themes are the Great October Socialist Revolution, victory, industrialization and the Constitution.

The cantata is written for two choruses, professional and amateur, and four orchestras—symphony, military, percussion and accordion bands. No less than 500 people are required for its performance.

It gave me great pleasure to write this cantata. The complex events reflected in it demanded a complex musical idiom. But I trust that the passion and sincerity of the music will make it accessible to our audiences.[1]

Another large work just completed is a suite for chorus, soloists and orchestra which I intend to entitle *Songs of Our Days*. It will be performed for the first time on January 5 in the Large Hall of the Moscow Conservatory. It is written to words by Lebedev-Kumach, Marshak and other texts translated from Ukrainian and Byelorussian folk-lore and published in *Pravda*. My melodies here are written in the style of the given nationality. I hope they will be easily understood and remembered.

I have also composed several marches for military band, some mass songs and romances to Pushkin's verse on the occasion of the centenary of his death. Unfortunately, the theatres have not made use of the incidental music I wrote for a number of Pushkin productions.[2]

---

1. This cantata was never performed. Part of the musical material was used for the *Ode on the End of the War*. [Shlifstein]
2. Reference to music for the projected productions of *Boris Godunov* and *Eugene Onegin* and for the film *The Queen of Spades*. Part of this music was used in other compositions; some of it went into the opera *War and Peace* (scene in Hélène's house) and the Fifth Symphony *(Adagio)*. [Shlifstein]

21 Dmitri Shostakovich

Dmitri Shostakovich (1906–1975) was one of the two most prominent Russian composers of the Soviet period (the other was Sergey Prokofiev). Like those of his compatriot, all of Shostakovich's writings published during his lifetime closely hewed to the Communist Party line. Following the composer's death, however, the Russian music critic Solomon Volkov, who emigrated to the United States in 1976, published *Testimony,* a book of memoirs based on material dictated to him by the composer in the early 1970s. Though efforts have been made to discredit this work, most Shostakovich scholars accept the material as authentic. Certainly it offers a view of Soviet musical life much different from and more critical than anything officially published in the U.S.S.R. The excerpt included here recounts the events surrounding one of the two most wide-reaching Soviet crackdowns on progressive music (the other being the 1936 review of Shostakovich's own *Lady Macbeth of the Mtsensk District,* see No. 19): the notorious 1948 attack on Vano Ilyich Muradeli's opera *The Great Friendship.* In a manner at once humorous yet bitterly sarcastic, Shostakovich tells of Muradeli's desperate efforts to regain status after his sudden fall from official favor.

FROM *Testimony*

One of the disgruntled was Muradeli,[1] a fact that is now forgotten. After the historic resolution "On the Opera *The Great Friendship,*" Muradeli seemed to walk among the victims, but actually Muradeli was never a victim, and he was planning to warm his hands on his *Great Friendship.*

And he wanted more than just personal glory, he hoped to pull formalism out by the roots from music. His subsequently infamous opera was accepted for production in 1947 by almost twenty opera companies, and most important, the Bolshoi was doing it, and they were planning it for an important occasion— the thirtieth anniversary of the October Revolution. They were going to open at the Bolshoi on November 7, with Stalin attending.

Muradeli walked around and blustered, "He Himself will invite me into his box! I'll tell him everything! I'll tell him the formalists have been blocking

TEXT: *Testimony: the Memoirs of Dmitri Shostakovich,* as related to and edited by Solomon Volkov, trans. by Antonina W. Bouis (New York: HarperCollins Publishers, Inc., 1979), pp. 142–47. Reprinted by permission of HarperCollins Publishers, Inc.

1. Vano Ilyich Muradeli (1908–1970), a composer whose place in the history of Russian music is assured because he was grouped with Shostakovich and Prokofiev as a "formalist." Of course Muradeli does have his own musical "record": a singing Lenin makes his first appearance in his opera *October* (1964). (A talking Lenin appeared in Soviet opera in 1939, in Khrennikov's *Into the Storm.*) [Volkov]

my way. Something has to be done!" Everything seemed to augur success for Muradeli. The plot had ideology, from the lives of the Georgians and Ossetians. The Georgian Commissar Ordzhonikidze was a character in the opera, he was cleaning up the Caucasus. The composer was also of Caucasian descent. What more could you ask?

But Muradeli had miscalculated terribly. Stalin disliked the opera. First of all, he didn't like the plot, he found a major political error in it. According to the plot, Ordzhonikidze convinces the Georgians and Ossetians not to fight with the Russians. Stalin, as you know, was an Ossetian himself (and not a Georgian, as is usually thought). He took offense on behalf of the Ossetians. Stalin had his own view of the matter. He despised the Chechens and Ingush, who were just then being moved out of the Caucasus. That was a simple thing to do in Stalin's day. They loaded two nations into wagons and took them away to the devil. So Muradeli should have blamed all the evildoing on the Chechens and Ingush, but he didn't display the necessary mental nimbleness.

And then there was Ordzhonikidze. Muradeli showed his naïveté once more. He thought that it would be a good idea to have Ordzhonikidze in the opera, he didn't think that reminding Stalin of him was like stepping on a corn. At the time, the country had been informed that Ordzhonikidze had died from a heart attack. Actually, Ordzhonikidze shot himself. Stalin drove him to it.

But the main problem was with the *lezghinka*.[2] The opera was based on life in the Caucasus, so Muradeli crammed it full of native songs and dances. Stalin expected to hear his native songs, but instead he heard Muradeli's own *lezghinka,* which he had composed in a fit of forgetfulness. And it was that original *lezghinka* that angered Stalin the most.

There were black clouds, a storm was brewing. It just lacked an excuse, the lightning needed an oak to strike, or at least a blockhead. Muradeli played the part of the blockhead.

But in the end, Muradeli didn't get burned by the historic resolution "On the Opera *The Great Friendship.*"[3] He was a clever man and he managed to profit even from the historic resolution.

As you know, the resolution drew heated interest among the toiling masses. Meetings and gatherings were held everywhere, in factories, communal farms, industrial cartels, and places of public food consumption. And the workers discussed the document with enthusiasm, since, as it turned out, the document

2. In the Stalin years, the sounds of the *lezghinka,* a national Georgian folk dance, as well as the melody "Suliko," Stalin's favorite Georgian folk song, were familiar to millions of Soviet people. [Volkov]

3. "The year 1948 is a historical, watershed year in the history of Soviet and world musical culture. The 'Resolution of the Central Committee of All-Union Communist Party (Bolshevik) of February 10, 1948, On the Opera *The Great Friendship* by V. Muradeli,' harshly condemning the anti-people formalist tendency in Soviet music, broke the decadent fetters that hobbled for so many years the creativity of many Soviet composers; for many years ahead the only correct path for the development of musical art in the U.S.S.R. has been determined." (From a collective work published in 1948 by the Composers' Union.) [Volkov]

echoed the spiritual needs of millions of people. These millions were united in their rejection of Shostakovich and other formalists. And so Muradeli added his babble to satisfy the spiritual interests of the workers ... for money, of course.

Muradeli began making appearances at various organizations. He came to the people and repented. I was a so-and-so, a formalist and cosmopolite. I wrote the wrong *lezghinka,* but the Party showed me the way in time. And now I, the former formalist and cosmopolite Muradeli, have stepped onto the righteous road of progressive realistic creativity. And in the future I'm determined to write *lezghinkas* that are worthy of our great epoch.

Muradeli said all this in an agitated manner, with Caucasian temperament. The only thing he didn't do was dance the *lezghinka.* And then he sat at the piano and played excerpts from his future, yet-to-be-written works, worthy of our great epoch. The excerpts were melodious and harmonious, quite like the harmony exercises from the conservatory textbook.

Everyone was satisfied, the workers saw a live formalist, they had something to tell their friends and neighbors. Muradeli earned good money and met the Composers' Union's plan on self-criticism.

Why am I spending so much time on Muradeli? In a musical sense he was a rather pathetic figure and as a man he was extremely malignant. An excess of temperament might lead Muradeli to perform a good deed, but only by accident. For instance, once he got the wild idea of reconciling Prokofiev and me. He decided that if Prokofiev and I sat down at a table and started drinking Georgian wines and eating shashlik, we would become great friends. We had to, for who could resist Georgian wines and shashlik? Naturally, nothing came of that idea.

However, Muradeli played an important role in the business with formalism, albeit an extremely deplorable one. This was the situation. There was Shostakovich, who needed to be put in his place, and there was Muradeli, whose opera *The Great Friendship* displeased Stalin. But the problem of formalism in music did not yet exist, the horrible picture of a formalist conspiracy had not yet formed. They could hit Shostakovich and hit Muradeli and be finished. Stalin might not have even taken aim at all of Soviet music.[4] The impetus to start a broadly based destruction of Soviet music came from Muradeli and him alone.

After the unhappy presentation of *The Great Friendship,* a meeting was called at the Bolshoi Theater, and at that meeting Muradeli repented and came up with the following theory: that he loved melody and understood melody and

4. In order to appreciate Shostakovich's commentaries, one must picture the ubiquity of the "discussions" of formalism in music instituted in 1948. Unlike the "antiformalist" campaign of 1936, which had struck at many victims but then paled before the mass repressions, the "formalism" theme of 1948 became the most important issue in the public life of the times and dominated every conversation. [Volkov]

he would be more than happy to write melody alone, including melodious and harmonious *lezghinkas,* but it seems that he was kept from writing melodious *lezghinkas* because the formalist conspirators were everywhere—in the conservatories, in the publishing houses, in the press. Everywhere. And they forced poor Muradeli to write a formalist *lezghinka* instead of a melodious and harmonious one. Muradeli's *lezghinka* was the direct result of a conspiracy of enemies of the people, formalists, and toadies to the West.

And this version from Muradeli interested Stalin, who was always interested in conspiracies, an unhealthy interest that always had unpleasant consequences. The unpleasant consequences were quick to follow in this instance as well. One provocateur—Muradeli—had been found. But that wasn't enough. They gathered the composers, who began hanging one another. It was a pathetic sight that I would rather not recall. Of course, almost nothing surprises me, but this is one thing that's too repugnant to think about. Stalin designated to Zhdanov the task of compiling a list of the "main offenders." Zhdanov worked like an experienced torturer—he set one composer against the other.

Of course, Zhdanov didn't have to work too hard; the composers chewed one another up with glee. No one wanted to be on the list, it wasn't a list for prizes but for possible extermination. Everything had significance here—your position on the list, for instance. If you were first, consider yourself gone. Last—there was still hope. And the citizen composers knocked themselves out to avoid the list and did everything they could to get their comrades on it.[5] They were real criminals, whose philosophy was: you die today, and I'll go tomorrow.

Well, they worked and worked on the list. They put some names on, crossed others off. Only two names had the top spots sewn up. My name was number one, and Prokofiev's number two. The meeting was over, and the historic resolution appeared. And after that . . .

Meeting upon meeting, conference upon conference. The whole country was in a fever, the composers more than anyone. It was like a dam breaking and a flood of murky, dirty water rushing in. Everyone seemed to go mad and anyone who felt like it expressed an opinion on music.

Zhdanov announced, "The Central Committee of Bolsheviks demands beauty and refinement from music." And he added that the goal of music was to give pleasure, while our music was crude and vulgar, and listening to it undoubtedly destroyed the psychological and physical balance of a man, for example a man like Zhdanov.

Stalin was no longer considered a man. He was a god and all this did not

5. The reference is in part to the desperate attempt by Dmitri Borisovich Kabalevsky (1904–1987) to replace his name in a blacklist, prepared by Zhdanov, of composers "who held formalistic, anti-People tendencies" with that of Gavriil Nikolayevich Popov (1904–1972). The attempt was successful. The final text of the Party's "historic resolution" does not mention Kabalevsky. The talented Popov eventually drank himself to death. [Volkov]

concern him. He was above it all. The leader and teacher washed his hands of it, and I think he did so consciously. He was being smart. But I only realized this later. At the time it seemed as though my end had come. Sheet music was reprocessed; why burn it? That was wasteful. But by recycling all the caco-phonic symphonies and quartets, they could save on paper. They destroyed tapes at the radio stations. And Khrennikov said, "There, it's gone forever. The formalist snake will never rear its head again."

All the papers printed letters from the workers, who all thanked the Party for sparing them the torture of listening to the symphonies of Shostakovich. The censors met the wishes of the workers and put out a blacklist, which named those symphonies of Shostakovich's that were being taken out of circula-tion. Thus I stopped personally offending Asafiev, that leading figure of musical scholarship, who complained, "I take the Ninth Symphony as a personal insult."

From now unto forever, music had to be refined, harmonious, and melodi-ous. They wanted particular attention devoted to singing with words, since singing without words satisfied only the perverted tastes of a few aesthetes and individualists.

Altogether this was called: The Party has saved music from liquidation. It turned out that Shostakovich and Prokofiev had wanted to liquidate music, and Stalin and Zhdanov didn't let them. Stalin could be happy. The whole country, instead of thinking about its squalid life, was entering mortal combat with for-malist composers.

22 Marian Anderson

The contralto Marian Anderson (1897–1993) was one of the first African-Ameri-can artists to be recognized as a major performer of Western concert music. After completing her training in the United States, Anderson began concertizing and won a major New York Philharmonic competition in 1925; but only after successful concert tours in Europe in the early 1930s did she begin to receive full recognition at home. Indeed, Anderson's Metropolitan Opera debut did not take place until 1955, when she was past her prime. In this passage from her 1956 autobiography, Anderson recounts the most famous and politically charged event of her career: the refusal by officials at Constitution Hall in Wash-ington, D.C. to allow her to perform there in 1939 (supposedly on orders from the Daughters of the American Revolution, the hall's owners) and the legendary free outdoor concert she presented at the Lincoln Memorial instead.

FROM *My Lord, What a Morning*
(1956)

The excitement over the denial of Constitution Hall to me did not die down. It seemed to increase and to follow me wherever I went. I felt about the affair as about an election campaign; whatever the outcome, there is bound to be unpleasantness and embarrassment. I could not escape it, of course. My friends wanted to discuss it, and even strangers went out of their way to express their strong feelings of sympathy and support.

What were my own feelings? I was saddened and ashamed. I was sorry for the people who had precipitated the affair. I felt that their behavior stemmed from a lack of understanding. They were not persecuting me personally or as a representative of my people so much as they were doing something that was neither sensible nor good. Could I have erased the bitterness, I would have done so gladly. I do not mean that I would have been prepared to say that I was not entitled to appear in Constitution Hall as might any other performer. But the unpleasantness disturbed me, and if it had been up to me alone I would have sought a way to wipe it out. I cannot say that such a way out suggested itself to me at the time, or that I thought of one after the event. But I have been in this world long enough to know that there are all kinds of people, all suited by their own natures for different tasks. It would be fooling myself to think that I was meant to be a fearless fighter; I was not, just as I was not meant to be a soprano instead of a contralto.

Then the time came when it was decided that I would sing in Washington on Easter Sunday. The invitation to appear in the open, singing from the Lincoln Memorial before as many people as would care to come, without charge, was made formally by Harold L. Ickes, Secretary of the Interior. It was duly reported, and the weight of the Washington affair bore in on me.

●　　●　　●　　●　　●

I studied my conscience. In principle the idea was sound, but it could not be comfortable to me as an individual. As I thought further, I could see that my significance as an individual was small in this affair. I had become, whether I liked it or not, a symbol, representing my people. I had to appear.

I discussed the problem with Mother, of course. Her comment was characteristic: "It is an important decision to make. You are in this work. You intend to stay in it. You know what your aspirations are. I think you should make your own decision."

Mother knew what the decision would be. In my heart I also knew. I could

TEXT: *My Lord, What a Morning* (New York: Viking Press, 1956), pp. 187–91. Copyright renewed 1984 by Marian Anderson. Used by permission of Viking Penguin, a division of Penguin Books USA Inc.

not run away from this situation. If I had anything to offer, I would have to do so now. It would be misleading, however, to say that once the decision was made I was without doubts.

•   •   •   •   •

We reached Washington early that Easter morning and went to the home of Gifford Pinchot, who had been Governor of Pennsylvania. The Pinchots had been kind enough to offer their hospitality, and it was needed because the hotels would not take us. Then we drove over to the Lincoln Memorial. Kosti was well enough to play,[1] and we tried out the piano and examined the public-address system, which had six microphones, meant not only for the people who were present but also for a radio audience.

When we returned that afternoon I had sensations unlike any I had experienced before. The only comparable emotion I could recall was the feeling I had had when Maestro Toscanini had appeared in the artist's room in Salzburg. My heart leaped wildly, and I could not talk. I even wondered whether I would be able to sing.

The murmur of the vast assemblage quickened my pulse beat. There were policemen waiting at the car, and they led us through a passageway that other officers kept open in the throng. We entered the monument and were taken to a small room. We were introduced to Mr. Ickes, whom we had not met before. He outlined the program. Then came the signal to go out before the public.

If I did not consult contemporary reports I could not recall who was there. My head and heart were in such turmoil that I looked and hardly saw, I listened and hardly heard. I was led to the platform by Representative Caroline O'Day of New York, who had been born in Georgia, and Oscar Chapman, Assistant Secretary of the Interior, who was a Virginian. On the platform behind me sat Secretary Ickes, Secretary of the Treasury [Henry] Morgenthau [Jr.], Supreme Court Justice [Hugo] Black, Senators [Robert] Wagner, [James] Mead, [Alben] Barkley, [D. Worth] Clark, [Joseph] Guffey, and [Arthur] Capper, and many Representatives, including Representative Arthur W. Mitchell of Illinois, a Negro. Mother was there, as were people from Howard University and from churches in Washington and other cities. So was Walter White, then secretary of the National Association for the Advancement of Colored People. It was Mr. White who at one point stepped to the microphone and appealed to the crowd, probably averting serious accidents when my own people tried to reach me.

I report these things now because I have looked them up. All I knew then as I stepped forward was the overwhelming impact of that vast multitude. There seemed to be people as far as the eye could see. The crowd stretched in a great semicircle from the Lincoln Memorial around the reflecting pool on to the shaft of the Washington Monument. I had a feeling that a great wave of good will poured out from these people, almost engulfing me. And when I

1. Kosti Vehanen, Anderson's Finnish accompanist.

stood up to sing our National Anthem I felt for a moment as though I were choking. For a desperate second I thought that the words, well as I know them, would not come.

I sang, I don't know how. There must have been the help of professionalism I had accumulated over the years. Without it I could not have gone through the program. I sang—and again I know because I consulted a newspaper clipping—"America," the aria "O mio Fernando," Schubert's "Ave Maria," and three spirituals—"Gospel Train," "Trampin'," and "My Soul Is Anchored in the Lord."

23 Cornelius Cardew

During the 1960s, the English composer Cornelius Cardew (1936–1981), like many other young composers of the time, began focusing his energies on developing a more explicit social role for music, especially the "possibilities for political music-making." In 1969 he cofounded the Scratch Orchestra, a cooperative organization consisting of both professional and amateur musicians "willing and eager to engage in experimental performance activities." Players, both skilled and unskilled, participated on equal terms; and all musical decisions regarding what was to be played and how were determined by mutual agreement. Though the Scratch Orchestra had a brief and turbulent history and was plagued by considerable internal strife, it came to typify efforts of the time to rethink the entire musical project in more socially activist terms. This excerpt from the orchestra's "draft constitution" contains a definition, a statement of intent, and descriptions of four of the five repertory categories (the draft also includes a fifth, called "Research Project," and four "appendices" listing compositions, improvisations, and special projects).

FROM A Scratch Orchestra: Draft Constitution
(1969)

Definition: A Scratch Orchestra is a large number of enthusiasts pooling their resources (not primarily material resources) and assembling for action (music-making, performance, edification).

TEXT: *Scratch Music*, ed. by Cornelius Cardew (Cambridge: MIT Press, 1972), p. 10.

Note: The word music and its derivatives are here not understood to refer exclusively to sound and related phenomena (hearing, *etc*). What they do refer to is flexible and depends entirely on the members of the Scratch Orchestra.

The Scratch Orchestra intends to function in the public sphere, and this function will be expressed in the form of—for lack of a better word—concerts. In rotation (starting with the youngest) each member will have the option of designing a concert. If the option is taken up, all details of that concert are in the hands of that person or his delegates; if the option is waived the details of the concert will be determined by random methods, or by voting (a vote determines which of these two). The material of these concerts may be drawn, in part or wholly, from the basic repertory categories outlined below.

1 SCRATCH MUSIC

Each member of the orchestra provides himself with a notebook (or Scratchbook) in which he notates a number of accompaniments, performable continuously for indefinite periods. The number of accompaniments in each book should be equal to or greater than the current number of members of the orchestra. An accompaniment is defined as music that allows a solo (in the event of one occurring) to be appreciated as such. The notation may be accomplished using any means—verbal, graphic, musical, collage, *etc*—and should be regarded as a period of training: never notate more than one accompaniment in a day. If many ideas arise on one day they may all be incorporated in one accompaniment. The last accompaniment in the list has the status of a solo and if used should only be used as such. On the addition of further items, what was previously a solo is relegated to the status of an accompaniment, so that at any time each player has only one solo and that his most recent. The sole differentiation between a solo and an accompaniment is in the mode of playing.

The performance of this music can be entitled *Scratch Overture, Scratch Interlude* or *Scratch Finale* depending on its position in the concert.

2 POPULAR CLASSICS

Only such works as are familiar to several members are eligible for this category. Particles of the selected works will be gathered in Appendix 1. A particle could be: a page of score, a page or more of the part for one instrument or voice, a page of an arrangement, a thematic analysis, a gramophone record, *etc*.

The technique of performance is as follows: a qualified member plays the given particle, while the remaining players join in as best they can, playing along, contributing whatever they can recall of the work in question, filling the gaps of memory with improvised variational material.

As is appropriate to the classics, avoid losing touch with the reading player (who may terminate the piece at his discretion), and strive to act concertedly rather than independently. These works should be programmed under their original titles.

3 IMPROVISATION RITES

A selection of the rites in *Nature Study Notes* will be available in Appendix 2. Members should constantly bear in mind the possibility of contributing new rites. An improvisation rite is not a musical composition; it does not attempt to influence the music that will be played; at most it may establish a community of feeling, or a communal starting-point, through ritual. Any suggested rite will be given a trial run and thereafter left to look after itself. Successful rites may well take on aspects of folklore, acquire nicknames, *etc.*

Free improvisation may also be indulged in from time to time.

4 COMPOSITIONS

Appendix 3 will contain a list of compositions performable by the orchestra. Any composition submitted by a member of the orchestra will be given a trial run in which all terms of the composition will be adhered to as closely as possible. Unless emphatically rejected, such compositions will probably remain as compositions in Appendix 3. If such a composition is repeatedly acclaimed it may qualify for inclusion in the Popular Classics, where it would be represented by a particle only, and adherence to the original terms of the composition would be waived.

· · · · ·

24 Ethel Smyth

Against seemingly insurmountable odds, Ethel Smyth (1858–1944) established herself as a composer and critical writer of considerable importance in late nineteenth- and early twentieth-century England, a time when professional opportunities were largely barred to women in the field of music. Smyth, who was also active in the women's suffrage movement, wrote sharp-penned prose that met with considerable critical and popular success. The following excerpt is from an article written shortly after World War I, a time when women, having recently acquired new freedom and mobility during the war, were suddenly thrust back into their former positions of subservience. Smyth argues for a resuscitation of the moribund postwar English orchestral life through an influx of feminine vitality, which she believes would bring a new richness and more robust spirit to performances. And as she also observes, taking this step would help create a musical atmosphere in which women musicians, including composers, would be able to compete on a more equal professional footing with men.

FROM *Streaks of Life*
(1921)

AN OPEN SECRET

I know few places more depressing nowadays than concert rooms, apart from their being too often half empty when the free list is suspended. Programme after programme is reeled off with scarce a semblance of fervour (even the critics, the least critical beings in the world, are beginning to notice it), and judging by appearances the audience are derelicts putting in time till something more interesting happens—a tea-party perhaps, or, if it is an evening concert, bed. Of course there are exceptions, but as a rule this is the situation.

It may be partly owing to war fatigue, and I fancy another factor is the disappearance of the Germans and German Jews who, whatever their faults, really do love music and disseminated an attitude towards it that counteracted our own fundamental indifference. But I also believe that the commercial principles we carry into everything, and which result in as many performances and as little rehearsing as possible, bring their own Nemesis. Spiritual aridity, the mead of all who industrialize sacred things, has overtaken languid performer and bored listener, and people who once cherished illusions on this subject are beginning to ask themselves whether we are a musical people—in the sense that we certainly are a sporting and an adventurous people. The exterior equipment, perhaps a heritage of the past, is there still—beautiful voices, exquisitely fine ears, and great natural technical facility; but the fire within burns low and capriciously.

The one element of hope lies, I think, in the gradual interpenetration of the life musical by women. I say this in no fanatical feminist spirit, but in all calmness, as the result of quiet and, I trust, sane observation of things in general, and of what is going on under my nose in particular. What is more, many thoughtful, knowledgeable men I know are saying the same; not openly, for moral courage is, I think, the rarest virtue in the world, but in corners!

Generally speaking I find women more capable of enthusiasm and devotion, readier to spend and be spent emotionally than men—as I noticed in my deal-

TEXT: *The Memoirs of Ethel Smyth*, abridged and introduced by Ronald Crichton (New York: Viking Penguin, Inc., 1987), pp. 339–42. Reprinted by permission of David Higham Associates.

ings with stage choruses long before the war. Their nerves, too, seem nearer the surface, more responsive to appeal, less deeply buried under that habitual resistance to the emotional appeal which is surely a post-Elizabethan trait. I cannot conceive of music being an Englishman's religion—that is, a thing pure of financial taint—but in the case of an Englishwoman I can conceive it. At this moment, too, women are the keener, the harder-working sex. All the world over men seem disinclined to put their backs into the job—war-weariness, it is called—and the responsible statesmen of Europe are unanimous in ascribing the slackness of trade in large measure to the slackness of the workers. But during the war woman *found out her powers*, glories in them now, and only asks to go on using them.

During the war it became impossible to carry on without admitting women into the orchestras, and few things more deeply impressed such as were capable of dispassionate judgement than the increased brilliance and warmth of tone. A new and refreshing spirit, too, was perceptible—in part the result, no doubt, of sex rivalry of the right sort. Well do I remember the transfiguration of a certain elderly violinist who seldom used more than half his bow, and who now was making it bite into the strings as it had not bitten for years in honour of the extremely capable maiden who was sharing his desk. But I think the main gain was the infusion of un-war-wearied feminine vitality, the "go" of keen young talents for the first time allowed scope.

It was generous-minded Sir Henry Wood, I think, who first started mixed bathing in the sea of music, and so successful was the innovation that many other orchestras followed suit. True, the London Symphony Orchestra, much to its disadvantage, in my opinion, still remained an all-male body, except of course as regards the harp (an immemorial concession, I imagine, to aesthetic promptings . . . this solitary, daintily clad, white-armed sample of womanhood among the black coats, as it might be a flower on a coal dump). One hoped however that in time the LSO would come to see the error of its ways and that one more selfish monopoly was a thing of the past.

But now, a bolt from the blue: it appears that the Hallé orchestra at Manchester, true to its Hun origin I suppose, has suddenly sacked its women members. Not in order to make way for fighting men whose places they had been occupying—no woman that breathes but gives way gladly in such case—but merely because of their sex!

Asked to justify this proceeding, the Committee give two reasons that remind one of the wonderful excuses put forward for opposing female Suffrage—excuses so feeble, so transparently bogus, that one almost pities the gentlemen who, unequal to higher flights of invention, imagine that this sort of thing will do!

The first excuse is that when on tour it is not always easy to find suitable hotel accommodation for "the ladies." Very sad—yet dramatic companies have not yet reverted to the Elizabethan practice of entrusting women's roles to men on that account!

But the second excuse is the supreme effort—as fine an instance of solemn pretentious humbug, in other words cant, as I have ever come across. It is in the interests of "Unity of Style," we are told, that the women have been shown the door!

Now will anyone bind a wet towel round his head (yes, *his* head, for only a man can expound the deeper workings of the male mind) and tell us what on earth this means? What, pray, is "unity of style" in this sense? When Joachim and Lady Hallé played the Double Concerto in the very town whence issues this precious pronouncement, did the fathers and uncles of the members of that Committee hand in their resignation? Did Bach turn in his grave with horror (although it is his own fault for not mentioning the sex question in his score)? Do the soprani and alti interfere with the "unity of style" in a chorus? Does the English Quartet, that is led by Miss Hayward, lack it?

No! You can talk of unity of style between static things, such as Italian violins, verses of a poem, houses in a street, bank clerks, priests, etc., but not in the case of a fluid force. Sex will not give it to forty men of different talent, temperament, habit, digestions and schools; that is the conductor's office. And two first-class artists of different sexes who respond subtly to his intention can more easily be welded by him into the "unity" he wants than a first-rate and fourth-rate male.

But a truce to poking about in the unsavoury dust-heap of man's disingenuous reasons for doing an ugly action. Let us rather see what that action leads to.

Apart from the more spiritual element which I know women will bring, as performers, to the making of music, their admission on equal terms with men to our orchestras has another aspect. As I am never weary of pointing out, orchestral playing is the finest training a young composer can have, and the cheapest. The whole of musical literature passes across your desk; you are learning form and instrumentation automatically; and even though much of your time be spent in what must be the hateful work of giving lessons, you are on the crest of the wave of music, where strong breezes refresh your spirit and keep it buoyant.

Finally, to wind up with a consideration of a practical order, once you are member of a well-known orchestra, you are entitled to ask good fees for private lessons.

All this was hitherto denied to woman; no wonder the sacred flame that burned in her bosom throughout her student years too often flickered out. I have always maintained that until we are in the rough and tumble of musical life as men are, there cannot possibly be many women composers worth talking about. Competition, environment, and the sort of chance you get all round, are to talent what sunshine and the less poetical activities of the gardener are to a flower. In a word, the general level of human circumstance determines what stature one particularly gifted being can be expected to attain, and if you have to hurl yourself upwards from the sea-level you may become a Tenerife, but improbably a Mount Everest.

Bullying and cowardice, meanness and jealousy, are not pretty qualities, and I wonder if men have a notion with what contempt women view these attempts to prevent them from earning their livelihood in any sphere for which they can prove themselves fitted? Meanwhile, as finishing touch, a certain group of young intellectuals are busy shedding crocodile's tears in any newspaper that will act as blotting paper over the paucity of female stars of the first magnitude, *the equality of their chances with men notwithstanding!* . . .

25 Eva Rieger

The participation of women in professional musical life has grown dramatically in the second half of the twentieth century and has encompassed all areas, including performance, composition, scholarship, and teaching. This growth has been achieved, however, only with considerable struggle, and since full equity is far from attained, that struggle continues. While many have argued for more active professional participation by women simply on the principle of equal opportunity for all, others have maintained that such participation is desirable because women bring unique qualities to the art, enhancing and enriching it. The latter, so-called essentialist, position is represented in this 1992 article (here somewhat condensed) by the Dutch musicologist Eva Rieger. Noting that "sex role is one of the most important determinants of human behavior," Rieger identifies and discusses characteristics she finds typical of much music composed by women.

"I Recycle Sounds": Do Women Compose Differently?
(1992)

No one would get worked up if one decided to study ethnological differences in music of people living in various geographical places, but when one suggests studying differences in music by people of opposed sex, musicologists get

TEXT: *Journal of the International League of Women Composers*, March 1992, pp. 22–25. The present text is a shortened version of the original, made with the author's approval.

extremely touchy. Yet sociologists teach us that gender is one of the most important determinants of human behavior. In our Western culture men and women have had different cultural fields assigned to them, and this tradition prevails in our thoughts and emotions. Pedagogical research has shown that girls prefer different musical instruments than boys, their musical preferences differ, and a German research project on children's drawings revealed that boys mostly draw instrumentalists standing on their own, whereas girls show them playing in a group. Yet the question whether women compose differently than men has been posed mainly by the feminist scene up to now. It is usually assumed that the musical style and development is something confined solely to aesthetic issues and has nothing to do with gender.

When discussing the subject of women aesthetics, someone is bound to protest and say "oh, but I know a male composer who composes exactly that way," or "I know a female composer who composes exactly opposite." This level of argument leads nowhere, as it is confined to personal experience. Yet my assumptions are also based on listening experience. Should I therefore bury the subject? I admit that it is well-nigh impossible to prove my points; they remain hypothetical. Yet if we on the other hand wanted to come to scientifically proven results we would have to study hundreds of pieces of music by women and just as many by men. We would have to take their age, their nationality, their opinions, their development just as much into account as their sex. Such a research project would need enormous personal and financial resources, and even then we would not really come to fixed results. Nevertheless, I am aware that one day such research will have to be undertaken in order to put the subject on a more reliable level. This paper serves only to spark a discussion on the subject.

I am not determined to prove by all means that women compose differently. That would be ideological. I am just taking the before-mentioned assumption seriously that sex role is one of the most important determinants of human behavior. In consequence it seems to me sensible to ask whether gender influences music, especially since other disciplines like the visual arts, film and literature have been posing these questions for years.

Although we must distinguish between the *theoretical* constructions of male and female, as can be found in ideologies and which have led to a distorted picture of women, and the *real* differences, I believe that the real differences, which are based on different biological, social, psychological and aesthetic experiences of women and men in patriarchal culture, are to an extent influenced by the theoretical constructions of female. By suggesting that women have adopted certain traits because of their roles, I do not intend to push them back to the confinement of the past. However, the more I realize that women cannot rid themselves of their traditions by a sheer act of will-power (our past is too much a part of our present), the question arises as to whether they should not redefine some of these traditions and derive strength from them, instead of ignoring or condemning them.

In the past women acquiesced to the male-defining music system, and their creations were absorbed into the masculine tradition, which resulted for instance in Clara Schumann speaking disparagingly of her own music. I do not agree with Elaine Showalter, who in her book *Feminist Criticism in the Wilderness* maintains that a woman's culture existed in the past. I doubt whether we can find an independent counter-tradition, but there are signs that women in the past had a different approach to music, and that some mutual bonds between women composers exist. If we compare Clara Schumann's piano variations on a theme by Robert Schumann with the variations of Johannes Brahms on the same theme, we find that whereas Clara Schumann's variations are closely connected with the original theme, Brahms creates a well-nigh new piece of work. He departs from the original theme and turns his music into Brahms' music. It seems to me typical for a woman of the nineteenth century that Clara Schumann was thinking more of Robert than of herself. But our culture will always define Brahms' variations as the more valuable, because in our aesthetic hierarchy the innovative effect is ranked highest of all.

It would be ridiculous to maintain that all women compose similarly or in a specific style. Women composers cannot be judged all on the same scale—they differ by age, nationality, talents, places of residence, state of maturity, experience, etc. All sorts of music ranging from uncritical adaptation and assimilation up to the search for specifically female modes of expression can be found. Yet when listening to music composed by women in the twentieth century I have very often found what seem to me remarkable similarities. I have not just listed them—that would be arbitrary—but have attempted to trace them back to specific social-historical conditions and facts. I shall state and discuss seven points which I find typical for a great deal of music written by women.

1. Many women have a special ability to create a maximum amount out of a minimum of material, a sort of "restricted aesthetics."

Although women have composed in all forms and genres, ranging from small piano pieces to the mass and the symphony, they were in the nineteenth century confined mainly to parlor music on account of their social status. (This of course led to the well-known prejudice that women were unable to compose large forms.) They are skilled in writing music which can be performed easily and are less experienced in writing music for its own sake. This tradition prevails: songs, piano and chamber music predominate in music written by women. It is difficult to judge whether women are struggling with a negative burden or whether their ability to make the most of limited circumstances can also be a specific talent which is linked to their social character. The striving of composers like Pauline Oliveros, Annea Lockwood, Anne Gillis, Joan La Barbara and others to intensify the act of listening by limiting the material should be seen in this light.

2. Many have a special preference for functional music.

Women were also allotted to the fields of church music, music for educational purposes and music for amateurs. This has to do with the jobs women could get in the nineteenth century; the main field open for them was the so-called "social mothering," meaning jobs as teachers, governesses and nurses.

Even today a large amount of music written by women is functional music, and once more we must ask whether women prefer this branch because they are particularly skilled, or because they have not rid themselves of the constraints of tradition. Whatever the reason may be, women have written excellent functional music. German composers like Erna Woll and Felicitas Kukuck are known for the high quality of their church and pedagogic music.

3. Communication is of primary concern to them.

A while ago the German feminist magazine EMMA organized a competition for female journalists. The jury announced later: "When women write, they don't ramble. They have a message to transmit." This attitude can often be found in many women composers. They often compose music that alludes to something or someone; they like to tell stories. They write music that can be played, performed, and understood and the contact to the audience is of primary concern to many of them. Sofia Gubaidulina has for instance written hardly any music without a title, a text, a ritual or some kind of instrumental "action."

The traditional view of the male gender role in Western societies emphasizes power, strength, aggressiveness, competitiveness and logic, while the female role involves nurturing, cooperativeness and emotion. The role of women as mothers has taught them to harmonize conflicts, to negotiate in family problems, to unite instead of separate. This has consequences for their artistic output. For instance, they often have the performers in mind while composing, prefer to talk to the instrumentalists beforehand and get acquainted with their way of handling their instruments, and this influences them when composing.

4. Women composers are more interested in constituent substance than in compulsive innovation.

The male desire for narcissistic self-celebration is frequently missing in women, so that they do not feel the impulse to create sensations with hitherto unheard-of music. Many male composers seem to have their careers foremost in mind when composing. They aspire to become famous, and their music is often a novelty which aims at publicity, possible notoriety. It is quite possible that women might one day imitate men's burning desire for becoming famous, but for women today it has not the same importance. This has to do with the tradition of the nineteenth century when no jobs were offered them and they composed for their own pleasure (amateur status vs. professional status). This is why they do not find the craze for novelty and uniqueness as important as men, and it may explain why composers like Louise Farrenc, Louisa Adolpha Le Beau or Emilie Mayer in the nineteenth century, or Ethel Smyth, Grazyna Bacewicz and others in the twentieth century did not crave to develop a new language but rather leaned back on tradition. I am certainly not suggesting that women have difficulties in creating novelties, but rather that they do not find it important to be novel just for novelty's sake. They stress the content more than the aspect of material development. The German Canadian composer Hildegard Westerkamp uses background music from the radio as material, and she says of herself: "I recycle sounds."

5. They often strive to overcome binary contrasts.

Myriam Marbe firmly believes there is no such thing as past and present, but rather that times melt into each other. We often find women composers or performers attempting to combine various traditions, as for instance Ushio Torikai or Jin Him Kim who integrates into her work elements that she has assimilated from traditional Korean music. Eliane Radigue converted to Tibetan Buddhism and writes music in a semi-religious style which is intended to slow down the listeners. This aptitude to turn back instead of straight ahead can be seen as a more cyclic preference, contrary to the dynamic straight-forward line preferred by many men.

6. The aspect of "Ganzheitlichkeit" [the quality of being complete] means that they wish to combine various fields of art, but also the whole of human being, body and soul, Mankind (or Womankind) and Nature.

This probably has to do with women's preference to combine rather than to tear apart, which again can be attributed to women's role in society for many centuries. Women musicians like the Japanese Ushio Torikai or Meredith Monk often include other arts such as theatre, dance and performance in their music. They find it adequate to express themselves by taking fragments of the cultural diversity surrounding them and moulding these fragments into a unity. The wish to combine music and the visual arts is also strong. In the USA Performance Art has been developed mainly by women. Women composers often express the wish to be at harmony with nature. The American composer and singer Candace Natvig has studied bird's singing and tries to prove that music of old societies is influenced by the sounds of nature.

7. They relate closely to their own bodies and the human voice.

Men are physically nonproductive, whereas the creative powers of women are experienced in their own bodies. They did not experience the rigid borderline between body and spirit as did men. The confinement of women to the home also led to their composing innumerable songs in the nineteenth century. This tradition has led to a close relationship of the woman composer with the human voice, and especially to the female voice. This voice tradition is very alive today. Contemporary composers like Meredith Monk, Pauline Oliveros, Laurie Anderson, Connie Beckley and others trod new ground with their voice experiments. Joan LaBarbara is renowned for her exploration of vocal techniques inspired by musical traditions throughout the world. She has developed a vocabulary of new techniques including multiphonics, circular breathing and guttural sounds.

Sometimes these points unite in one composer, as for instance in the case of Oliveros or Gubaidulina. Pauline Oliveros need not be mentioned in detail as her striving to intensify the experience of listening, to abolish the linear structure of Western music and to unite many disparate elements in her music is well known. Sofia Gubaidulina is not interested in feminism, yet she composes as if she were a feminist: she is open towards all material. She is not stylistically bound, but concentrates on the contents of music. For her religion and music are just as much a unity as music and language, music and scenes. She combines folkloristic instruments like the bajan with classical instruments (violoncello); she is concerned with improvisation, is not interested in originality for its own sake, wishes to convert her audience from their "staccato" life style to a more meditative attitude, and she often stresses the unity of mankind with nature.

When one listens to music one cannot judge whether it has been written by a man or woman, one can only guess. It is possible, however, to trace female mentality and experience in the music of women. This is easy for instance in music of someone like Ruth Anderson, who in her piece, *I come out of your sleep,* uses electronic music to create the sound of breathing, which has a soothing effect on her listeners. On the other hand you will find that someone as rational-minded as Elisabeth Lutyens prefers to change time signatures, as she feels rhythm is more akin to breathing and spontaneous movement than to the military march. The music styles of Anderson and Lutyens differ hugely and prove that it would be useless to define a feminine aesthetic in the same sense of similarity; but we can trace their convictions back to their female experience.

I believe that women composers should get involved with women's traditions because they could then derive power and energy from them instead of ignoring or negating them. As to theorists and feminists, we should not forget that our Western culture is made to fit male requirements. If we continue to evaluate music written by women by male standards, we would have to define much of it as "deficient." As long as symphonic music is looked upon as more prestigious than chamber music, as long as functional music counts less than absolute (abstract) music, as long as the product is looked on as more valuable than the act of production, as long as music is defined by qualities such as loudness, virtuosity and greatest input instead of emphasizing heightened awareness and sensibility, as long as binary contrast such as body/soul, pop music/classical music, tradition/progression, functional music/absolute music etc. persist, music written by men will be looked on as superior. It will be necessary to attack conventional hierarchies and search for other values in which women can be represented. This can only be done satisfactorily, of course, if women's role is put on an equal basis with men's in society. In the meantime there are signs that male composers are changing their attitudes towards the role of music in society, and that they are taking over "feminine" traits in their music. So the challenge goes to both sexes, and it looks as if some exciting music is in store for us in the future.

26 William Grant Still

William Grant Still (1895–1978) was the first black composer to gain wide-spread recognition as a writer of American concert music. After receiving a degree in music from Oberlin College, Still moved to New York, where he studied privately with Edgard Varèse and became a leading figure in the Harlem Renaissance Movement of the 1920s. Still's pioneering role in American music is reflected in numerous accomplishments: he was the first African-American to write a symphony and have it performed by a major orchestra, the first to conduct a major symphony orchestra, the first to compose an opera produced by a major American company, and the first to produce music for radio, film, and television. In this autobiographical passage from an address delivered at UCLA in 1957, Still discusses the diverse influences he encountered as a young black composer and speaks of his wish—contrary to the advice of those advocating a more traditional concert style or more emphasis on ethnic and vernacular materials—to remain receptive to all of them.

FROM Horizons Unlimited

(1957)

I speak as a composer who has, in a very real sense, been through the mill. In my early days, I studied at Conservatories with Conservatory-trained teachers. There I learned the traditions of music and acquired the basic tools of the trade. If I had stopped there, the sort of music I later composed might have been quite different. But necessity forced me to earn a living, so I turned to the field of commercial music.

Back in the days when America became aware of the "Blues," I worked with W. C. Handy in his office on Beale Street in Memphis. This certainly would not seem to be an occupation nor a place where anything of real musical value could be gained. Nor would nearby Gayoso Street, which was then a somewhat disreputable section. But, in searching for musical experiences that might later help me, I found there an undeniable color and a musical atmosphere that stemmed directly from the folk.

Any alert musician could learn something, even in that sordid atmosphere. W. C. Handy listened and learned—and what he learned profited him financially and in other ways in the succeeding years. He, of course, belongs in the popular field of music. But if a popular composer could profit by such contacts with folk music, why couldn't a serious composer? Instead of having a feeling

TEXT: *William Grant Still and the Fusion of Cultures in American Music*, ed. by Robert Bartlett Haas (Los Angeles: Black Sparrow Press, 1975), pp. 114–16. Reprinted by permission of William Grant Still Music.

of condescension, I tried to keep my ears open so that I could absorb and make mental notes of things that might be valuable later.

As the years went on, and I went from one commercial job to another, there were always people who tried to make me believe that the commercial field was an end in itself, and who argued that I should not waste my time on what is now often called "long-hair" music. In this, I disagreed. I felt that I was learning something valuable, but only insofar as I could use it to serve a larger purpose.

The next important step was my study with Edgard Varèse. He might be classed as one of the most extreme of the ultramodernists. He took for himself, and encouraged in others, absolute freedom in composing. Inevitably, while I was studying with him, I began to think as he did and to compose music which was performed; music which was applauded by the avant-garde, such as were found in the International Composers' Guild. As a matter of fact, I was so intrigued by what I learned from Mr. Varèse that I let it get the better of me. I became its servant, not its master. It followed as a matter of course that, after freeing me from the limitation of tradition, it too began to limit me.

It took me a little while to realize that it *was* limiting me, and that the ultra-modern style alone (that is to say, in its unmodified form) did not allow me to express myself as I wished. I sought then to develop a style that debarred neither the ultra-modern nor the conventional.

Certain people thought this decision was unwise, and tried to persuade me to stay strictly in the ultra-modern fold. I didn't do it, but at the same time, the things I learned from Mr. Varèse—let us call them the horizons he opened up to me—have had a profound effect on the music I have written since then. The experience I gained was thus most valuable even though it did not have the result that might have been expected.

After this period, I felt that I wanted for a while to devote myself to writing racial music. And here, because of my own racial background, a great many people decided that I ought to confine myself to that sort of music. In that too, I disagreed. I was glad to write Negro music then, and I still do it when I feel so inclined, for I have a great love and respect for the idiom. But it has certainly not been the *only* musical idiom to attract me.

Fortunately for me, nobody tried to talk me out of the two things that strikingly influenced my musical leanings, possibly because those influences were not the sort which make themselves known to outsiders as readily as others. The first was my love for grand opera, born around 1911 when my stepfather bought many of the early Red Seal recordings for our home record library. I knew then that I would be happy only if someday I could compose operatic music, and I have definitely leaned toward a lyric style for that reason.

The second influence had to do with writing for the symphony orchestra, something which has deeply interested me from the very start of my musical life. Many years ago, I began to evolve theories pertaining to orchestration, and to experiment with them from time to time. Applying those theories has tended to modify, perhaps even to curtail, the development of a contrapuntal style as it is known today. However, their use has enabled me to better achieve the result I sought.

Today the music I write stems in some degree from all of my experiences, but it is what *I* would like to write, not what others have insisted that I write. Some people have been kind enough to say that I have developed a distinctly personal style of musical expression. I hope they are right, and if they are, I'm sure it has come from keeping an open mind, meanwhile making an effort to select what is valuable and to reject what is unimportant, in my estimation.

27 Olly Wilson

In contrast to the relatively conciliatory tone taken by William Grant Still regarding his relationship to American music at large (see pp. 151–52), Olly Wilson (b. 1937), some forty years younger and writing in 1972 at the height of the civil rights movement, adopts a more aggressive, even accusatory manner. Traditionally trained, with degrees in music from major universities, and holding a professorship at the University of California at Berkeley, Wilson puts forward a somewhat bifurcated position. On the one hand, he responds to the historical suppression of black culture through racism with an essentialist stance (compare the essay by Eva Rieger, pp. 145–50), arguing that the black composer has a unique voice shaped by sources that lie "deeply embedded in the collective consciousness of his people" (Wilson himself studied music in Africa during 1971 and 1972). On the other hand, he eschews parochialism, encouraging black composers to make use of all the technical resources they have available in order to write music that, while culturally specific, is universal in reach.

The Black American Composer
(1972)

At a time when the collective consciousness of black people has been raised to a renewed awareness of the power and significance of their culture, the black composer finds himself in a vital though demanding position. The role of any artist is to reinterpret human existence by means of the conscious transformation of his experience. He does this by ordering the media that he has chosen in such a manner that his fellow men gain new perspectives on their shared

TEXT: *Readings in Black American Music*, 2nd ed., compiled and edited by Eileen Southern (New York: W. W. Norton, 1983), pp. 327–32.

experiences; that they realize new dimensions of perception and expression and thereby broaden the scope of their existence.

The black composer (or any black artist) is unique because, unlike his white counterpart, his cultural history has been plagued by an exploitive racism as damnable as any ever to exist in the history of mankind. This obviously has a profound effect on the way he reinterprets the world; his reality is different from that of someone who has not had his experience. He sees the world from a unique point of view.

To paraphrase something that Leroi Jones wrote several years ago (in his set of essays entitled *Home*), the view from the top of the hill is significantly differ- ent from that of the bottom, and in most cases each viewer is unaware of the existence of another perspective. The latter part of that statement is particu- larly important because all too often one's concept of reality is held to be abso- lute. Thus positions that do not conform to that reality are seen as incorrect. People whose world view is different from that of Blacks, for example, fre- quently see such concepts as black music, black art, black theater, or black anything—where the emphasis is on black as a distinctive factor—as an aber- rant or distorted concept. The usual rejoinder to the claims of a special world view is that there is no such thing as black art or black music—there is simply music and art.

I call your attention to a recent review of a recording by the black pianist Natalie Hinderas. The recording, entitled *Natalie Hinderas Plays Compositions by Black Composers*, was reviewed by Irving Kolodin in the *Saturday Review* magazine. Kolodin took exception to the idea of a recording by black compos- ers on the grounds that he could not define what constituted black music. Since he could not determine what constituted black music, he felt there was not a meaningful distinction to be made. In his view, therefore, the notion of black music was an absurdity. It was absurd because his perspective was devoid of anything which would allow him to be aware of those unique elements which united all of those pieces. Because his frame of reference did not include those elements, he assumed they did not exist.

Kolodin's attitude very frequently has been manifest historically in the white American psyche. One of its most dramatic exhibitions occurred in the pseudo- scholarly investigations of the origin of the Negro Spirituals. As others before him, but without the trappings of scholarship, George P. Jackson (a white musi- cologist) developed a theory that the Negro spiritual was in fact derived from southern white Gospel songs. Briefly, his basic proposition was that in view of the fact that many Negro spirituals have text and notated melodies similar to those of white gospel songs, the Negro Spiritual must have been derived from the gospel song.

It was outside his range of possibilities that the African exiles and their prog- eny brought with them a sophisticated musical tradition, which flourished in this country in adapted forms both as religious and secular music. It was out- side his range of possibilities because he subscribed to the conventional wisdom of the time which held that there was no significant African musical tradition. Therefore, he was incapable of dealing adequately with black music because of his limited perspective—limited in the same sense as was Kolodin's. In both cases there was no recognition of a black music because the scope of the viewer was blurred by both ignorance and cultural bias.

The black composer, on the other hand, approaches his task from a different perspective—a perspective from which he is consciously aware of the black music tradition. In transforming his experience, he draws upon a wide spectrum of musical expression which includes much not normally regarded as a part of the Euro-American tradition. Paradoxically, much of that Euro-American tradition itself was derived from the Afro-American tradition. It is this black tradition and the black composer's individual interpretation of it that makes his work unique. It is this special tradition that enables him to project human experience in a unique and meaningful manner.

At the same time it must be recognized that the universality of his work is not diminished. Universality in art does not stem from a denial of individual differences. It is not based upon a universal homogeneity of expression. It stems, rather, from the recognition of the similarity of the human condition which transcends important differences between cultures. The form and character of the work itself, however, is derived from strong cultural bases. The source of Verdi's music, for example, lies deeply imbedded in the collective sensibilities of the Italian people. It is deeply infected with the love of drama, with passionate emotions, surface clarity, and disarming candor.

The source of the black composer's music lies deeply embedded in the collective consciousness of his people. Along with a heightened sensitivity to motion, qualitative rhythm, and immediateness of expression, it includes a dimension which encompasses the wordless moans of a mid-week poorly attended prayer meeting, the Saturday-night ecstatic shrieks of a James Brown, the relentless intensity of the modal excursions of a John Coltrane, and the tonal word-songs of the teenage brothers "rapping" on the corner, full of the pride of new-found self respect.

The means by which the black composer brings these things to bear on his music are of individual concern. These means are as diverse as are the composers. In the work of many black composers, for example, the elements easily identified with the black experience are features of the foreground of their music. That is, they are clearly distinguishable since they form the external as well as internal aspects of the musical events shaped by the composer.

In other works these factors may be more subtle, but nonetheless are equally as important. They are used to determine internal factors, such as pacing, intensity, and formal development. In the works of such composers as T. J. Anderson, David Baker, and Wendell Logan may be found examples of this.

In this regard, it may be instructive to cite the work of the contemporary black painter Romare Bearden. Superficially, Bearden's work appears to have been influenced by the cubists (who, paradoxically, were strongly influenced by African sculpture). But a closer examination of Bearden's work reveals a sense of ritual, a sense of color, and a sense of motion which I do not detect in the works of most cubists. I attribute my response to factors which reside in Bearden's singular conception.

Nevertheless, I also sense some of these feelings when listening to the work of the above-named fellow composers. In short, the black composer brings with him cultural baggage, just as his African ancestors did. It is my contention that this cultural baggage will be manifest if the artist honestly follows the dictates of his musical imagination. The manifestation may take different forms and may not always be immediately obvious, but it will always exist.

It should not be deduced from what I have said that the black American composer is uninfluenced by music that comes from non-black traditions. Nothing could be further from the truth. The black composer is like any contemporary composer who is constantly stimulated by a bombardment of diverse musical sources. As a matter of fact, one of the general characteristics of twentieth-century music of any type is the pervasiveness of cross-cultural influences. This has led one observer of contemporary music to refer to this eclectic period as one in which the norm was one of constant stylistic diversity—or a period of "fluctuating stasis." There is no such thing in the world of today as complete cultural isolation. One need only turn on the radio to hear the mixtures of various musical cultures. Aretha Franklin is "big" in Japan, Indian ragas are popular on American college campuses, the Edwin Hawkins singers were a smashing success in Europe.

Nevertheless, the many influences that bear upon a black composer are so adapted as to project his personal conception from a black perspective. Any compositional technique or instrumental innovation may be used as long as the composer is controlling it. As long as he is shaping it, it will reflect him. A few years ago I began using the electronic media in some of my compositions. Some of my associates accused me of copping out, of using a white man's machine to try to express my black humanity—an endeavor which they felt was intrinsically contradictory.

My response, in some despair, was to point out to my brothers that for several hundred years now since our forefathers' involuntary departure from the homeland, black people have been adapting machines in the American environment to suit their purposes. Everything from food and dress to language and religion has been adapted to conform to an essentially African way of doing things. Nowhere has this adaptation been truer than in music. After all the Belgian Adolph Sax invented the saxophone and Jimmie Smith's last name was not Hammond. The point here is that, as in African Bantu philosophy, a thing is given meaning only by the will of a human being. The media is a vehicle of expression, not the substance of expression. Since the substance stems from the well springs of the individual, the media may be derived therefore from any source.

My approach to the electronic media is similar to my approach to any musical media. I use it as a means of projecting the musical idea I am trying to convey in a particular piece. It is as illogical to assume that different composers using the same media will produce similar works, as it is to assume that different artists using the same plastic media will produce works that look alike. Both Scott Joplin and Arnold Schoenberg wrote pieces for the piano about the same time, but there any similarity ends. Each man was expressing something out of his personal experience, and those experiences were culturally light-years apart. Nevertheless, each man created something that was universal in that it reflected universal sentiments from a discernible cultural perspective. My approach to electronic media, like my approach to the orchestra or any instrument, carries with it the sensibilities of a black man in the latter half of the twentieth century.

The attitude I hold toward media is also applicable to my approach to compositional techniques. I will use any technique or device which will enable me to project my musical ideas. It is debilitating to limit oneself a priori to any one system or style. For me, questions of musical technique are meaningless outside the context of a specific piece and should not limit one's appreciation of the musical ideas. A response to any music ultimately must be on the basis of the communicability of that music. One should ask himself, "Does this affect me in a meaningful way?," not "Does it use this or that technique?"

In conclusion, I would like to make a final statement on the role of the black composer in the struggle for Black Liberation. I am sometimes asked by students and others how I am able to justify my activity as a composer at this crucial historical moment. The question betrays a fundamental lack of understanding of the role of music in the traditional black community, both in the United States and in Africa. In traditional West African cultures music is not an abstraction, separate from life, a distillation of experience. It is, rather, a force by which man communicates with other men, the gods, and nature. In this sense it is obligatory and vital to existence.

The ideal I strive toward as a composer is to approach music as it is approached in traditional African cultures. In that sense my music is directly related to the struggle in that it aspires to inform, motivate, and humanize my fellow men in their aspirations.

V

EXTENDING WESTERN MUSIC'S BOUNDARIES

28 Claude Debussy

Claude Debussy (1862–1918) is considered by many the most important composer of the early twentieth century in establishing an esthetic orientation independent of Romanticism. Employed as a writer and critic throughout much of his career, Debussy actively espoused the need for widespread renewal in music. The first of these three pieces, dating from 1902, responds to a question posed in the first issue of a new periodical, *Musica:* "Is it possible to predict where the music of tomorrow will be?" The second and third, both written in 1913 for a prominent French music journal, *La revue musicale S.I.M.,* cover a broad spectrum of ideas. Collectively, these writings articulate many of Debussy's principal esthetic positions: that traditional training leads to standardization; that music should not slavishly imitate nature but evoke its fluidity, freedom, and mystery; that composers should adopt innovative approaches, such as techniques borrowed from cinematography; and that they should seek inspiration in music by earlier composers, such as François Couperin, and in music beyond the Western tradition, such as that of Java and Indochina.

Three Articles for Music Journals

[I]
(1902)

The best thing one could wish for French music would be to see the study of harmony abolished as it is practiced in the conservatories. It is the most ridiculous way of arranging notes. Furthermore, it has the severe disadvantage of standardizing composition to such a degree that every composer, except for a few, harmonizes in the same way. We can be sure that old Bach, the essence of all music, scorned harmonic formulae. He preferred the free play of sonorities whose curves, whether flowing in parallel or contrary motion, would result in an undreamed of flowering, so that even the least of his countless manuscripts bears an indelible stamp of beauty.

That was the age of the "wonderful arabesque," when music was subject to laws of beauty inscribed in the movements of Nature herself. Rather will our time be remembered as the era of the "age of veneer"—although here I am speaking generally and not forgetting the isolated genius of certain of my colleagues.

Contemporary dramatic music, however, embraces everything from Wagnerian metaphysics to the trivialities of the Italians—not a particularly French orientation. Perhaps in the end we will see the light and achieve conciseness of expression and form (the fundamental qualities of French genius). Will we

TEXT: *Debussy on Music,* ed. by François Lesure, trans. and ed. by Richard Langham Smith (New York: Alfred A. Knopf, 1977), pp. 84–85, 277–79, 295–98. Reprinted by permission of Alfred A. Knopf, Inc.

rediscover that abundant fantasy of which music alone is capable? It seems to have been forgotten under the pretext of research, which at first sight makes it seem as if the days of music are numbered.

Art is the most beautiful deception of all! And although people try to incorporate the everyday events of life in it, we must hope that it will remain a deception lest it become a utilitarian thing, sad as a factory. Ordinary people, as well as the élite, come to music to seek oblivion: is that not also a form of deception? The Mona Lisa's smile probably never existed in real life, yet her charm is eternal. Let us not disillusion anyone by bringing too much reality into the dream. . . . Let us content ourselves with more consoling ways: such music can contain an everlasting expression of beauty.

[II]
(1913)

Our symphonic painters do not pay nearly enough attention to the beauty of the seasons. Their studies of Nature show her dressed in unpleasantly artificial clothes, the rocks made of cardboard and the leaves of painted gauze. Music is the art that is in fact the closest to Nature, although it is also the one that contains the most subtle pitfalls. Despite their claims to be true representationalists, the painters and sculptors can only present us with the beauty of the universe in their own free, somewhat fragmentary interpretation. They can capture only one of its aspects at a time, preserve only one moment. It is the musicians alone who have the privilege of being able to convey all the poetry of night and day, of earth and sky. Only they can re-create Nature's atmosphere and give rhythm to her heaving breast. . . . We know that it is a privilege they do not abuse. It is a rare thing when Nature wrings from them one of those sincere love cries of the kind that make certain pages of *Der Freischütz* so wonderful; usually her passion is somewhat tamed because they portray her green beauty in such a lifeless way. It comes out like pressed leaves festering in dreary old books. Berlioz made do with such an approach all his life; otherwise sweet delights were soured because he insisted on patronizing artificial flower shops.

The music of our time has learned how to free itself from the romantic fancies of this literary view of things, but other weaknesses remain. During the past few years we have seen it tending toward an indulgence in the mechanical harshness of certain combinations of landscape. We can certainly do without the naïve aesthetics of Jean-Jacques Rousseau, but all the same we can learn great things from the past. We should think about the example Couperin's harpsichord pieces set us: they are marvelous models of grace and innocence long past. Nothing could ever make us forget the subtly voluptuous perfume, so delicately perverse, that so innocently hovers over the *Barricades mystérieuses*.

Let us be frank: those who really know the art of expressing themselves symphonically are those who have never learned how to do it. There is no conservatoire or music school that holds the secret. The theater offers a happy

alternative, however, in its resources of gesture, dramatic cries, and movements; they come to the aid of many a perplexed musician. Pure music offers
no such easy way out: one should either have a natural gift for evocation or
give up the struggle. And in any case, where did the symphonic music of our
country come from? Who are those ancestors who urge us toward this form of
expression? . . . First of all, our musicians willingly allowed themselves to be
inspired by the symphonic poems of Liszt and of Richard Strauss. And note,
furthermore, that any attempts at emancipation were soon forcibly quelled.
Each time anyone tried to break free from this inherited tradition he was
brought to order, crushed beneath the weight of the more illustrious examples.
Beethoven—who ought really be permitted to take a well-earned rest from
criticism—was brought to the rescue. Those severe old critics passed judgment
and threatened terrible punishments for breach of the classical rules whose
construction—they should have realized—was nothing less than mechanical.
Did they not realize that no one could ever go further than Bach, one of their
judges, toward freedom and fantasy in both composition and form?

Why, furthermore, did they not so much as try to understand that it really
would not be worthwhile having so many centuries of music behind us, having
benefited from the magnificent intellectual heritage it has bequeathed us, and
trying childishly to rewrite history? Is it not our duty, on the contrary, to try
and find the symphonic formulae best suited to the audacious discoveries of
our modern times, so committed to progress? The century of aeroplanes has a
right to a music of its own. Let those who support our art not be left to waste
away in the lowest ranks of our army of inventors, let them not be outdone by
the genius of engineers!

Dramatic music is also directly involved in this change in symphonic ideals;
its fate is governed by that of pure music. If it is suffering at the moment it is
because it has wrongly interpreted the Wagnerian ideal and tried to find in it a
formula. Such a formula could never be in tune with the French spirit. Wagner
was not a good teacher of French.

Let us purify our music! Let us try to relieve its congestion, to find a less
cluttered kind of music. And let us be careful that we do not stifle all feeling
beneath a mass of superimposed designs and motives: how can we hope to
preserve our finesse, our spirit, if we insist on being preoccupied with so many
details of composition? We are attempting the impossible in trying to organize
a braying pack of tiny themes, all pushing and jostling each other for the sake
of a bite out of the poor old sentiment! If they are not careful the sentiment
will depart altogether, in an attempt to save its skin. As a general rule, every
time someone tries to complicate an art form or a sentiment, it is simply
because they are unsure of what they want to say.

But we must first understand that our fellow countrymen have no love of
music. Composers are therefore discouraged from doing battle or starting
afresh. Music is simply not liked in France; if you doubt this, just listen to the
tone in which the critics speak of her. How obvious it is that they feel no love
for her at all! They always seem to be taking it out on the poor unfortunate

creature, assuaging some nasty deep-seated hatred. Such a feeling is not pecu-liar to our own time. Beauty has always been taken by some as a secret insult. People instinctively feel they need to take their revenge on her, defiling the ideal that humiliates them. We should be grateful to those few critics who do not hate her: for the scrupulous severity of Sainte-Beuve, who himself cared passionately for literature, and for Baudelaire, who was not only a critic with a unique understanding but a fine artist as well.

There remains but one way of reviving the taste for symphonic music among our contemporaries: to apply to pure music the techniques of cinematography. It is the film—the Ariadne's thread—that will show us the way out of this disquieting labyrinth. M. Léon Moreau and Henry Février have just supplied the proof of this with great success.[1] Those hordes of listeners who find them-selves bored stiff by a performance of a Bach *Passion,* or even Beethoven's *Missa Solemnis,* would find themselves brought to attention if the screen were to take pity on their distress. One could even provide a film of what the com-poser was doing while composing the piece.

How many misunderstandings would thus be avoided! The spectator is not always to be blamed for his mistakes! He cannot always prepare for each new piece he listens to as if he were engaged on a piece of research, for the normal routine of an ordinary citizen is not well suited to include matters of aesthetics. In this way the author would no longer be betrayed; we would be free from any false interpretations. At last we would know the truth with certainty—the truth, the whole truth, and nothing but the truth!

Unfortunately we are too set in our ways. We are reluctant to renounce the boring! On we go in the same old way, imitating one another.

What a pity Mozart was not French. He would have really been worth imi-tating!

[III]
(1913)

In these times, when we are so preoccupied with trying out various different ways of educating people, we are gradually losing our sense of the mysterious. The true meaning of the word "taste" is also bound to be lost.

In the last century, having "taste" was merely a convenient way of defending one's opinions. Today the word has come to mean much more than that: it is now used in many different ways. It generally signifies something that involves the kind of argument usually settled with knuckle-dusters; one makes one's point, but in a way somewhat lacking in elegance. The natural decline of a "taste" concerned with nuance and delicacy has given way to this "bad taste," in which colors and forms fight each other. . . . But then perhaps these reflec-tions are rather too general, for here I am only supposed to be concerned with music—a difficult enough task in itself.

1. Debussy refers to a film directed by Louis Feuillade, *L'Agonie de Byzance.* [Tr.]

Geniuses can evidently do without taste: take the case of Beethoven, for example. But on the other hand there was Mozart, to whose genius was added a measure of the most delicate "good taste." And if we look at the works of J. S. Bach—a benevolent God to whom all musicians should offer a prayer before commencing work, to defend themselves from mediocrity—on each new page of his innumerable works we discover things we thought were born only yesterday—from delightful arabesques to an overflowing of religious feeling greater than anything we have since discovered. And in his works we will search in vain for anything the least lacking in "good taste."

Portia in *The Merchant of Venice* speaks of a music that everyone has within them: "The man that hath no music in himself . . . let no such man be trusted." Those people who are only preoccupied with the formula that will yield them the best results, without ever having listened to the still small voice of music within themselves, would do well to think on these words. And so would those who most ingeniously juggle around with bars, as if they were no more than pathetic little squares of paper. That is the kind of music that smells of the writing desk, or of carpet slippers. (I mean that in the special sense used by mechanics who, when trying out a badly assembled machine, say, "That smells of oil.") We should distrust the *writing* of music: it is an occupation for moles, and it ends up by reducing the vibrant beauty of sound itself to a dreadful system where two and two make four. Music has known for a long time what the mathematicians call "the folly of numbers."

Above all, let us beware of systems that are designed as dilettante traps.

There used to be—indeed, despite the troubles that civilization has brought, there still are—some wonderful peoples who learn music as easily as one learns to breathe. Their school consists of the eternal rhythm of the sea, the wind in the leaves, and a thousand other tiny noises, which they listen to with great care, without ever having consulted any of those dubious treatises. Their traditions are preserved only in ancient songs, sometimes involving dance, to which each individual adds his own contribution century by century. Thus Javanese music obeys laws of counterpoint that make Palestrina seem like child's play. And if one listens to it without being prejudiced by one's European ears, one will find a percussive charm that forces one to admit that our own music is not much more than a barbarous kind of noise more fit for a traveling circus.

The Indochinese have a kind of embryonic opera, influenced by the Chinese, in which we can recognize the roots of the *Ring*. Only there are rather more gods and rather less scenery! A frenetic little clarinet is in charge of the emotional effects, a tam-tam invokes terror—and that is all there is to it. No special theater is required, and no hidden orchestra. All that is needed is an instinctive desire for the artistic, a desire that is satisfied in the most ingenious ways and without the slightest hints of "bad taste." And to say that none of those concerned ever so much as dreamed of going to Munich to find their formulae— what could they have been thinking of?

Was it not the professionals who spoiled the civilized countries? And the accusation that the public likes only simple music (implying bad music)—is that not somewhat misguided?

The truth is that real music is never "difficult." That is merely an umbrella term that is used to hide the poverty of bad music. There is only one kind of music: music whose claim to existence is justified by what it actually is, whether it is just another piece in waltz time (for example, the music of the *café-concert*) or whether it takes the imposing form of the symphony. Why do we not admit that, of these two cases, it is very often the waltz that is in better taste? The symphony can often only be unraveled with great difficulty—a pompous web of mediocrity.

Let us not persist in exalting this commonplace invention, as stupid as it is famous: taste and color should be beyond mention. On the other hand, let us discuss, rediscover our own taste; it is not as if we have completely lost it, but we have stifled it beneath our northern eiderdowns. That would be a step forward in the fight against the barbarians, who have become much worse since they started parting their hair in the center. . . .

We should constantly be reminding ourselves that the beauty of a work of art is something that will always remain mysterious; that is to say one can never find out exactly "how it is done." At all costs let us preserve this element of magic peculiar to music. By its very nature music is more likely to contain something of the magical than any other art.

After the god Pan had put together the seven pipes of the syrinx, he was at first only able to imitate the long, melancholy note of the toad wailing in the moonlight. Later he was able to compete with the singing of the birds, and it was probably at this time that the birds increased their repertoire.

These are sacred enough origins, and music can be proud of them and preserve a part of their mystery. In the name of all the gods, let us not rid it of this heritage by trying to "explain" it. . . . Let it be enhanced by delicately preserving our "good taste," the guardian of all that is secret.

29 Béla Bartók

In addition to being a leading composer of the first half of the twentieth century, Béla Bartók (1881–1945) was a pioneer in the study of folk music, helping establish the discipline now known as ethnomusicology. The two aspects of his professional life were intimately connected, as Bartók drew upon his knowledge of native music for both technical and expressive enrichment of his own work. In the following two articles, Bartók considers relationships between folk music and twentieth-century concert music. In the first, dating from 1931, he discusses the use of folk music as an aid to breaking away from traditional musical conceptions and the different ways such music can be incorporated into contemporary works: through quotation, imitation, or—most ideally—total stylistic absorption. In the second, written a decade earlier, Bartók expresses his disdain for the use of folk materials merely to provide an "exotic" effect—covering the surface of a traditional substance with "foreign" color—thus destroying the essential nature of the borrowed materials.

FROM Two Articles on the Influence of Folk Music

THE INFLUENCE OF PEASANT MUSIC ON MODERN MUSIC
(1931)

There have always been folk music influences on the higher types of art music. In order not to go back too far into hardly known ages, let us begin by referring to the pastorals and musettes of the seventeenth and eighteenth centuries, which are nothing but copies of the folk music of that time performed on the bagpipe or the hurdy-gurdy.

It is a well-known fact the Viennese classical composers were influenced to a considerable extent by folk music. In Beethoven's Pastoral Symphony, for instance, the main motive of the first movement is a Yugoslav dance melody. Beethoven obviously heard this theme from bagpipers, perhaps even in Western Hungary; the *ostinato*-like repetition of one of the measures, at the beginning of the movement, points to such an association.

But it was only a number of so-called "national" composers who yielded deliberately and methodically to folk music influences, such as Liszt (Hungarian Rhapsodies) and Chopin (Polonaises and other works with Polish characteristics). Grieg, Smetana, Dvořák, and the late nineteenth-century composers continued in that vein, stressing even more distinctly the racial character in their works. In fact, Moussorgsky is the only composer among the latter to yield completely and exclusively to the influence of peasant music, thereby forestalling his age—as it is said. For it seems that the popular art music of the eastern and northern countries provided enough impulse to the other "blatantly nationalistic" composers of the nineteenth century, with very few exceptions. There is no doubt that such music also contained quite a number of peculiarities missing till then in the higher types of Western art music, but it was mixed—as I have said previously—with Western hackneyed patterns and Romantic sentimentality.

TEXT: *Béla Bartók Essays*, ed. by Benjamin Suchoff (London: Faber & Faber, 1976), pp. 322–23, 340–44. Reprinted by permission of Faber & Faber Ltd. and the University of Nebraska Press.

At the beginning of the twentieth century there was a turning point in the history of modern music.

The excesses of the Romanticists began to be unbearable for many. There were composers who felt: "this road does not lead us anywhere; there is no other solution but a complete break with the nineteenth century."

Invaluable help was given to this change (or let us rather call it rejuvenation) by a kind of peasant music unknown till then.

The right type of peasant music is most varied and perfect in its forms. Its expressive power is amazing, and at the same time it is devoid of all sentimentality and superfluous ornaments. It is simple, sometimes primitive, but never silly. It is the ideal starting point for a musical renaissance, and a composer in search of new ways cannot be led by a better master. What is the best way for a composer to reap the full benefits of his studies in peasant music? It is to assimilate the idiom of peasant music so completely that he is able to forget all about it and use it as his musical mother tongue.

In order to achieve this, Hungarian composers went into the country and made their collections there. It may be that the Russian Stravinsky and the Spaniard Falla did not go on journeys of collection, and mainly drew their material from the collections of others, but they too, I feel sure, must have studied not only books and museums but the living music of their countries.

In my opinion, the effects of peasant music cannot be deep and permanent unless this music is studied in the country as part of a life shared with the peasants. It is not enough to study it as it is stored up in museums. It is the character of peasant music, indescribable in words, that must find its way into our music. It must be pervaded by the very atmosphere of peasant culture. Peasant motives (or imitations of such motives) will only lend our music some new ornaments; nothing more.

Some twenty to twenty-five years ago well-disposed people often marvelled at our enthusiasm. How was it possible, they asked, that trained musicians, fit to give concerts, took upon themselves the "subaltern" task of going into the country and studying the music of the people on the spot. What a pity, they said, that this task was not carried out by people unsuitable for a higher type of musical work. Many thought our perseverance in our work was due to some crazy idea that had got hold of us.

Little did they know how much this work meant to us. We went into the country and obtained first-hand knowledge of a music that opened up new ways to us.

The question is, what are the ways in which peasant music is taken over and becomes transmuted into modern music?

We may, for instance, take over a peasant melody unchanged or only slightly varied, write an accompaniment to it and possibly some opening and concluding phrases. This kind of work would show a certain analogy with Bach's treatment of chorales.

Two main types can be distinguished among works of this character.

In the one case accompaniment, introductory and concluding phrases are of secondary importance, and they only serve as an ornamental setting for the precious stone: the peasant melody.

It is the other way round in the second case: the melody only serves as a 'motto' while that which is built round it is of real importance.

All shades of transition are possible between these two extremes and sometimes it is not even possible to decide which of the elements is predominant in any given case. But in every case it is of the greatest importance that the musical qualities of the setting should be derived from the musical qualities of the melody, from such characteristics as are contained in it openly or covertly, so that melody and all additions create the impression of complete unity.

At this point I have to mention a strange notion widespread some thirty or forty years ago. Most trained and good musicians then believed that only simple harmonizations were well suited to folk melodies. And even worse, by simple harmonies they meant a succession of triads of tonic, dominant and possibly subdominant.

How can we account for this strange belief? What kind of folk songs did these musicians know? Mostly new German and Western European songs and so-called folk songs made up by popular composers. The melody of such songs usually moves along the triad of tonic and dominant; the main melody consists of a breaking up of these chords into single notes, for example, the opening measures of "O du lieber Augustin" and "Kutya, kutya tarka." It is obvious that melodies of this description do not go well with a more complex harmonization.

But our musicians wanted to apply the theory derived from this type of song to an entirely different type of Hungarian song built up on pentatonic scales.

It may sound odd, but I do not hesitate to say: the simpler the melody the more complex and strange may be the harmonization and accompaniment that go well with it. Let us for instance take a melody that moves on two successive notes only (there are many such melodies in Arab peasant music). It is obvious that we are much freer in the invention of an accompaniment than in the case of a melody of a more complex character. These primitive melodies moreover, show no trace of the stereotyped joining of triads. That again means greater freedom for us in the treatment of the melody. It allows us to bring out the melody most clearly by building round it harmonies of the widest range varying along different keynotes. I might almost say that the traces of polytonality in modern Hungarian music and in Stravinsky's music are to be explained by this possibility.

Similarly, the strange turnings of melodies in our Eastern European peasant music showed us new ways of harmonization. For instance the new chord of the seventh which we use as a concord may be traced back to the fact that in our folk melodies of a pentatonic character the seventh appears as an interval of equal importance with the third and the fifth. We so often heard these intervals as of equal value in the succession, that nothing was more natural than that we should try to make them sound of equal importance when used simultaneously. We sounded the four notes together in a setting which made us feel it not necessary to break them up. In other words: the four notes were made to form a concord.

The frequent use of fourth-intervals in our old melodies suggested to us the use of fourth chords. Here again what we heard in succession we tried to build up in a simultaneous chord.

Another method by which peasant music becomes transmuted into modern music is the following: the composer does not make use of a real peasant melody but invents his own imitation of such melodies. There is no true difference between this method and the one described above.

Stravinsky never mentions the sources of his themes. Neither in his titles nor in footnotes does he ever allude to whether a theme of his is his own invention or whether it is taken over from folk music. In the same way the old composers never gave any data: let me simply mention the beginning of the Pastoral Symphony. Stravinsky apparently takes this course deliberately. He wants to demonstrate that it does not matter a jot whether a composer invents his own themes or uses themes from elsewhere. He has a right to use musical material taken from all sources. What he has judged suitable for his purpose has become through this very use his mental property. In the same manner Molière is reported to have replied to a charge of plagiarism: "Je prends mon bien où je le trouve." In maintaining that the question of the origin of a theme is completely unimportant from the artist's point of view, Stravinsky is right. The question of origins can only be interesting from the point of view of musical documentation.

Lacking any data I am unable to tell which themes of Stravinsky's in his so-called "Russian" period are his own inventions and which are borrowed from folk music. This much is certain, that if among the thematic material of Stravinsky's there are some of his own invention (and who can doubt that there are) these are the most faithful and clever imitations of folk songs. It is also notable that during his "Russian" period, from *Le Sacre du Printemps* onward, he seldom uses melodies of a closed form consisting of three or four lines, but short motives of two or three measures, and repeats them "à la *ostinato*." These short recurring primitive motives are very characteristic of Russian music of a certain category. This type of construction occurs in some of our old music for wind instruments and also in Arab peasant dances.

This primitive construction of the thematic material may partly account for the strange mosaic-like character of Stravinsky's work during his early period.

The steady repetition of primitive motives creates an air of strange feverish excitement even in the sort of folk music where it occurs. The effect is increased a hundredfold if a master of Stravinsky's supreme skill and his precise knowledge of dynamic effects employs these rapidly chasing sets of motives.

There is yet a third way in which the influence of peasant music can be traced in a composer's work. Neither peasant melodies nor imitations of peasant melodies can be found in his music, but it is pervaded by the atmosphere of peasant music. In this case we may say, he has completely absorbed the idiom of peasant music which has become his musical mother tongue. He masters it as completely as a poet masters his mother tongue.

In Hungarian music the best example of this kind can be found in Kodály's work. It is enough to mention *Psalmus Hungaricus,* which would not have been written without Hungarian peasant music. (Neither, of course, would it have been written without Kodály.)

THE RELATION OF FOLK SONG TO THE DEVELOPMENT OF THE ART MUSIC OF OUR TIME
(1921)

•   •   •   •   •

Peasant music, in the strict sense of the word, must be regarded as a natural phenomenon; the forms in which it manifests itself are due to the instinctive *transforming power* of a community entirely devoid of erudition. It is just as much a natural phenomenon as, for instance, the various manifestations of Nature in fauna and flora. Correspondingly it has in its individual parts an absolute artistic perfection, a perfection in miniature forms which—one might say— is equal to the perfection of a musical masterpiece of the largest proportions. It is the classical model of how to express an idea musically in the most concise form, with the greatest simplicity of means, with freshness and life, briefly yet completely and properly proportioned. This is quite sufficient to account for the fact that peasant music, in the strict sense of the word, is not generally understood by the average musician. He finds it empty and inexpressive; popular art music suits his taste much better. This latter derives from individual composers, known or unknown, who possess a certain musical erudition. With us in Eastern Europe, it comes from amateurs of gentle birth who satisfy the creative impulse of their slender musical talents by the composition of more or less simple tunes. Their music is partly made up of elements of Western European art music—a jumble of commonplaces in this respect—but it also bears traces of the peasant music of their own country. This is what lends their music a certain exotic flavour by which even men like Liszt, Brahms, and Chopin felt themselves attracted. Nevertheless the outcome of this mixture of exoticism and banality is something imperfect, inartistic, in marked contrast to the clarity of real peasant music with which it compares most unfavourably. At all events it is a noteworthy fact that artistic perfection can only be achieved by one of the two extremes: on the one hand by peasant folk in the mass, completely devoid of the culture of the town-dweller, on the other by creative power of an individual genius. The creative impulse of anyone who has the misfortune to be born somewhere between these two extremes leads only to barren, pointless and misshapen works. When peasants or the peasant classes lose their naïvety and their artless ignorance, as a result of the conventional culture, or more accurately half-culture, of the town-dwelling folk, they lose at the same time all their artistic transforming power. So that in western countries it is a long while since there was any real peasant music in the strict sense of the word.

In Eastern Europe about a hundred years ago or even earlier many popular art melodies were appropriated by the peasant classes, who, by means
of alterations, in a greater or lesser degree, have given them a new lease of
life in a new *milieu;* but these tunes have not led to the formation of a new style
of peasant music, nor indeed have they contributed anything towards it. The
greater the alteration, or rather the more complete the process of perfection
that they have undergone at the hands of their peasant appropriators has been,
the more nearly do they approximate to the true style of peasant music; at the
same time it is impossible to regard them as representative peasant melodies.

•   •   •   •   •

30 Darius Milhaud

Of the diverse ways in which twentieth-century composers reacted against the
perceived pretensions of Romanticism, none was more characteristic than the
turn from a view of the art as a deeply "spiritual," even quasi-religious phenomenon to one with a more "materialistic," ordinary perspective. This tendency
took many different forms, two of which are found in this brief autobiographical
passage by Darius Milhaud (1892–1974), a member of *Les Six,* a group of
French composers closely linked with Erik Satie at the end of World War I.
Milhaud first recounts a joint attempt with Satie to create a truly "everyday"
music (compare the entry by Cocteau, pp. 20–24), indeed a music so ordinary
that it would not—or so Milhaud and Satie hoped—be "listened to" at all: what
they called *musique d'ameublement,* or "furniture music." He then discusses
two notorious instances of anti-Romantic "objectivity" evident in text setting:
his own two song cycles based on unadorned listings of items chosen from
commercial catalogues.

FROM *Notes without Music*
(1949)

MUSIQUE D'AMEUBLEMENT AND CATALOGUE MUSIC

Just as one's field of vision embraces objects and forms, such as the pattern
on the wallpaper, the cornice of the ceiling, or the frame of the mirror, which
the eye sees but to which it pays no attention, though they are undoubtedly

TEXT: *Notes without Music* (New York: Alfred A. Knopf, 1953), pp. 122–24.

there, Satie thought that it would be amusing to have music that would not be listened to, *"musique d'ameublement,"* or background music that would vary like the furniture of the rooms in which it was played. Auric and Poulenc disapproved of this suggestion, but it tickled my fancy so much that I experimented with it, in cooperation with Satie, at a concert given in the Galerie Barbazange. During the program, Marcelle Meyer played music by Les Six, and Bertin presented a play by Max Jacob called *Un Figurant au théâtre de Nantes,* which required the services of a trombone. He also sang Stravinsky's *Berceuses du chat* to the accompaniment of three clarinets, so Satie and I scored our music for the instruments used in the course of these various items on the program. In order that the music might seem to come from all sides at once, we posted the clarinets in three different corners of the theater, the pianist in the fourth, and the trombone in a box on the balcony floor. A program note warned the audience that it was not to pay any more attention to the ritornellos that would be played during the intermissions than to the candelabra, the seats, or the balcony. Contrary to our expectations, however, as soon as the music started up, the audience began to stream back to their seats. It was no use for Satie to shout: "Go on talking! Walk about! Don't listen!" They listened without speaking. The whole effect was spoiled. Satie had not counted on the charm of his own music. This was our one and only public experiment with this sort of music. Nevertheless Satie wrote another *"ritournelle d'ameublement"* for Mrs. Eugene Meyer, of Washington, when she asked him, through me, to give her an autograph. But for this *Musique pour un cabinet préfectoral* to have its full meaning, she should have had it recorded and played over and over again, thus forming part of the furniture of her beautiful library in Crescent Place, adorning it for the ear in the same way as the still life by Manet adorned it for the eye. In any case, the future was to prove that Satie was right: nowadays, children and housewives fill their homes with unheeded music, reading and working to the sound of the radio. And in all public places, large stores and restaurants the customers are drenched in an unending flood of music. In America cafeterias are equipped with a sufficient number of machines for each client to be able, for the modest sum of five cents, to furnish his own solitude with music or supply a background for his conversation with his guest. Is this not *"musique d'ameublement,"* heard, but not listened to?

We frequently gave concerts in picture galleries. At Poiret's, Auric and I gave the first performance of Debussy's *Épigraphes antiques* for piano duet. At the Galerie la Boétie, Honegger played his violin sonatas with Vaurabourg, and the pianist André Salomon pieces by his friend Satie. Delgrange conducted my *Machines agricoles.*

I had written musical settings for descriptions of machinery taken from a catalogue that I had brought back from an exhibition of agricultural machinery which I had visited in company with Mme de B. and Mlle de S., who wanted to choose a reaper for their estate in the Bordeaux area. I had been so impressed by the beauty of these great multicolored metal insects, magnificent modern brothers to the plow and the scythe, that the idea came to me of celebrating them in music. I had put away in a drawer a number of catalogues, that I came across in 1919. I then composed a little suite for singer and seven solo instruments in the style of my little symphonies; the titles were *"La Faucheuse"* (reaper), *"La Lieuse"* (binder), *"La Déchaumeuse-Semeuse-Enfouisseuse"* (harrow, seeder, and burier), *"La Moissonneuse Espigadora"* (harvester), *"La Fouilleuse-Draineuse"* (subsoil and draining plow), *"La Faneuse"* (tedder). A few months later I used the same group of instruments for settings to some delightful poems by Lucien Daudet inspired by a florist's catalogue: *Catalogue de fleurs.*

Not a single critic understood what had impelled me to compose these works, or that they had been written in the same spirit as had in the past led composers to sing the praises of harvest-time, the grape harvest, or the "happy plowman," or Honegger to glorify a locomotive, and Fernand Leger to exalt machinery. Every time anyone wanted to prove my predilection for leg-pulling and eccentricity he cited *Les Machines agricoles.* I have never been able to fathom why sensible beings should imagine that any artist would spend his time working, with all the agonizing passion that goes into the process of creation, with the sole purpose of making fools of a few of them.

31 Wanda Landowska

Although the nineteenth century experienced a growing sense of historical consciousness, as evident in music as in other areas, when compositions of the more distant past were performed, they were normally transcribed so as to be rendered more acceptable to contemporary taste. During the course of the twentieth century, however, performers tried increasingly to approach earlier music on its own terms. The Polish harpsichordist Wanda Landowska (1879–1959) took a leading role in this development in the early years of the century, playing Bach's keyboard works on the harpsichord rather than the piano, which had by then become the long-preferred medium for this music. This excerpt from her groundbreaking 1909 book *Music of the Past,* here as condensed and revised for a subsequent publication, speaks for the importance of older music and for its capacity to enrich contemporary musical life. The so-called early music movement, which Landowska helped pioneer and which in recent years has attained truly remarkable currency, represents one of numerous efforts in the present century to establish a more encompassing conception of musical culture.

The Return to the Music of the Past
(1909)

I have insisted on the fallacy of progress in music because I consider it to be the principal cause of ignorance about our past and of most errors in the interpretation of our ancient masters. Because of this prejudice, blown up almost to the importance of a religion, the true beauties of music—as numerous as those of other arts—are still very poorly revealed. We remain deaf to these miracles of beauty, so marvelously remote; yet they should uplift the soul by their melodious echo, and, from century to century, they should link sympathetic hearts with a divine tie.

If sometimes we tire of grandiosity and if we lack air in the thick atmosphere of exaggerated romanticism, we need only to open wide the windows on our magnificent past; it will refresh our soul. We wish to participate in all emotions, in all ecstasies at the whim of our fancy. No longer shall we believe that while all the arts flourished marvelously in the past, music alone, although admired, was like a frail and sickly plant that could hardly break through the ground. Even supposing that music was in its cradle, we may be as sensitive to the charm of a prattling child as to the most skillful speech of a seasoned orator. If, on the contrary, music is afflicted with old age, we know how to admire the beauty of a lined face. No, the genius of the composers of the past was not a mere flash in the pan; it is an eternal flame, softly warming. It will never perish.

Yes, but one must go along with one's own time. Let new beauties be created, and we shall like them; but, at the same time, let us not relegate to darkness the works of the masters who were our models. They are not wolves; they will not, as Gounod said, devour the new masterpieces.

And in the name of what prejudice shall we continue to be suspended from the tiny spot we occupy in space instead of extending our view afar, instead of being contemporaries of all men? Only when we are strong enough to withstand that prejudice shall we really belong to our epoch. The great merit of the last half of the nineteenth century was that it awakened a taste for retrospection, a sense of comparison, and made us delight in that which is old, an "old" that is often newer than the new. A passion has been kindled in us; it does not encompass superior civilizations alone, but also those that our computer of taste had rated childish, decadent, or barbaric.

There is an evergrowing interest in the music of the past. But this would prove little in itself, since at all times the greatest musicians bowed before the works of the geniuses that preceded them. "We are not recapturing the

TEXT: *Landowska on Music*, ed. and trans. by Denise Restout and Robert Hawkins (New York: Stein and Day, 1964), pp. 159–60. Reprinted with permission of Denise Restout.

masterpieces," said Jules Janin; "the masterpieces themselves are recapturing us." Sooner or later, everyone will understand that a work of Josquin des Prés is well worth a Breughel. People of refined taste will feel that a Magnificat of Pachelbel, a chanson of Jannequin, a cantata of Bach, and a motet of Palestrina are worth more than the songs of modern sirens and of all the machines of speed. Then they will help us to erect a museum where we shall be able to hear and admire all our Titians, our Velasquezes, and our Raphaels, just as painters are able to admire theirs. And then we shall be able to enhance our lives with the memory of times that are gone.

32 Harry Partch

Not only did the traditional system of Western harmonic tonality come into question during the twentieth century, so did its underlying basis in equal temperament. In this 1940 article, originally intended (though later discarded) as an introduction for his book *A Genesis of Music,* the American composer Harry Partch (1901–1976) argues for a more flexible and subtly modulated tone system encompassing microtonal divisions. For Partch this proposal formed an essential part of his lifelong effort to undermine the rationalistic foundations of Western art in order to create an alternative, more ritualistically conceived music incorporating theater, dance, and costume, as well as specially constructed instruments that themselves took on the function of theatrical sets.

Patterns of Music
(1940)

He is an artist. Before him is a scale of colors, and in his mind he approaches the reds. For his brush's immediate use he sees a carmine, a vermilion, a scarlet, a crimson, a cerise, a garnet, a ruby, and verging off into other color values are an orchid and a magenta, a nasturtium and an orange, and a sienna, a rust, and an ochre.

He ponders leisurely. No, the exact shade he envisions—despite the great variety at hand—isn't here. With the assurance born of a life spent in being able to get what he wants, he then mixes—in just the right proportions—a bit of white, rust, and cerise to his vermilion, and—there! He has it!

TEXT: *Bitter Music,* ed. by Thomas McGeary (Urbana: University of Illinois Press, 1991), pp. 159–61.

Consider the writer of music. Before him is also a scale. It holds seven white keys and five black ones. In his mind he approaches C-sharp, one of the five blacks. He approaches it, and he lands on it. His action is direct, simple, predetermined.

There are no shades of C-sharp, no shades of red, for him. The one shade that his gods will allow him to use is before him. He is taught that that is enough; it is good, traditional, and proper, and he feels a vague sense of immorality in even wondering about those possible bastard C-sharps.

The present-day musician might observe: "If he doesn't like C-sharp he has D," which paraphrases: "He has yellow; why must he be so difficult as to also want vermilion?"

With the disquietude born of a life getting substitutes for nearly everything he really wants, the composer yearns for the streaking shades of sunset. He gets red. He longs for geranium, and gets red. He dreams of tomato, but he gets red. He doesn't want red at all, but he gets red, and is presumed to like it. But does he?

Another picture. It is that of a poet in torment over a line, and—to particularize—let us conjure a vision of Hart Crane laboring over the handful of words which, referring to the ocean, end: "Her undinal vast belly moonward bends."

There is no intention here to divine the thought processes of Crane in coming at last to this particular beauty of word cadence. But—were Hart Crane a composer of music—it would be exceedingly easy to unravel his processes, and, because his medium wouldn't allow him subtle and unusual shadings, he would never, never arrive at—"Her undinal vast belly moonward bends."

He would tentatively write: "The deep blue ocean moonward bends—"

Or: "With the moon rolls the boundless deep—"

Or, if he wanted to be modern: "Mooncalls sea-ocean bluedeep rolling—"

"Deep blue ocean" was and is used to excess by every writer of music since Palestrina. "The boundless deep" dates from Schubert and John Field, and is still widely used, and the last version is a fair literary paraphrase of most modern tonality—a cliché hash.

Before he ever writes a note the most brilliant composer is doomed to a system that is not capable of growth at his hands—or even of elasticity—and thus to a weary sea of worn-out forms, phrases, progressions, cadences, and chords.

Perhaps better than in any other way the two pictures above explain the reason for my musical heresy. The wayward trail began eighteen years ago, and, having traveled it all—inch by inch—I would not recommend it to others too heartily.

The great cathedral of modern music, erected in trial and labor and pain through most of the Christian era, is a safe and beautiful sanctuary. Its one sad aspect is that it seems to be finished—there is so little, if anything, that is significant that can be added to it. On the other hand, in the wild, little-known country of subtle tones beyond the safe cathedral, the trails are old and dim, they disappear completely, and there are many hazards.

The zealot driving into this wilderness should have more than one life to give: one to create instruments within the tyranny of the five-fingered hand, to play the tones he finds; one that will wrestle with notation and theory, so that he can make a record of what he finds, and give it understandable exposition; still another that will create and re-create significant music for his new-old instruments and in his new-old media; and, finally, another that will perform it, give it—as a revelation—to the general wealth of human culture.

It is not so simple as the few minutes' work of dabbing colors together from the already rich language of color. It is not so simple as combining a few choice words from the already rich language of words. It is the long, painful process of making less poor the pathetically impoverished language of tone.

The present book shows how the bonds of the composer might be, and are being, burst—how that which is too limited is being delimited. It is not a new trail in itself. It is only a survey—but a survey of all trails, both old and projected, and of one particular new trail.

Hence, *Patterns of Music.*

33 Bruno Nettl

Aided by developments in communication and transportation, the boundaries of Western musical culture have been extended dramatically in recent years, embracing music and musical practices from all parts of the globe. One result of this development toward "multiculturalism" has been an interest in reexamining Western musical culture from a more detached, "non-native" point of view: to pry beneath its surface manifestations (particular compositions, stylistic group-ings, performers, best-selling records, and the like) in search of its ideological foundations. At first evident mainly in the work of feminist writers and of socially, politically, and gender-oriented critics, the tendency has subsequently had a considerable impact on music studies in general. The field of ethnomusi-cology is especially interesting in this connection, as its practitioners are by nature concerned with the role of music in its larger socio-ideological frame-work. Historically, the discipline has been applied almost exclusively to non-Western cultures, a tradition that is broken in this 1992 article by the American scholar Bruno Nettl (b. 1930).

FROM Mozart and the Ethnomusicological Study of Western Culture

An Essay in Four Movements
(1992)

In works such as this, it is common to begin by defining ethnomusicology. I shall give three definitions and use them all: the comparative study of musical systems and cultures; the study of music in or as culture; the study of a musical culture from an outsider's perspective. None of these excludes the art-music culture of Western society, but few ethnomusicological studies have actually been devoted to it. I would like to deal with this topic, speaking at times as an American ethnomusicologist, at other times pretending to be an outsider, and sometimes acting as the native informant of this study. For comparative perspective I shall turn to one or two other societies with whose musical cultures I have become acquainted. I doubt that this essay states anything new. It is intended to provide food for thought, but it is also—by implication, at least— a critique of ethnomusicological approaches.

I. ADAGIO: WE BEGIN IN MONTANA

GUIDING PRINCIPLES

As this paper is also presented in homage to Mozart, the most special of composers, it follows, in its attempt to establish interplay of ideas and cultures, the form of an eighteenth-century symphony. And as the first movement may begin with an introduction quite removed, at least on the surface, from the main subject matter of the movement, I take the liberty of beginning an essay about Mozart with an excursion to the Blackfoot people of Montana.

After working with them for a time, I came to believe—influenced by a series of recent musical ethnographies published in the wake of significant works by Alan Merriam[1]—that the system of ideas about music held in each society, however small, is complex but coherent and that it informs importantly about both music and culture. It became clear to me, for example, that the principal unit of musical thought in Blackfoot culture is the song, an indivisible unit which is thought by Blackfoot people not to undergo change or variation and which is identified by use and secondarily by persons and events with which it is associated. The musical universe of the Blackfoot is capable of infinite expansion, as new songs can always come into existence although their

---

TEXT: *Disciplining Music: Musicology and its Canons,* ed. by Katherine Bergeron and Philip V. Bohlman (Chicago: University of Chicago Press, 1992), pp. 137–45.

1. Alan P. Merriam, *The Anthropology of Music* (Evanston: Northwestern University Press, 1964) and *Ethnomusicology of the Flathead Indians* (Chicago: Aldine, 1967).

style may not be new. One melody dreamed separately by two seekers of visions is in certain respects considered to be two songs. The concepts of composition and learning are closely related, as new songs are seen as extant musical units learned from an outside source. Most important, songs are significant mediators among groups of beings—between groups of humans and between humans and supernatural forces.

It became clear also that in Blackfoot culture, certain things about music and not others are evaluated. A person may say that he likes or dislikes genres of song, such as gambling songs or Grass Dance songs, and a singer or a singing group may be praised for the totality of their performance. But most individual songs, and individual performances, are not verbally evaluated. People say, "I like hand-game songs," "That's a good singing group," and "He's a good singer," but not "That is a fine song" or "I like the way they sang that particular song." And they do not say things like "That group is good because they work so hard" or "I like this group of songs because it must have taken a long time to make them."[2]

ALLEGRO ASSAI: ETHNOGRAPHY OF THE MUSIC BUILDING

FIRST THEME: A VISITOR FROM MARS

This summary may be a guide to the kinds of things that a perfect stranger in Western art music culture might note and investigate. When I teach courses in the anthropology of music, one of my favorite figures is an "ethnomusicologist from Mars" who has the task of discerning the basics of Western art music culture as manifested by the community of denizens of a fictitious (well, maybe not so fictitious) Music Building. Would the visitor's experiences be a bit like mine in a Blackfoot community? We can imagine him or her (or it?) on arrival looking in the windows of the little practice rooms, seeing people playing on various instruments to themselves, and being told by a bystander, "He's a very talented young man, practicing Mozart, but until recently he used to play only bluegrass." A woman turns on the radio, there is music, and she says, "Aha, it's Mozart" (or Brahms, maybe; but not, for instance, "Aha, it's piano music" or "It's Heifetz," or "Thank heavens, a rondo!"). The Martian is told that he simply *must* hear the symphony orchestra that evening, or the opera—but he is confused when he is told that he shouldn't bother with the day's soap operas or the evening TV's "Grand Ole Opry." He is urged to go to a concert of student compositions, told that what he may hear will surely be wonderfully new and experimental, even though it actually might sound quite awful.

Walking around the Music Building, he sees names engraved in stone around the top: Bach, Beethoven, Haydn, Palestrina (on Smith Memorial Hall

---

2. For explanations in more detail, see Bruno Nettl, *Blackfoot Musical Thought: Comparative Perspectives* (Kent, Ohio: Kent State University Press, 1989).

in Urbana); or a more hierarchical, much longer list clearly featuring Beethoven, Mozart, Bach, Haydn, and Wagner (in Bloomington). No names are found
on the English Building, and no Franz Boas or Claude Lévi-Strauss or Margaret Mead at Social Sciences. And he hears of no music buildings with "Concerto," "Symphony," "Oratorio." Seeking a score at the library, he must look
under "Mozart." "Symphony," "long pieces," "loud pieces," "sad" or "meditative," "C minor" and "Dorian" won't do.

There is no need to belabor the impact that the initial experiences may have
on any newcomer to a culture. Confronting the Music Building, one is quickly
exposed to a number of guiding principles of Western art music.[3] Importantly,
they include the concept of hierarchy—among musical systems and repertories
and, within art music, among types of ensembles and composers. There is a
pyramid, at the top one of two or three composers. There is the preeminence
of large ensembles and grand performances, and their metaphorical extensions
to other grand, dramatic events in life. Talent and practicing go together in a
way, but they are also opposing forces, the one both practically and philosophically a possible complement for the other. There is the great value placed on
innovation, but it is the old and trusted, the music of the great masters of the
past, that is most respected. In particular, our visitor is struck by the enormous
significance of the concept of the master composer, a concept of which the
figure of W. A. Mozart is paradigmatic.

SECOND THEME: AMADEUS

In his stay, our Martian friend runs into the concept of Mozart in many
guises; and having read Merriam,[4] Steven Feld,[5] Lorraine Sakata,[6] and others,
he realizes that one way to do good fieldwork is to pursue a concept wherever
it leads you. What he pursues, of course, is the Mozart of today; and so he is
doing—and I want to do—something quite different from what is done by the
many scholars (prominent among whom was my father) who have studied the
Mozart who lived in the eighteenth century. The two are closely related and
depend on each other, but they are not identical. In suggesting that the study
of today's Mozart may be a task for ethnomusicology, I must add that what I
say here is at best suggestive, that I have not really done much research and
have little hard data. My claim to authority is really that I am speaking as the
Martian's native informant in the culture.

So far he has been confronted by Mozart as a composer or, perhaps more
properly, Mozart as a group of pieces. A second, perhaps relatively minor form

3. For anthropological studies of schools of music, see Catherine Cameron, "Dialectics of the Arts"
   (Ph.D. diss., University of Illinois, 1982) and Henry Kingsbury, *Music, Talent, Performance: A
   Conservatory Cultural System* (Philadelphia: Temple University Press, 1988).
4. See note 1 above.
5. Steven Feld, *Sound and Sentiment: Birds, Weeping, Poetics, and Song in Kaluli Expression*
   (Philadelphia: University of Pennsylvania Press, 1983).
6. Hiromi Lorraine Sakata, *Music in the Mind* (Kent, Ohio: Kent State University Press, 1983).

of Mozart is the composer as a person. Denizens of the Music Building think of a composer in these two forms, forms that are partly congruent but that sometimes also conflict. It is in this context that the ethnomusicologist encounters the play *Amadeus* by Peter Shaffer.[7]

Let me now leave our imaginary colleague and talk about musicologists. The literary and dramatic merits of the play have been widely debated, and I can surely not contribute to this discussion. But musicologists have, in writing but in talking even more, taken an essentially critical position. The point is this, I believe: *Amadeus* involves the depiction of Mozart as a thoroughly ludicrous figure who is nevertheless able to compose incredible music—although only his enemy, the composer Antonio Salieri, recognizes it. Obviously, the play is not about the historical Mozart but uses him as a metaphor for the concept of the genius, the man loved by God; and Salieri for the hardworking, competent musician who is not a genius and therefore feels betrayed by God. Some musicologists who were put off by the play said that history was falsified, but there are other works of fiction about Mozart,[8] partly about the mystery of his death, and they are not usually the subject of heated criticism. The critical view of *Amadeus* has, I suggest, other bases. Mozart was made to look ridiculous, the kind of person who could not possibly be taken seriously as a great master of music. The response was similarly heated when Beethoven, in a psychoanalytical study, was made to look weak, impotent, petty.[9] The Music Building denizens are concerned about the *kinds* of persons to whom they have accorded the great-master status, but they have not resolved certain dilemmas. Are great composers great souls, and does the music come from divine inspiration, or are they just excellent technicians? Is it better to be a genius who comes to his accomplishments effortlessly or someone who achieves by the sweat of his brow? Who should properly be loved by God? In some societies the matter has been resolved. In Madras I was told, "Tyagaraja was such a great composer *because* he was such a holy man;" and a Blackfoot composer received his songs directly from the supernatural, a source above criticism.

DEVELOPMENT AND RECAPITULATION: THE GREAT MASTERS

In real life, these two themes are mixed and intertwined; let me briefly develop and eventually recapitulate them, returning to the ethnography of the Music Building and the centrality of the "great masters"—a dozen or so figures who are the deities of the culture. As geniuses, they exist on a different plane from other musicians. In the symphonic and chamber repertory, their works

7. Peter Shaffer, *Amadeus* (New York: Harper & Row, 1981).
8. For example, Eduard Friedrich Mörike, *Mozart auf der Reise nach Prag* (Vienna: Schroll, 1855), Alexander Pushkin, *Mozart and Salieri,* trans. R. M. Hewitt (Nottingham: University College, 1938; originally published as *Motsart i Salieri,* 1831), and Marcia Davenport, *Mozart* (New York: Charles Scribner's Sons, 1932).
9. Edith Sterba and Richard Sterba, *Beethoven and His Nephew* (New York: Pantheon, 1954).

occupy some 65 percent of performance time, a bit less in piano and choral concerts. An elite within a segment of musical culture already elite, they stand out because they wrote only great music, and when they did not, it must be explained. Beethoven's works are accorded universal status as masterworks, and when a *Wellington's Victory* appears, special excuses have to be made: He didn't mean it, was playing games, composed the work only for money. Although there are borderline composers, for those individuals not in this group, one or two major works are regarded as masterworks while the rest are essentially ignored.

The great masters wrote great music, but opinion is sometimes divided on the basis of their personalities. The music of Richard Wagner, a man with tremendous ego and little regard for his fellow humans, so one is given to understand, is disliked by many for precisely that reason. Richard Strauss, an occasional Nazi sympathizer, was widely ignored as a composer. J. S. Bach's obviously profamily attitude has helped his music to be extolled, while Chopin's slightly outré lifestyle, Tchaikovsky's homosexuality, and Schumann's psychiatric history have lowered their status a bit. To the denizens of the Music Building, music lives in their conception of the principal units of musical thought—the persons of the great composers.

In musicology as well, the selection of research topics often revolves about a person; one is a "Mozart scholar," "Bach scholar," "Liszt scholar." Successful research on a minor composer depends to a considerable extent on the scholar's ability to show relationship to or influence from or upon a member of the great-master elite. The coherence of the corpus of creations by a composer is a paramount issue to scholars. To know the person who composed a piece is to know the most important thing about it. To find a new piece by a great master can give you the musicological equivalent of the Nobel Prize. To learn that a piece "by" Beethoven is actually by Friedrich Witt would today get you on the front pages of the *New York Times*. Such a piece, a bit like the song dreamed by two Blackfoot visionaries, is somehow no longer the same piece if Beethoven did not write it. And that it be truly a *piece* on its own terms, without excessive relationship to others, represents another value of the Music Building: the great importance of innovation.

The Music Building is in North America, but its denizens don't worry that the great masters are not Americans but, indeed, largely ethnic Germans. Their concept of art music is supranational, more so perhaps than in the case of visual art or literature. The emblem of this concept is the use of a single notation system which enables musicians who cannot speak to each other to play in the same orchestra. (This is not so everywhere; note the many systems operative in Japanese traditional music.) Furthermore, there is a universal terminology, derived from Italian, which has only recently begun to give way to national vernaculars. Why it should be Italian, in a repertory dominated by Germans, moves us to another guiding principle of Western art music, that of the musician as stranger. Deep in the roots of European culture is an ambivalence about music, suspicion of it, a belief that somehow the musician, often a strangely behaving person who can perform incredible feats, is in league with the devil. The musician is permitted, even required, to be a strange, unconventional person, wear his hair long, speak with an accent, be absent minded. The mad, inexplicable genius, perhaps; but he may also be thought to have a deviant lifestyle, to be a habitual drunkard, drug addict, debtor, homosexual, womanizer, but then also a foreigner. It is, I suggest, the idea of keeping music at arm's length that results in a foreign terminology for music, motivates denizens of the Music Building to be so much attracted to foreign teachers, and causes orchestras to seek foreign conductors (while never promoting, say, the first clarinettist to that post).

And so, while Austrians make much of *their* Mozart, and Germans of Beethoven, nations throughout the world, including some where their works have rarely if ever been heard, put their likenesses on postage stamps.

II. ANDANTE: MYTHOLOGICAL VARIATIONS

THEME: THE MYTH OF BEAVER

Our Martian observer has noted a number of guiding principles, foremost among which are hierarchies headed by a pantheon of great masters. If they are the deities, their character may be explained by myths widely told, if not rationally believed. Can one gain important insights into musical culture from the reading of myths? It is an approach well established in anthropology, and ethnomusicologists have begun to join it. Steven Feld, in *Sound and Sentiment* (1983), builds the interpretation of an entire musical culture on a single central myth about a boy who became a bird. Could one show the Music Building's system of ideas about music as the function of a mythic duel between Mozart and Beethoven? Let me show you what I mean by recalling an important myth of the Blackfoot people.

It concerns the interaction of a human family and the figure of the beaver, who is a kind of lord of the part of the world below the surface of the water, a sort of underworld. A great human hunter has killed a specimen of each animal and bird, and their dressed skins decorate his tent. While he is hunting, a beaver comes to visit his wife and seduces her, and she follows him into the water. After four days she returns to her husband, and in time gives birth to a beaver child. In Blackfoot society, such an affair would have been severely punished, but the hunter continues to be kind to his wife and particularly to the child. One day the beaver visits the wife again and, expressing pleasure at the way his child is treated, says that he wants to give the hunter some of his supernatural power as a reward. He asks for certain ritual preparations to be made and then visits the hunter. They smoke together and then the beaver begins to sing, song after song, each song containing a request for a particular bird or animal skin. The hunter gives the skin and in return receives the song. At the end, the hunter has received the songs of the beaver and their supernatural power—and with them the principal ritual of Blackfoot religion.[10]

This myth imparts many important things about Blackfoot music. Here is a brief summary. Songs come to humans and exist as whole units, and they are learned in one hearing. They are objects that can be traded, as it were, for physical objects. The musical system reflects the cultural system, as each being in the environment has its song. Music reflects and contains supernatural power. It is something which only men use and perform, but women are instrumental in bringing its existence about. Music is given to a human who acts morally, gently, in a civilized manner. It is the result of a period of dwelling with the supernatural, after which a major aspect of culture is brought, so in a way it symbolizes humanness and Blackfootness, a role that music has in some other Native American myths. Music has specific roles and functions and is used in a prescribed ritual. There is more, despite the fact that this is not specifically a myth of the origins of music.

Two Variations: Myths of Mozart and Beethoven

The mythology of the Music Building has more characters, and facts and fancy are intertwined in its stories. Yet they are myths in the sense that they explain complex reality to the ignorant and the young. We now hear a native consultant telling about his childhood in a family of denizens of the Music Building, though on another continent. He hears an attractive piece of music and is told it "is" Mozart, and, in bits of pieces, learns this: Mozart was a young boy with incredible talent and ability; no one could explain his feats. He composed without much in the way of lessons. His father took him to show him off to the royalty of Europe, but he seemed not to appreciate these advantages and eventually got along badly with his father. Later he tried to make his living as a composer but was always poor. He was not appreciated in his own city of Salzburg, and also not very much in Vienna; only in the somewhat foreign city of Prague was he understood. Very important: He could compose without trying, his music came full-blown into his mind and had only to be written down. He could hear a piece of music and play it back unerringly by ear, and he was a superb improviser. He had a ribald sense of humor. He was disliked by his rival Salieri and died very young, a mysterious death. When he was terminally ill, someone came to ask him to write a requiem, and he had the notion that it was for his own funeral but died before he could finish it. His accomplishments were the result of some kind of supernatural power; thus the great attention to his mysterious death. He was born a genius—a traditional European notion, related to social immobility and the belief in elites. (And indeed, Mozart is, I

---

10. For a more detailed account, see John Ewers, *The Blackfeet, Raiders on the Northwestern Plains* (Norman, Okla.: University of Oklahoma Press, 1958).

think, held in even higher esteem in Europe than in North America, as his kind of life fits better into the older, European notion of the relationship of art and life.)

Mozart, a composer whom a child could understand. But there is a second variation, as the informant soon hears about another composer, his music better for older people: Beethoven. He was a different kind of person; like his music, difficult, hard to get along with. In various ways, he was quite the opposite of Mozart. As Mozart had a mystery about his death, Beethoven had one about his birth; was he Dutch, German, maybe exotic, and was he aristocratic or lower class? He had a dark and brooding look. He suffered greatly, was frequently disappointed, never found the right woman, and of course there was the tragedy of his deafness. His music didn't come easily, you could tell he had to work hard to write it, you had to work hard to listen to it. His humor was ponderous. But he is said to be the man who "freed music" (from the likes of Mozart?). He had no children, but a nephew on whom he doted but who disappointed him.

For adults, the myth is elaborated: Beethoven, the master of serious music, had a hard life; his deafness dominates our idea of him. He worked hard, sketched his works for years before getting them right, is seen as a struggler against many kinds of bonds—musical, social, political, moral, personal. He is thought to have seen himself as a kind of high priest, giving up much for the spiritual aspects of his music. He was a genius, but he had to work hard to become and be one. It is perhaps no coincidence that he has been, to Americans, the quintessential great master of music—for this is, after all, the culture in which hard work was once prized above all, labor rewarded; the culture in which you weren't born to greatness but were supposed to struggle to achieve it.

These are the myths that this native informant pieced together in early years; they correspond, I believe, in general nature if not in detail to those perceived by that part of society that is involved with this music, the denizens of the Music Building. The two composers represent complementary values, they are the opposites in a Lévi-Straussian diagram, and they reflect the tensions that are the subject of the debates airing the most general issues of art and life.

Of course, speaking now as a musicology professor, I know that these two men were not all that different in their work habits, that Mozart was a workaholic and an innovator and did some sketching, while Beethoven was not just a grind and a firebrand. The point is that in looking at the popular conceptions of a population of musicians, ferreting out myths from various sources, we can learn about the relationship of the musical system to the rest of culture.

And so, as the Blackfoot beaver myth shows us important things about the way Blackfoot people conceive of their songs, the ideas we—today—have about Mozart and Beethoven reveal some of the values of our musical culture. Genius must suffer. There is conflict between inspiration and labor and between consistency and innovation. The great composer has supernatural connections or is a stranger. Music is mysterious; its great practitioners come, in some sense, from outside the culture. The "composers" are the main units of musical thought and recognition. Their configuration illuminates major structural principles of Western music and society such as hierarchy and duality.

•   •   •   •   •

VI

CONCERT LIFE, RECEPTION, AND THE CULTURE INDUSTRY

34 Alban Berg

Arnold Schoenberg's Society of Private Musical Performances, founded in Vienna in 1918, offers a pointed early indication of twentieth-century music's separation from general concert life and thus of its isolation from the greater musical public. In this statement of aims, written by Schoenberg's former pupil Alban Berg shortly after the organization's founding, we can see the extraordinary efforts made to avoid normal concert trappings in order to allow the music that was performed to be experienced as "purely" as possible. No publicity, no critics, and no applause were permitted, and no names of pieces were announced in advance. Consistent with the society's "semi-pedagogical" purpose, emphasis was placed upon well-rehearsed renderings so as to make the music as "comprehensible" as possible. One notes the society's self-proclaimed "private"—today one might say "elitist"—character: only members and out-of-town guests were welcome at the concerts.

FROM Society for Private Music Performances in Vienna

A Statement of Aims

(1919)

The Society was founded in November, 1918, for the purpose of enabling Arnold Schoenberg to carry out his plan to give artists and music-lovers a real and exact knowledge of modern music.

The attitude of the public toward modern music is affected to an immense degree by the circumstance that the impression it receives from that music is inevitably one of obscurity. Aim, tendency, intention, scope and manner of expression, value, essence, and goal, all are obscure; most performances of it lack clarity; and specially lacking in lucidity is the public's consciousness of its own needs and wishes. All works are therefore valued, considered, judged, and lauded, or else misjudged, attacked, and rejected, exclusively upon the basis of one effect which all convey equally—that of obscurity.

This situation can in the long run satisfy no one whose opinion is worthy of consideration, neither the serious composer nor the thoughtful member of an audience. To bring light into this darkness and thus fulfill a justifiable need and desire was one of the motives that led Arnold Schoenberg to found this society.

To attain this goal three things are necessary:

1. Clear, well-rehearsed performances.

TEXT: Nicolas Slonimsky, *Music Since 1900*, 4th ed. (New York: Charles Scribner's Sons, 1971), pp. 1307–1308. Trans. by Stephen Somervell. Reprinted with permission of Schirmer Books, an imprint of Macmillan Publishing Company.

2. Frequent repetitions.

3. The performances must be removed from the corrupting influence of publicity; that is, they must not be directed toward the winning of competitions and must be unaccompanied by applause, or demonstrations of disapproval.

Herein lies the essential difference revealed by a comparison of the Society's aims with those of the everyday concert world, from which it is quite distinct in principle. Although it may be possible, in preparing a work for performance, to get along with the strictly limited and always insufficient number of rehearsals hitherto available, for better or worse (usually the latter), yet for the Society the number of rehearsals allotted to works to be performed will be limited only by the attainment of the greatest possible clarity and by the fulfillment of all the composer's intentions as revealed in his work. And if the attainment of these minimum requirements for good performance should necessitate a number of rehearsals that cannot be afforded (as was the case, for example, with a symphony of Mahler, which received its first performance after twelve four-hour rehearsals and was repeated after two more), then the work concerned should not, and will not, be performed by the Society.

In the rehearsal of new works, the performers will be chosen preferably from among the younger and less well-known artists, who place themselves at the Society's disposal out of interest in the cause; artists of high-priced reputation will be used only so far as the music demands and permits; and moreover that kind of virtuosity will be shunned which makes of the work to be performed not the end in itself but merely a means to an end which is not the Society's, namely, the display of irrelevant virtuosity and individuality, and the attainment of a purely personal success. Such things will be rendered automatically impossible by the exclusion (already mentioned) of all demonstrations of applause, disapproval, and thanks. The only success that an artist can have here is that (which should be most important to him) of having made the work, and therewith its composer, intelligible.

While such thoroughly rehearsed performances are a guarantee that each work will be enabled to make itself rightly understood, an even more effective means to this end is given to the Society through the innovation of weekly meetings[1] and by frequent repetitions of every work. Moreover, to ensure equal attendance at each meeting, the program will not be made known beforehand.

Only through the fulfillment of these two requirements—thorough preparation and frequent repetition—can clarity take the place of the obscurity which used to be the only impression remaining after a solitary performance; only thus can an audience establish an attitude towards a modern work that bears any relation to its composer's intention, completely absorb its style and idiom, and achieve that intimacy that is to be gained only through direct study—an

---

1. At that time, every Sunday morning from 10 to 12, in the Society's small concert hall. [Slonimsky]

intimacy with which the concert-going public can be credited only with respect to the most frequently performed classics.

The third condition for the attainment of the aims of the Society is that the performances shall be in all respects private; that guests (foreign visitors excepted) shall not be admitted, and that members shall be obligated to abstain from giving any public report of the performances and other activities of the Society, and especially to write or inspire no criticisms, notices, or discussions of them in periodicals.

This rule, that the sessions shall not be publicized, is made necessary by the semipedagogic activities of the Society and is in harmony with its tendency to benefit musical works solely through good performance and thus simply through the good effect made by the music itself. Propaganda for works and their composers is not the aim of the Society.

For this reason no school shall receive preference and only the worthless shall be excluded; for the rest, all modern music—from that of Mahler and Strauss to the newest, which practically never, or, at most, rarely, is to be heard—will be performed.

In general the Society strives to choose for performance such works as show their composers' most characteristic and, if possible, most pleasing sides. In addition to songs, pianoforte pieces, chamber music, and short choral pieces, even orchestral works will be considered, although the latter—since the Society has not yet the means to perform them in their original form—can be given only in good and well-rehearsed 4-hand and 8 hand arrangements. But the necessity becomes a virtue. In this manner it is possible to hear and judge a modern orchestral work divested of all the sound-effects and other sensuous aids that only an orchestra can furnish. Thus the old reproach is robbed of its force—that this music owes its power to its more or less opulent and effective instrumentation and lacks the qualities that were hitherto considered characteristic of good music—melody, richness of harmony, polyphony, perfection of form, architecture, etc.

A second advantage of this manner of music-making lies in the concert style of the performance of these arrangements. Since there is no question of a substitute for the orchestra but of so rearranging the orchestral work for the piano that it may be regarded, and should in fact be listened to, as an independent work and as a pianoforte composition, all the characteristic qualities and individualities of the piano are used, all the pianistic possibilities exploited. And it happens that in this reproduction—with different tone quality—of orchestral music, almost nothing is lost. Indeed, these very works, through the sureness of their instrumentation, the aptness of their instinctively chosen tone-colors, are best able to elicit from the piano tonal effects that far exceed its usual expressive possibilities.

·   ·   ·   ·   ·

35 Theodor W. Adorno

Theodor W. Adorno (1903–1969) was a leading German philosopher and social critic who devoted a significant portion of his work to music, most notably his book *Philosophy of New Music.* Trained as a composer under Alban Berg, Adorno was especially concerned with how music reflects and is influenced by larger social and intellectual issues. In this essay, written in 1945 when he was a refugee in the United States, Adorno examines the effects of mass media—specifically radio—on music and the musical experience. While openly betraying the exclusively "high-art" orientation of his thought (evident in his contemptuous dismissal of popular music and jazz), Adorno raises issues that continue to be seriously debated: the growing commodification and standard-ization of music, the detrimental effect of electronic transmission on listening (in particular the tendency toward "atomization"—dwelling on the part rather than the whole)—and the power of mass media to instill its audiences with a sense of "smugness and self-satisfaction."

FROM A Social Critique of Radio Music
(1945)

Some would approach the problem of radio by formulating questions of this type: If we confront such and such a sector of the population with such and such a type of music, what reactions may we expect? How can these reactions be measured and expressed statistically? Or: How many sectors of the population have been brought into contact with music and how do they respond to it?

What intention lies behind such questions? This approach falls into two major operations:

(a) We subject some groups to a number of different treatments and see how they react to each.

(b) We select and recommend the procedure which produces the effect we desire.

The aim itself, the tool by which we achieve it, and the persons upon whom it works are generally taken for granted in this procedure. The guiding interest behind such investigations is basically one of *administrative* technique: how to manipulate the masses. The pattern is that of market analysis even if it appears to be completely remote from any selling purpose. It might be research of an *exploitive* character, i.e. guided by the desire to induce as large a section of the population as possible to buy a certain commodity. Or it may be what Paul F. Lazarsfeld calls *benevolent* administrative research, putting questions such as, "How can we bring good music to as large a number of listeners as possible?"

I would like to suggest an approach that is antagonistic to exploitive and at least supplementary to benevolent administrative research. It abandons the form of question indicated by a sentence like: How can we, under given conditions, best further certain aims? On the contrary, this approach in some cases questions the aims and in all cases the successful accomplishment of these aims under the given conditions. Let us examine the question: how can good music be conveyed to the largest possible audience?

What is "good music"? Is it just the music which is given out and accepted as "good" according to current standards, say the programs of the Toscanini concerts? We cannot pass it as "good" simply on the basis of the names of great composers or performers, that is, by social convention. Furthermore, is the goodness of music invariant, or is it something that may change in the course of history with the technique at our disposal? For instance, let us take it for granted—as I do—that Beethoven really is good music. Is it not possible that this music, by the very problems it sets for itself, is far away from our own situation? That by constant repetition it has deteriorated so much that it has ceased to be the living force it was and has become a museum piece which no longer possesses the power to speak to the millions to whom it is brought? Or, even if this is not so, and if Beethoven in a musically young country like America is still as fresh as on the first day, is radio actually an adequate means of communication? Does a symphony played on the air remain a symphony? Are the changes it undergoes by wireless transmission merely slight and negligible modifications or do those changes affect the very essence of the music? Are not the stations in such a case bringing the masses in contact with something totally different from what it is supposed to be, thus also exercising an influence quite different from the one intended? And as to the large numbers of people who listen to "good music": *how* do they listen to it? Do they listen to a Beethoven symphony in a concentrated mood? Can they do so even if they want to? Is there not a strong likelihood that they listen to it as they would to a Tchaikovsky symphony, that is to say, simply listen to some neat tunes or exciting harmonic stimuli? Or do they listen to it as they do to jazz, waiting in the introduction of the finale of Brahms's First Symphony for the solo of the French horn, as they would for Benny Goodman's solo clarinet chorus? Would not such a type of listening make the high cultural ideal of bringing good music to large numbers of people altogether illusory?

These questions have arisen out of the consideration of so simple a phrase as "bringing good music to as large an audience as possible." None of these or similar questions can be wholly solved in terms of even the most benevolent research of the administrative type. One should not study the attitude of listeners without considering how far these attitudes reflect broader social behavior patterns and, even more, how far they are conditioned by the structure of society as a whole. This leads directly to the problem of a social critique of radio music, that of discovering social position and function. We first state certain axioms.

(a) We live in a society of commodities—that is, a society in which production of goods is taking place, not primarily to satisfy human wants and needs, but for profit. Human needs are satisfied only incidentally as it were. This basic condition of production affects the form of the product as well as the human interrelationships.

(b) In our commodity society there exists a general trend toward a heavy concentration of capital which makes for a shrinking of the free market in favor of monopolized mass production of standardized goods; this holds true particularly of the communications industry.

(c) The more the difficulties of contemporary society increase as it seeks its own continuance, the stronger becomes the general tendency to maintain, by all means available, the existing conditions of power and property relations against the threats which they themselves breed. Whereas on the one hand standardization necessarily follows from the conditions of contemporary economy, it becomes, on the other hand, one of the means of preserving a commodity society at a stage in which, according to the level of the productive forces, it has already lost its justification.

(d) Since in our society the forces of production are highly developed, and, at the same time, the relations of production fetter those productive forces, it is full of antagonisms. These antagonisms are not limited to the economic sphere where they are universally recognized, but dominate also the cultural sphere where they are less easily recognized.

How did music become, as our first axiom asserts it to be, a commodity? After music lost its feudal protectors during the latter part of the 18th Century it had to go to the market. The market left its imprint on it either because it was manufactured with a view to its selling chances, or because it was produced in conscious and violent reaction against the market requirements. What seems significant, however, in the present situation, and what is certainly deeply connected with the trend to standardization and mass production, is that *today the commodity character of music tends radically to alter it*. Bach in his day was considered, and considered himself, an artisan, although his music functioned as art. Today music is considered ethereal and sublime, although it actually functions as a commodity. Today the terms ethereal and sublime have become trademarks. Music has become a means instead of an end, a fetish. That is to say, music has ceased to be a human force and is consumed like other consumers' goods. This produces "commodity listening," a listening whose ideal it is to dispense as far as possible with any effort on the part of the recipient—even if such an effort on the part of the recipient is the necessary condition of grasping the sense of the music. It is the ideal of Aunt Jemima's ready-mix for pancakes extended to the field of music. The listener suspends all intellectual activity when dealing with music and is content with consuming and evaluating its gustatory qualities—just as if the music which tasted best were also the best music possible.

Famous master violins may serve as a drastic illustration of musical fetishism. Whereas only the expert is able to distinguish a "Strad" from a good modern fiddle, and whereas he is often least preoccupied with the tone quality of the fiddles, the layman, induced to treat these instruments as commodities, gives them a disproportionate attention and even a sort of adoration. One radio company went so far as to arrange a cycle of broadcasts looking, not primarily to the music played, nor even to the performance, but to what might be called an acoustic exhibition of famous instruments such as Paganini's violin and Chopin's piano. This shows how far the commodity attitude in radio music goes, though under a cloak of culture and erudition.

Our second axiom—increasing standardization—is bound up with the commodity character of music. There is, first of all, the haunting similarity between most musical programs, except for the few non-conformist stations which use recorded material of serious music; and also the standardization of orchestral performance, despite the musical trademark of an individual orchestra. And there is, above all, that whole sphere of music whose lifeblood is standardization: popular music, jazz, be it hot, sweet, or hybrid.

The third point of our social critique of radio concerns its ideological effect. Radio music's ideological tendencies realize themselves regardless of the intent of radio functionaries. There need be nothing intentionally malicious in the maintenance of vested interests. Nonetheless, music under present radio auspices serves to keep listeners from criticizing social realities; in short, it has a soporific effect upon social consciousness. The illusion is furthered that the best is just good enough for the man in the street. The ruined farmer is consoled by the radio-instilled belief that Toscanini is playing for him and for him alone, and that an order of things that allows him to hear Toscanini compensates for low market prices for farm products; even though he is ploughing cotton under, radio is giving him culture. Radio music is calling back to its broad bosom all the prodigal sons and daughters whom the harsh father has expelled from the door. In this respect radio music offers a new function not inherent in music as an art—the function of creating smugness and self-satisfaction.

The last group of problems in a social critique of radio would be those pertaining to social antagonisms. While radio marks a tremendous technical advance, it has proved an impetus to progress neither in music itself nor in musical listening. Radio is an essentially new technique of musical reproduction. But it does not broadcast, to any considerable extent, serious modern music. It limits itself to music created under pre-radio conditions. Nor has it, itself, thus far evoked any music really adequate to its technical conditions.

The most important antagonisms arise in the field of so-called musical mass-culture. Does the mass distribution of music really mean a rise of musical culture? Are the masses actually brought into contact with the kind of music which, from broader social considerations, may be regarded as desirable? Are the masses really participating in music culture or are they merely forced consumers of musical commodities? What is the role that music actually, not verbally, plays for them?

Under the aegis of radio there has set in a retrogression of listening. In spite of and even because of the quantitative increase in musical delivery, the psychological effects of this listening are very much akin to those of the motion picture and sport spectatoritis which promotes a retrogressive and sometimes even infantile type of person. "Retrogressive" is meant here in a psychological and not a purely musical sense.

An illustration: A symphony of the Beethoven type, so-called classical, is one of the most highly integrated musical forms. The whole is everything; the part, that is to say, what the layman calls the melody, is relatively unimportant. Retrogressive listening to a symphony is listening which, instead of grasping that whole, dwells upon those melodies, just as if the symphony were structurally the same as a ballad. There exists today a tendency to listen to Beethoven's Fifth as if it were a set of quotations from Beethoven's Fifth. We have developed a larger framework of concepts such as atomistic listening and quotation listening, which lead us to the hypothesis that something like a musical children's language is taking shape.

As today a much larger number of people listen to music than in pre-radio days, it is difficult to compare today's mass-listening with what could be called the elite listening of the past. Even if we restrict ourselves, however to select groups of today's listeners (say, those who listen to the Philharmonics in New York and Boston), one suspects that the Philharmonic listener of today listens in radio terms. A clear indication is the relation to serious advanced modern music. In the Wagnerian period, the elite listener was eager to follow the most daring musical exploits. Today the corresponding group is the firmest bulwark against musical progress and feels happy only if it is fed Beethoven's Seventh Symphony again and again.

In analyzing the fan mail of an educational station in a rural section in the Middle West, which has been emphasizing serious music at regular hours with a highly skilled and resourceful announcer, one is struck by the apparent enthusiasm of the listeners' reception, by the vast response, and by the belief in the highly progressive social function that this program was fulfilling. I have read all of those letters and cards very carefully. They are exuberant indeed. But they are enthusiastic in a manner that makes one feel uncomfortable. It is what might be called standardized enthusiasm. The communications are almost literally identical: "Dear X, Your Music Shop is swell. It widens my musical horizon and gives me an ever deeper feeling for the profound qualities of our great music. I can no longer bear the trashy jazz which we usually have to listen to. Continue with your grand work and let us have more of it." No musical item was mentioned, no specific reference to any particular feature was made, no criticism was offered, although the programs were amateurish and planless.

It would do little good to explain these standard responses by reference to the difficulty in verbalizing musical experience: for anybody who has had profound musical experiences and finds it hard to verbalize them may stammer and use awkward expressions, but he would be reluctant, even if he knew no other, to cloak them in rubber stamp phrases. I am forced to another explanation. The listeners were strongly under the spell of the announcer as the personified voice of radio as a social institution, and they responded to his call to prove one's cultural level and education by appreciating this good music. But they actually failed to achieve that very appreciation which stamped them as cultured. They took refuge in repeating, often literally, the announcer's speeches in behalf of culture. Their behavior might be compared with that of the fanatical radio listener entering a bakery and asking for "that delicious, golden crispy Bond Bread."

•   •   •   •   •

36 Lawrence Gilman

The commercialization of music referred to by Theodor Adorno in the previous entry is reflected in this talk by the American music writer Lawrence Gilman (1878–1939), presented during the intermission of Arturo Toscanini's final radio broadcast with the NBC Symphony on April 26, 1938. Gilman, music critic for the *New York Tribune* (later *Herald-Tribune*) from 1923 until his death, was a pioneering author in the field later known as "music appreciation." Among his books were *Stories of Symphonic Music* (New York, 1907), *Aspects of Modern Opera* (New York, 1909), and *Nature in Music and Other Studies* (New York, 1914). In this address Gilman praises Toscanini as being no less than "vicar of the Immortals" and "music-lover *in excelsis*." Such adulation helped shape the "star system" that has become so characteristic of twentieth-century concert life and that provides one essential component of the packaging of music for mass consumption. The following excerpts present the opening and closing portions of Gilman's address.

FROM Intermission Talk for Toscanini's Final Radio Concert

(1938)

Today's concert is Mr. Toscanini's farewell to the radio audience. Many of you have sent him letters of gratitude and appreciation with the thought of letting him know what his leadership of these concerts has meant to you, and I should like to add my own inadequate tribute to those that he has already received from you.

I have been wondering what it is about Toscanini that makes him unique as an artist; and I think the answer probably is that he represents with peculiar completeness the perfect type and example of the music-lover.

Of all the musicians I have known and observed as interpretive artists, I have never known one who loved music with the concentrated, fanatical, devastating intensity that is characteristic of Toscanini. As Shelley, one might say, is the perfect type of the poet, the poet *in excelsis,* and Mozart the music-maker *in excelsis,* and Napoleon the military genius *in excelsis,* so Toscanini will be known, I think, as the music-lover *in excelsis.*

Toscanini has many great qualities as an interpretive musician. But the one that transcends and animates them all is a passion for music so imperious and ungovernable that it will not let him rest until he has shared with us, through the medium of the instruments that he commands and inspires, his image of the ideal beauty that possesses him.

A great scholastic philosopher of an earlier century said that the influence of inspired men is to be explained in several ways. First, he said, because they have an undistorted vision of reality. Second, because they are receptacles of light; third, because they know, and make us know, that the reality which they see is identical with beauty. Fourth, because they are distinguished by what he called "an excess of love." They have in themselves, he concluded, "an inextinguishable light, illuminating others."

I think that this describes all men, all artists, who are vehicles of what we call, for want of a better name, inspiration. Their perception is undistorted; they receive and shed illumination; they see beauty as the supreme reality of the spirit; and their love of it is boundless, unquenchable, and creative.

•   •   •   •   •

Toscanini is leaving us; and we who have listened to him discerningly, season after season, are well aware of what we are about to lose. But we must face the fact with all possible fortitude and philosophy. We are confronted, as an Ameri-

TEXT: Typescript, New York Public Library, Library and Museum of the Performing Arts at Lincoln Center, NBC Archives, Toscanini Clipping Files.

can statesman once observed, with a condition and not a theory. Mr. Toscanini, vicar of the Immortals, is bound by mortal laws. He has served the Immortals long and gloriously, and with incomparable devotion; and now he would lighten his burden. He is sixty-nine years old. He would conduct when he chooses—not when conducting becomes burdensome and exhausting. And so we must do without him.

To minimize his loss would be an act of treachery toward our assumed allegiance to that ideal of lofty and self-effacing service which this great artist has exemplified. It would be an act of gross ingratitude to an interpreter who has re-created the music of the masters with unforgettable beauty and fidelity.

37 Roland Barthes

The literary and cultural critic Roland Barthes (1915–1980) was a leading figure in both the structuralist and poststructuralist schools of late twentieth-century French literary and philosophical thought. In this essay, written in 1970 and one of a number Barthes devoted to music, he considers certain features of contemporary musical life. He notes the replacement of the traditional "amateur," who recreated music "manually" and "muscularly" at a piano or some other instrument, by listeners who respond "passively" and "receptively" to music heard in concert, on record, and over the radio. For Barthes this transformation is tied to musical specialization, particularly to the development of the performing technician, who "relieves the listener of all activity." Yet Barthes closes by considering changes in the reception of Beethoven's works that reflect this same process more positively, fostering a response to music that requires "writing it anew." This idea of what he elsewhere terms the "readerly" text, which must be reconstructed actively by the reader/listener to be adequately comprehended (and which is especially characteristic of contemporary art), is of central importance to Barthes' later literary criticism.

Musica Practica
(1970)

There are two musics (at least so I have always thought): the music one listens to, the music one plays. These two musics are two totally different arts, each with its own history, its own sociology, its own esthetics, its own erotic;

TEXT: *Image, Music, Text*, ed. and trans. by Stephen Heath (New York: Hill and Wang, 1977), pp. 149–54. Reprinted by permission of Hill and Wang, a division of Farrar, Straus, & Giroux, Inc.

the same composer can be minor if you listen to him, tremendous if you play him (even badly)—such is Schumann.

The music one plays comes from an activity that is very little auditory, being above all manual (and thus in a way much more sensual). It is the music which you or I can play, alone or among friends, with no other audience than its participants (that is, with all risk of theater, all temptation of hysteria removed); a muscular music in which the part taken by the sense of hearing is one only of ratification, as though the body were hearing—and not "the soul"; a music which is not played "by heart": seated at the keyboard or the music stand, the body controls, conducts, coordinates, having itself to transcribe what it reads, making sound and meaning, the body as inscriber and not just transmitter, simple receiver. This music has disappeared; initially the province of the idle (aristocratic) class, it lapsed into an insipid social rite with the coming of the democracy of the bourgeoisie (the piano, the young lady, the drawing room, the nocturne) and then faded out altogether (who plays the piano today?). To find practical music in the West, one has now to look to another public, another repertoire, another instrument (the young generation, vocal music, the guitar). Concurrently, passive, receptive music, sound music, has become *the* music (that of concert, festival, record, radio): playing has ceased to exist; musical activity is no longer manual, muscular, kneadingly physical, but merely liquid, effusive, "lubrificating," to take up a word from Balzac. So too has the performer changed. The amateur, a role defined much more by a style than by a technical imperfection, is no longer anywhere to be found; the professionals, pure specialists whose training remains entirely esoteric for the public (who is there who is still acquainted with the problems of musical education?), never offer that style of the perfect amateur the great value of which could still be recognized in a Lipati or a Panzera, touching off in us not satisfaction but desire, the desire to *make* that music. In short, there was first the actor of music, then the interpreter (the grand Romantic voice), then finally the technician, who relieves the listener of all activity, even by procuration, and abolishes in the sphere of music the very notion of *doing*.

The work of Beethoven seems to me bound up with this historical problem, not as the straightforward expression of a particular moment (the transition from amateur to interpreter) but as the powerful germ of a disturbance of civilization, Beethoven at once bringing together its elements and sketching out its solution; an ambiguity which is that of Beethoven's two historical roles: the mythical role which he was made to play by the whole of the nineteenth century and the modern role which our own century is beginning to accord him (I refer here to Boucourechliev's study).[1]

For the nineteenth century, leaving aside a few stupid representations, such as the one given by Vincent d'Indy who just about makes of Beethoven a kind of reactionary and anti-Semitic hypocrite, Beethoven was the first man of music

1. André Boucourechliev, *Beethoven* (Paris: 1969). [Au.]

to be *free*. Now for the first time the fact of having several successive *manners*
was held to the glory of an artist; he was acknowledged the right of metamor-
phosis, he could be dissatisfied with himself or, more profoundly, with his language, he could change his codes as he went through life (this is what is
expressed by Lenz's naive and enthusiastic image of Beethoven's three different
manners).[2] From this moment that the work becomes the trace of a movement,
of a journey, it appeals to the idea of fate. The artist is in search of his "truth"
and this quest forms an order in itself, a message that can be read, in spite of
the variations in its content, over all the work or, at least, whose readability
feeds on a sort of totality of the artist: his career, his loves, his ideas, his character, his words become traits of meaning; a Beethovian biography is born (one
ought to be able to say a bio-mythology), the artist is brought forward as a
complete hero, endowed with a discourse (a rare occurrence for a musician), a
legend (a good ten or so anecdotes), an iconography, a race (that of the Titans
of Art: Michelangelo, Balzac) and a fatal malady (the deafness of he who creates for the pleasure of our ears). Into this system of meaning that is the
Romantic Beethoven are incorporated truly structural features (features which
are ambiguous, at once musical and psychological): the paroxysmal development of contrasts in intensity (the signifying opposition of the *piano* and the
forte, an opposition the historical importance of which is perhaps not very
clearly recognized, it characterizing after all only a tiny portion of the music of
the world and corresponding to the invention of an instrument whose name is
indicative enough, the *piano-forte*), the shattering of the melody, taken as the
symbol of restlessness and the seething agitation of creativeness, the emphatic
redundancy of moments of excitement and termination (a naive image of fate
dealing its blows), the experience of limits (the abolition or the inversion of the
traditional parts of musical speech), the production of musical chimera (the
voice rising out of the symphony)—and all this, which could easily be transformed metaphorically into pseudo-philosophical values, nonetheless musically
acceptable since always deployed under the authority of the fundamental code
of the West, tonality.

    Further, this romantic image (the meaning of which finally is a certain *dis-
cord*) creates a problem of performance: the amateur is unable to master Beethoven's music, not so much by reason of the technical difficulties as by the very
breakdown of the code of the former *musica practica.* According to this code,
the fantasmatic (that is to say corporal) image which guided the performer was
that of a song ("spun out" inwardly); with Beethoven, the mimetic impulse
(does not musical fantasy consist in giving oneself a place, as subject, in the
scenario of the performance?) becomes orchestral, thus escaping from the
fetishism of a single element (voice or rhythm). The body strives to be total,
and so the idea of an intimist or familial activity is destroyed: *to want* to play

---

2. Barthes refers to Wilhelm von Lenz (1809–1883), a Russian official of German descent, whose
   study *Beethoven et ses trois styles* (*Beethoven and his Three Styles*) appeared in 1852.

Beethoven is to see oneself as the conductor of an orchestra (the dream of how many children? the tautological dream of how many conductors, a prey in their conducting to all the signs of the panic of possession?). Beethoven's work forsakes the amateur and seems, in an initial moment, to call on the new Romantic deity, the interpreter. Yet here again we are disappointed: who (what soloist, what pianist?) can play Beethoven well? It is as though this music offers only the choice between a "role" and its absence, the illusion of demiurgy and the prudence of platitude, sublimated as "renunciation."

The truth is perhaps that Beethoven's music has in it something *inaudible* (something for which hearing is not the *exact* locality), and this brings us to the second Beethoven. It is not possible that a musician be deaf by pure contingency or poignant destiny (they are the same thing). Beethoven's deafness designates the lack wherein resides all signification; it appeals to a music that is not abstract or inward, but that is endowed, if one may put it like this, with a tangible intelligibility, with the intelligible as tangible. Such a category is truly revolutionary, unthinkable in the terms of the old esthetics; the work that complies with it cannot be received on the basis of pure sensuality, which is always cultural, nor on that of an intelligible order of (rhetorical, thematic) development, and without it neither the modern text nor contemporary music can be accepted. As we know since Boucourechliev's analyses, this Beethoven is exemplarily the Beethoven of the *Diabelli Variations* and the operation by which we can grasp this Beethoven (and the category he initiates) can no longer be either performance or hearing, but reading. This is not to say that one has to sit with a Beethoven score and get from it an inner recital (which would still remain dependent on the old animistic fantasy); it means that with respect to this music one must put oneself in the position or, better, in the activity of an operator, who knows how to displace, assemble, combine, fit together; in a word (if it is not too worn out), who knows how to structure (very different from constructing or reconstructing in the classic sense). Just as the reading of the modern text (such at least as it may be postulated) consists not in receiving, in knowing or in feeling that text, but in writing it anew, in crossing its writing with a fresh inscription, so too reading this Beethoven is *to operate* his music, to draw it (it is willing to be drawn) into an unknown *praxis*.

In this way may be rediscovered, modified according to the movement of the historical dialectic, a certain *musica practica*. What is the use of composing if it is to confine the product within the precinct of the concert or the solitude of listening to the radio? To compose, at least by propensity, is *to give to do,* not to give to hear but to give to write. The modern location for music is not the concert hall, but the stage on which the musicians pass, in what is often a dazzling display, from one source of sound to another. It is we who are playing, though still it is true by proxy; but one can imagine the concert—later on?—as exclusively a workshop, from which nothing spills over—no dream, no imaginary, in short, no "soul" and where all the musical art is absorbed in a praxis *with no remainder.* Such is the utopia that a certain Beethoven, who is not played, teaches us to formulate—which is why it is possible now to feel in him a musician with a future.

38 Steven Connor

In this excerpt from his book *Postmodernist Culture* (1989), the English cultural critic Steven Connor examines the nature of live performance in an age dominated by new technologies of representation. Though Connor develops his argument mainly in connection with rock music, it applies equally to many aspects of music in general. Connor is particularly interested in the way such "reproductive" innovations as film, recordings, and television have increased the public's desire for face-to-face contact. He also discusses the related pull between the producers of commercial music interested in supplying a marketable object and the public searching for a kind of immediate experience that is by nature ephemeral. Connor explores the tensions inherent in the notion of "presence" in a mass-media context, evident in efforts to package "live" experience itself (suitably enhanced through technological extensions), and suggests that the line between the "real" and the "representational" has been rendered largely illusory.

FROM *Postmodernist Culture*
(1989)
• • • • •

The dread of being frozen into a commodity brings about the contradictory response described by Henry Sayre as the 'mythology of presence' with which performance and such things as the oral poetry movement have surrounded themselves.[1] To highlight the fugitive intensity of the 'liberated' performance is to deny and downgrade any attempt to provide documentary records of such performances in galleries, museums and books, even as it simultaneously creates an ever more intense desire for such records (and opportunities for different kinds of packaging and display, in tapes, photographs and archives of

TEXT: *Postmodernist Culture: An Introduction to Theories of the Contemporary* (Cambridge: Basil Blackwell, 1989), pp. 148–55.

1. Henry Sayre, "The Object of Performance: Aesthetics in the Seventies," *Georgia Review* 37:1 (1983): 177. [Au.]

performance). Sayre is right to emphasize as he does the parasitic relationship between free performance and exploitable commodity, for it is in fact never possible to abstract one pole of the opposition and simply set it against the other, to insist on performance against text. For our intuition of the immediacy of performance is always a second-degree intuition, itself formed within a context of habits and expectations. What is more, the desire for noncommodifiable immediacy, for free theatrical experience, is no more immune from the operations of commodification than practices which yield an obvious object. In fact, the fixation of much postmodern performance theory upon the opposition of the commodity and of free experience draws, in an oddly anachronistic way, upon the language and concepts more appropriate to an earlier period in the development of capitalism. Late capitalism, organized in new ways around vastly enhanced networks of information, communication and reproduction, seems effectively to have dissolved the simple opposition of dead commodity-as-thing and live performance-as-process. The problem may then be not so much that performance always risks falling into the dead residue of objecthood in reproduction (photographs, audio- and video-recordings) as that performance and reproduction have become intertwined in complex ways.

This can best be exemplified, not in the more restricted field of avant-garde drama and performance, but in the much larger and culturally more pervasive area of rock music.[2] (This is not to deny the significant forms of connection between the two realms in the work of artists like Andy Warhol, Peter Gabriel and Laurie Anderson, of course.) Rock music, with its recurrent display of the values enshrined in performance, along with its extraordinary generation of new reproductive technologies, instances in a particularly powerful way the mutations undergone by those conceptual opposites, performance and text. The late 1970s and 1980s have seen a return in rock music to the "primitive" value and vitality of "live" performance, after the retreat of the largest and most influential bands like The Beatles and Pink Floyd into the technological delights of the studio. It is striking that the most powerful and successful artists over the last ten years have all felt obliged to demonstrate their capacity to engage with audiences in the direct contact of live performance as well as via albums and video recordings—the most familiar examples being Bruce Springsteen, Dire Straits and Michael Jackson. It is perhaps Springsteen whose career projects most unassailably the values associated with live performance, and because of this, the Springsteen mythology provides the most useful and interesting place to begin analysing the problematic status of the concept of the 'live' in postmodern mass culture. It needs to be said at this point that not many people would be inclined to see Bruce Springsteen's work as

2. I use the term "rock music" to distinguish the popular music of the 1960s onwards from the larger field of popular music in this century; the former would begin with rock and roll, Elvis Presley and the Beatles, the latter would include artists like Bing Crosby and Frank Sinatra and would extend back at least until the 1920s. [Au.]

itself postmodernist in style or expressive content; but, the ways in which his work is taken up, dispersed and distributed provide a way of understanding the contemporary conditions with which a theory of postmodern culture has to deal.

The most important part of the Springsteen mythology has always been his reputation as a live performer, one who works hard to give himself with energy and enthusiasm to his enormous audiences. To see Springsteen live is to be in the presence of a mythical figure, to enjoy a certain erotic closeness. Springsteen is most authentically "himself" when he is on stage, and the ecstasy generated by the sudden shrinking of distance between fan and star is at its most extreme in live performance. This ecstasy of desired identification is a comparatively recent phenomenon in mass culture and turns out to depend oddly upon the technology of mass reproduction and communication; for it is only when the means exist to provide audiences with various kinds of substitute for the presence of the star—films, records, tapes, pictures—that this ecstatic yield of pleasure can be obtained from being in his actual presence. In fact, the success of the rock industry, which has taken over from the film industry in the business of star-manufacture, depends upon the kinds of desire that high fidelity reproduction stimulates, the itch for more, for more faithful reproductions of the "real thing," the yearning to move ever closer to the "original."

There is a drama of possession and control acted out through this. To own a record is, in a limited sense, to be able to control the music that it encodes, for, with certain exclusions, one purchases with the record the freedom to reproduce and replay it wherever and whenever one wishes, at home, in the street, in the car. This repeatability is what seems to guarantee the consumer's possession and control of the commodity; but it also encloses a hidden deficiency. If recorded music is infinitely repeatable, then this is precisely because it is a form of copy, which must always stand at one remove from its original. So paradoxically, at the moment of its greatest yielding, the commodity always holds something back; the more the record is played, the more it confirms the possession and control of the consumer, the more it displays its failure to be the real thing. What guarantees the possibility of the consumer's control is an intrinsic shortfall in the commodity, the fact that it can never be the original of itself.

These factors connect with the more general issues which have been the subject of intensified debate within postmodern cultural theory in recent years. As Deleuze, Derrida and others have argued, we continue to depend upon an opposition between things which are felt to be immediate, original and "real" on the one hand, and the representations of those things, which we conceive of as secondary, derived and therefore "false" on the other. Repetition plays a crucial part in sustaining our sense of the real, since repetition is always, as Deleuze argues, tied to the conception of a return of the Same, and the threat posed by repetition and replication to the authority of original and universal ideas is only ever a temporary threat, which customarily reverts to the service of origins.[3]

In the light of the fantastic proliferation of processes for the replication of products, texts and information, many cultural theorists, from Walter Benjamin to Jean Baudrillard, have seen a diminution in the authority of ideas of original-ity, Benjamin arguing that the "aura" of the original work of art is lost with the predominance of mechanical reproduction, and Baudrillard proclaiming that the very opposition between original and copy has been lost in an age of simula-cra, or repetitions without originals.[4] At the same time, it is possible to see how the proliferation of reproductions actually intensifies the desire for origin, even if that origin is increasingly sensed as an erotic lack rather than a tangible and satisfying presence. In Baudrillard's terms, the real is ceaselessly manufactured as an intensified version of itself, as hyperreality.

For the rock fan, it is above all the live show which seems to offer this unfalsifiably real corporeal presence, for here—apparently—are to be found life, music, the body themselves, naked and unignorable, unobscured by barri-ers of reproduction or representation. But what kind of live experience charac-terizes contemporary rock music? In the case of Bruce Springsteen it is an experience of manufactured mass closeness. Whereas audiences at the great pop festivals of the 1970s had to make do with the sight of tiny figures per-forming inconsequentially on a stage half a mile away ("Is that Dylan in the hat?"), and a sound system that worked efficiently only with a following wind, Springsteen's appearances on his world tour in 1985, which were rarely to fewer than 50,000 people, made sure that no member of the vast audience could escape the slightest nuance of music or voice. Behind him, an enormous video screen projected claustrophobically every detail of his agonized facial expressions in a close-up which at one and the same time abolished and re-emphasized the actual distance between him and his audience.

Intimacy and immediacy on this scale can only be achieved by massively conspicuous acts of representation. Enormous amplification, hugely expanded images; these are the forms which reproduction takes in the context of the live. Sound and image are simultaneous with the "real" music that is being per-formed (although, of course, in the case of most contemporary music the "origi-nal" sound is usually itself only an amplified derivation from an initiating signal), even if it remains obvious that what is most real about the event is precisely the fact that it is being projected as mass experience. The normal condition for Springsteen's performances is an ecstatic, somatic excess that spills over into and is constituted by an excess of representations at the very heart of the live experience.

3. See Giles Deleuze, *Différence et répétition* (Paris: Presses Universitaires de France, 1968). [Au.]
4. Walter Benjamin, "The Work of Art in the Age of Mechanical Reproduction," in *Illuminations,* trans. Harry Zohn (London: Fontana, 1970), pp. 219–54; Jean Baudrillard, "The Precession of Simulacra," in *Simulations,* trans. Paul Foss, Paul Patton, and Philip Bleitchman (New York: Semiotext(e), 1983), pp. 1–80. [Au.]

It is for this reason that audiences of 80,000 or more now regularly attend concerts to watch videos, albeit "live" videos; the ecstasy of experience is turned into what Baudrillard calls an "ecstasy of communication," a fantastic, barely-controllable excess of images and representations.[5] This was well borne out during the Live Aid concerts in 1985 when Phil Collins, after playing in London, absurdly travelled across the Atlantic on Concorde in order to play in Philadelphia later that day, during the same global transmission of the concert, in a monstrously inflated version of the prank in which a schoolchild runs from one end to the other of a serial school photograph in order to be photographed in two places. But Phil Collins travelled 3,000 miles not in order to be visible in the flesh, but to provide an image to be projected on to the video-screen which projected close-up images of him to the audience in the stadium and round the world.

During the Live Aid concerts, video screens allowed the easy incorporation of other, recorded material into the live spectacle. David Bowie and Mick Jagger had originally planned to sing "Dancing in the Street" simultaneously in Philadelphia and London, but the unavoidable half-second delay in transmission made this impossible; so they came together in a video recording which was fitted seamlessly into the experience of the live concerts—and the fact that the song and the dance routines in the video exemplified the theme of spontaneous, *en plein air* celebration only added ironic piquancy to the blending of the real and the represented. The audience were also closely involved in this process of willed simulation. Often, the viewer of the spectacle at home was shown the audience watching an image of themselves on the giant video screen, so that when we subsequently saw shots of the audience at home, we were not sure whether it was the audience itself that we were seeing, or the image of the audience projected on to the video-screen at the event—whether we were watching them, in other words, or watching them watching themselves.

What emerges from all this is not so much the abolition of the desire for originality and presence in the performing instant, as the inversion of the structural dependence of copies upon originals. In the case of the "live" performance, the desire for originality is a secondary effect of various forms of reproduction. The intense "reality" of the performance is not something that lies behind the particulars of the setting, the technology and the audience; its reality consists in all of that apparatus of representation.

We should not be surprised, therefore, at the success of that postmodernist oxymoron, the "live recording." Of course many of the protocols of live performance derive from the familiarity of audience and performer alike with representations of other live performances. This is confirmed by the aesthetic conventions that determine the ways in which live recordings, in that evocative

---

5. "The Ecstasy of Communication," in *Postmodern Culture*, ed. Hal Foster (London and Sydney: Pluto Press, 1985), pp. 126–34. [Au.]

contemporary term, are "produced." After recording a live album, most artists have to spend considerable amounts of time in the studio, reworking sections, altering the balance, overdubbing vocals, adding instruments, correcting mistakes and, indeed, sometimes, roughing up a sound that may be too smooth in actual performance. (Once this becomes known, it can produce a primitivist reflex, as with Dire Straits' *Alchemy* album, which made a selling point of the fact that the 'original' sound had not been tampered with in any way.)

Increasingly, then, the experience of the "live" is itself being commodified, "produced" as a strategic category of the semiotic, even though its function *within* semiotic systems may be to embody that which remains authentically and dangerously outside the distortions of the commodity and of signification itself. The live is always in a sense the quotation of itself—never the live, always the "live." Paradoxically, the desire for original and authentic experience exists alongside the recognition that there can never be any such thing, at least in contemporary rock music. The increasing sophistication of studio technology, and the consequent multiplication of versions of a single song, in remixes and extended twelve-inch versions, combined more recently with the cult of "sampling," or the appropriation and re-editing of snatches of music from other songs, means the loss of a sense that there can be such a thing as an original version of a song. Nowadays, the title of a song names a diverse and theoretically endless range of embodiments and performances, or versions of performances, since one performance may be mixed and reassembled in any number of ways. This means that the opposition between the live and the reproduced which is sustained within studio recordings themselves—promotional videos often show the studio as a sort of substitute scene of the "live," discovering in the instant of recording a kind of immediacy which the technology of recording disseminates—is jeopardized. This recalls Walter Benjamin's argument that the abandonment of "real time" continuity in film-making with the chopping up of the narrative into discontinuous segments for the purpose of filming, results in a loss of "aura," since the narrative that is eventually synthesized has never been acted out anywhere all at once. Something similar happens in the modern studio recording, which assembles a performance which has never had any existence all at once anywhere except on the producer's console.

These points may be considerably generalized. Everywhere the world of the mass media holds out the possibility and desirability of "live" experience, and embraces "process" while discrediting fixity of definition. The economics of mass culture, far from requiring the freezing of freely contingent human experiences into commodifiable forms, consciously promotes these forms of transient intensity, since it is, in the end, much easier to control and stimulate demand for experiences which are spontaneously (nothing of the kind, of course) sensed as outside representation. From rock music to tourism to television and even education, advertising imperatives and consumer demand are no longer for goods, but for experiences.

Here, as elsewhere, postmodern theory has a complicated and ambivalent relationship to this process. Postmodern theories of performance, whether inversive (asserting the presence of performance against the inauthenticity of representation) or deconstructive (examining the mutual implications of performance and text) simultaneously stand aside from and form part of this semiotic terrain. In the attempt to think through the complexities of performance, and the ways in which it reproduces authoritative structures of thought, postmodern theory aligns itself with what it describes, and perhaps secretly designates itself in its descriptions of the subversive mission of avant-garde art. But, at the same time, it can function as an imaginative and institutional filtering of its own vision of the subversive sublime of pure performance. The more successful the intellectual paradigm of postmodern performance becomes, the tighter is the circuit of exchange between the self-acknowledging and unmistakable energies of performance and the exemplary or demonstrative function that such free energies perform for the paradigm. The freedom of performance, of the "live," is mortgaged to the theory and, of course, the cultural codes and assumptions, which accredit it in advance *as* freedom. The postmodern theory of a performance that escapes the museum, the script, or the recording, is the discursive form which precisely legislates the conditions of that escape.

VII

PLURALISM

39 Erik Satie

No composer of the early twentieth century did more than the Frenchman Erik Satie (1866–1925) to deflate the artistic pretensions of the immediate past, something he accomplished with a detached, ironic tone that was itself an important aspect of his new esthetic. The stark simplicity of Satie's music, his humorous indications to the performer ("very seriously silent"), and the absurd titles of his works ("Three Pieces in the Form of a Pear") all mock the expressive and programmatic excesses of the nineteenth century. These three brief prose pieces, originally written between 1912 and 1914, for the French periodical *La revue musicale S.I.M.* and later collected in the characteristically titled "Memoirs of an Amnesiac," brilliantly display the proto-surrealistic quality of Satie's mind, revealing his delight in satirizing the artistic enterprise and his refusal to take even himself too seriously.

FROM Memoirs of an Amnesiac

WHAT I AM
(1912)

Everyone will tell you that I am not a musician. That is correct.

From the very beginning of my career I classed myself as a phonomotrographer. My work is completely phonometrical. Take my *Fils des étoiles,* or my *Morceaux en forme de poire,* my *En habit de cheval* or my *Sarabandes*—it is evident that musical ideas played no part whatsoever in their composition. Science is the dominating factor.

Besides, I enjoy measuring a sound much more than hearing it. With my phonometer in my hand, I work happily and with confidence.

What haven't I weighed or measured? I've done all Beethoven, all Verdi, etc. It's fascinating.

The first time I used a phonoscope, I examined a B-flat of medium size. I can assure you that I have never seen anything so revolting. I called in my man to show it to him.

On my phono-scales a common or garden F-sharp registered 93 kilos. It came out of a fat tenor whom I also weighed.

Do you know how to clean sounds? It's a filthy business. Stretching them out is cleaner; indexing them is a meticulous task and needs good eyesight. Here, we are in the realm of phonotechnique.

On the question of sound explosions, which can often be so unpleasant, some

TEXT: *The Writings of Erik Satie,* ed. and trans. by Nigel Wilkins (London: Eulenburg Books, 1980), pp. 58–59, 62. Reprinted by permission of Nigel Wilkins.

cotton-wool in the ears can deaden their effect quite satisfactorily. Here, we are in the realm of pyrophony.

To write my *Pièces froides,* I used a caleidophone recorder. It took seven minutes. I called in my man to let him hear them.

I think I can say that phonology is superior to music. There's more variety in it. The financial return is greater, too. I owe my fortune to it.

At all events, with a motodynamophone, even a rather inexperienced phono-metrologist can easily note down more sounds than the most skilled musician in the same time, using the same amount of effort. This is how I have been able to write so much.

And so the future lies with philophony.

THE MUSICIAN'S DAY
(1913)

An artist must organize his life.

Here is the exact timetable of my daily activities:

Get up: 7.18 am; be inspired: 10.23 to 11.47 am. I take lunch at 12.11 pm and leave the table at 12.14 pm.

Healthy horse-riding, out in my grounds: 1.19 to 2.53 pm. More inspiration: 3.12 to 4.07 pm.

Various activities (fencing, reflection, immobility, visits, contemplation, swimming, etc. . . .): 4.21 to 6.47 pm.

Dinner is served at 7.16 and ends at 7.20 pm. Then come symphonic readings, out loud: 8.09 to 9.59 pm.

I go to bed regularly at 10.37 pm. Once a week (on Tuesdays) I wake up with a start at 3.19 am.

I eat only white foodstuffs: eggs, sugar, scraped bones; fat from dead animals; veal, salt, coconuts, chicken cooked in white water; mouldy fruit, rice, turnips; camphorated sausage, things like spaghetti, cheese (white), cotton salad and certain fish (minus their skins).

I boil my wine and drink it cold mixed with fuchsia juice. I have a good appetite, but never talk while eating, for fear of strangling myself.

I breathe carefully (a little at a time). I very rarely dance. When I walk, I hold my sides and look rigidly behind me.

Serious in appearance, if I laugh it is not on purpose. I always apologize about it nicely.

My sleep is deep, but I keep one eye open. My bed is round, with a hole cut out to let my head through. Once every hour a servant takes my temperature and gives me another.

I have long subscribed to a fashion magazine. I wear a white bonnet, white stockings and a white waistcoat.

My doctor has always told me to smoke. Part of his advice runs:

—Smoke away, my dear chap: if you don't, someone else will.

PERFECT SURROUNDINGS
(1914)

Living in the midst of wonderful Works of Art is one of the greatest joys anyone can know. Among the precious monuments to human thought which my limited fortune has obliged me to choose as my life companions, I would single out a magnificent fake Rembrandt, wide and deep, so good to press with one's eyes, like a fat but unripe fruit.

You could also see, in my study, a canvas of undeniable beauty, a unique object of admiration: the delicious "Portrait attributed to an Unknown Artist."

Have I told you about my imitation Téniers? It's adorable, a lovely thing and a real rarity.

Aren't those divine, those gems mounted in hardwood? Aren't they?

And yet, there is something which surpasses these masterly works; which crushes them beneath the colossal weight of its majestic genius; which makes them grow pale with its dazzling radiance—it is a forged Beethoven manuscript (a sublime apocryphal Symphony by the Master) piously purchased by myself ten years ago, I think.

Of all the works of this grandiose composer, this 10th Symphony, which nobody knows, is one of the most sumptuous. Its proportions are on a palatial scale; its ideas are fresh and plentiful; the developments are exact and appropriate.

This Symphony had to exist: the number 9 just wouldn't suit Beethoven. He liked the decimal system: "I have ten fingers," he used to explain.

Certain admirers who came dutifully to take in this masterpiece with thoughtful and attentive ears, quite wrongly felt it to be one of Beethoven's inferior works and went so far as to say so. They even went further than that.

In no way can Beethoven be inferior to himself. His form and technique are always portentous, even in his slightest works. In his case the word rudimentary cannot be used. As an artist he can easily stand up to any counterfeit attributed to him.

Would you think that an athlete, who had been famous for years and whose skill and strength had been acknowledged in many a public triumph, was made any the less worthy because he was easily able to carry a bouquet of mixed tulips and jasmine? Would he be any less admirable if a child helped him as well?

Of course not.

40 Nadia Boulanger

The Frenchwoman Nadia Boulanger (1887–1979) had an important influence on the development of American music during the first half of the century. Though a composer, conductor, and keyboard player of considerable accomplishment, Boulanger was best known as a brilliant and demanding teacher of composition and musicianship. Many of the leading American composers of the generation that reached maturity between the two world wars—among them Aaron Copland, Roy Harris, Virgil Thomson, and Elliott Carter—studied with her. Closely associated with Stravinsky and the neoclassical movement, and conscious of the special burden of working in an era in which "everything is in question," Boulanger emphasized discipline and the establishment of compositional limits. In these two excerpts from interviews conducted near the end of her life, she focuses upon matters with which she was particularly concerned: teaching composition and the development of American musicians.

FROM Two Interviews

(1980)

A MENTOR

Do you know that text of Valéry's: "In the past, one imitated mastery, today one searches for singularity."

It is cruel, for one is singular because one cannot be like everyone else. One isn't singular by choice.

I desperately try to make a pupil understand that he must express what he wants; I don't mind whether he agrees with me or not, so long as he can tell me: "This is what I want to say, this is what I love, this is what I'm looking for." Today, we are at a fascinating point because everything is in question. Those who provide an answer are those who find a new language which isn't to be discussed, or approved, or rejected: it simply exists. We know already that there are some who make themselves understood and others who seek to do so, and others who haven't much to say and are looking for something to say. But that has been the case in the past, too. The difference is that previously there was such an established style that if the music was trivial, it was nevertheless intelligible; whereas in a time of experiment, when language is handled by people

TEXT: *Mademoiselle: Conversations with Nadia Boulanger*, ed. by Bruno Monsaingeon, trans. by Robyn Marsack (Boston: Northeastern University Press, 1988), pp. 60–62, 72–73. Reprint by permission of Carcanet Press Limited.

who don't know what they're doing, it makes for the vague, the uncertain in the uncertain.

When my students compose, I prefer them to be mistaken if they must make mistakes, but to remain natural and free rather than wishing to appear other than what they are. I remember a day when Stravinsky was dining here. He took his neighbor at the table by the lapels, violently! His neighbor, crushed, said to him; "But Monsieur Stravinsky, I don't know why we're talking like this, I agree with you." And Stravinsky exclaimed furiously, "Yes, but not for the right reasons, so you are wrong."

You can have good or bad reasons for searching. If you search in order to hide your inadequacy, you're wrong. If you are looking in order to say what you really want to say, you're right. And so it's very important for a teacher first of all to let his pupil play as he wishes, write as he wishes; and then to be ruthless on questions of discipline.

The student who has completely assimilated Hindemith's book, *Elementary Training for Musicians*—a pedagogical masterpiece—cannot be stumped by any question of rhythm, harmony or counterpoint. It is a book of pure theory, indispensable to all musicians and containing remarkable exercises. Hindemith knew about music in such an amazing way that sometimes it is difficult to distinguish the composer from the teacher. The whole of his work is made up of very beautiful writing and the most exquisite combinations. But despite his very curious and analytic mind, I wonder whether his teaching hasn't influenced his work as a composer. Certainly there is a difference between the Hindemith of *Mathis der Maler* and that of *Marienleben,* but the development isn't very marked. The second version of *Marienleben* seems to me, in some of the pieces that I love deeply, a betrayal of his original thought. I say this in all humility.

He himself said of his educational books that they had led to bad Hindemith being written by many young composers, and sometimes by himself. On the necessity and danger of convention: without conventions, you don't have a framework, and without a framework you're lost, you lose your balance. But you fall over too if you abandon yourself to convention or to fashion.

A great work, I believe, is made out of a combination of obedience and liberty. Such a work satisfies the mind, together with that curious thing which is artistic emotion. Stravinsky said, "If I were permitted everything, I would be lost in the abyss of liberty." On the one hand he knew the limits, on the other he ceaselessly extended them.

If we look at the history of human production we note that there is a kind of tacit and profound accord between what has been achieved and what has been transcended. Take a work of the importance of Bach's *Well-Tempered Clavier;* the obedience is such that when Bach makes a decision, it always corresponds to a rule, to a convention that can be explained in clear terms. Thus he begins by obeying. But within that obedience, he is absolutely free. He doesn't submit to obedience, he chooses it.

PUPILS FROM THE NEW WORLD

I have had a lot of American pupils, that's true. It's easy to forget that fifty years ago, no one knew of American music, it wasn't an expression you used. There's been an enormous change since then, and today Mr. Copland comes to conduct in London, in Rome, in Paris; Mr. Bernstein conducts, and his works are played all over the world.

The term "American musician" is no longer unusual. It was unknown before for specific reasons: a number of foreign musicians had settled in America, but no musicians had been trained entirely there. This situation was linked to political, religious and racial questions; the artistic culture of America developed relatively late. The amalgam of these elements seems to have been achieved first in America through popular music, supplied by black men who had a particular talent for music but were hardly American in origin.

Of course, very few of us are pure French for generations back without any dilution; most of us are descended from parents of diverse origins, there's a mixture. But this mixing has gone on for such a long time that, as a wine that's quite old is more itself, more recognizable than an absolutely new wine, we can easily assert our identity. A tree has roots that establish themselves deep in the earth and the process requires time. The musical heritage of black Americans still constitutes an essential compost. Beginning from that, and little by little, American musicians have created an entirely new concept by using old methods. America has managed to generate a very advanced civilization without roots; it had to create simultaneously the fruit and the root; it has, I believe, succeeded to a very great extent.

41 Constant Lambert

Though well known in his day as a composer and conductor, the Englishman Constant Lambert (1905–1951) is perhaps now best remembered as the author of a brilliant and opinionated 1934 book on early twentieth-century music, *Music Ho! A Study of Music in Decline.* Here Lambert takes a jaundiced view of the whole modern compositional scene, letting fly with his own quirky yet stimulating views on whatever happens to have come across his field of hearing. In the following section he examines a characteristic feature of the period following World War I: the tendency to create new compositions based on stylistic simulations of older music. For Lambert this practice reflects an age that has lost faith in its own voice: the first era in which the music of the past is deemed superior to that of the present. He decries the use of "pastiche"—the making of

something new out of fragments of borrowed material—not simply as a "curiosity" but "as a chosen medium for self-expression" (though he takes no account
of similar practices in medieval and Renaissance music).

FROM *Music Ho!*
(1934)

THE AGE OF PASTICHE

To describe the present age in music as one of pastiche may seem a sweeping
generalization but, like the description of the Impressionist period as one of
disruption, it is a generalization with a strong basis in fact. There are many
contemporary composers of note who stand to some extent outside this classi-
fication, just as there were many composers who stood outside the Impressionism of the pre-war period, but the dominant characteristic of post-war music
is either pastiche or an attempted consolidation that achieves only pastiche.

Pastiche has existed in music for many years, but it is only since the war that
it has taken the place of development and experiment. In the nineteenth century a number of minor composers turned out their suites in the olden style,
but these mild pièces d'occasion[1] no more affected the main course of music
than an Olde Worlde Dunne Shoppe affects the architectural experiments of
Corbusier and Mallet-Stevens. Apart from these studio pieces, pastiche has
always existed in the form of stage decoration as, for example, the Mozartean
divertissement in Tchaikovsky's *Queen of Spades*, or the music off stage in the
second act of Puccini's *Tosca*. It need hardly be pointed out, though, that these
touches of dramatic colour indicated no change of heart on the part of the
composer. Tchaikovsky did not write symphonies modelled on Haydn any more
than Puccini set out to imitate Rossini or Mercadante.

The deliberate and serious use of pastiche, not as a curiosity or as a pièce
d'occasion but as a chosen medium for self-expression, is the property of the
post-war period alone.

The idea that music of an earlier age can be better than the music of one's
own is an essentially modern attitude. The Elizabethans did not tire of their
conceits and go back to the sweet simplicity of Hucbald, any more than the
late Caroline composers deserted the new and airy Italian style for the grave
fantasias of Dowland. Burney's *History of Music* is an astonishing example of
the complete satisfaction with its own period so typical of the eighteenth century. To him the earlier composers were only of interest as stepping-stones to
the glorious and unassailable music of his own day. Passages in the earlier

TEXT: *Music Ho! A Study of Music in Decline* (London: Faber & Faber, 1966), pp. 66–71.

1. "Occasional pieces," here implying "light music."

music which do not display the smoothness of texture that the eighteenth century looked on as technical perfection were dismissed as crudities due to lack of taste and skill.

The nineteenth century was to carry this smug attitude one stage further. The eighteenth-century masters were admired not so much for their own sake as for being precursors of the romantic school which through its sheer position in time was naturally an improvement. Once Beethoven's Symphonies were accepted they were considered as being superior to Mozart's in the way that a six-cylinder car is preferred to a four-cylinder car, or a talking to a silent film. Schumann, it is true, admired Scarlatti, but with a touch of the patronage displayed by a Lady Bountiful visiting the village, and Clara Schumann simply could not understand how Brahms could take any interest in composers earlier than Bach. Wagner's followers did not look upon *The Ring* as a way of writing operas that was different from Bellini's, but as a way that clearly was a much better one.

Even in the early twentieth century, when the attitude towards music of a past age was broader and more cultured, showing at times a certain humility, the direction taken, not only by composers but by the public and critics, was progressive in the mechanical sense of the word. Those who were swept off their feet by Strauss and, later, by Scriabin—and they included some of our most levelheaded critics—-thought nothing of referring to Mozart as a snuffbox composer in comparison with these cosmic masters; and it is clear that the more fervent admirers of Debussy and Stravinsky regarded their music as not only a reaction against Wagner, but as the death of Wagner.

That is not to say that music until the present has proceeded in a mechanical series of reactions. It is not until Stravinsky that a new movement in music is held to have automatically wiped out all traces of the preceding one (of which the wretched followers, like Babylonian courtiers, are forcibly immolated on the tomb of their master). The new music from Italy undoubtedly changed the course of Purcell's musical thought, but the Elizabethan spirit and technique displayed in his early string fantasias is not entirely banished from his later work, which, though experimental to a degree, and in no way reactionary, yet has a distinct connection with the work of previous generations.

Revolutionary, in fact, is an unsuitable word with which to describe the experimental periods of past ages. The revolutionaries of the seventeenth century were hardy pioneers who struck out boldly across undiscovered plains and cultivated the virgin soil. The revolutionaries of today are no more hardy than the man who takes a ticket on the Inner Circle, and is at liberty to travel in either direction, knowing that eventually he will arrive at the station which the fashion of the day has decreed to be the centre of the town. The modern musical revolutions are revolutions in the meanest sense of the word—the mere turning of a stationary wheel.

A great deal of pre-war music may have sounded, to use a dear old phrase, "like nothing on earth," but that at least is a negative merit from the revolutionaries' point of view. Most music of today sounds only too reminiscent of something that has previously been in existence.

Comparison to an earlier composer, at one time a well-known form of musician-baiting, is now come to be a delicate compliment. If you had told Wagner that you admired his operas because they were "like"' Cimarosa he would probably have kicked you out of the house, and I doubt if Liszt would have been pleased if you had said that his *Études transcendentales* were charming because they were "like" Couperin.

But today every composer's overcoat has its corresponding hook in the cloakroom of the past. Stravinsky's concertos (we have it on the composer's own authority) are "like" Bach and Mozart; Sauguet's music is admired because "c'est dans le vrai tradition de Gounod";[2] another composer's score is praised because in it "se retrouvent les graces étincellantes de Scarlatti."[3] The composer can no longer pride himself on being true to himself—he can only receive the pale reflected glory of being true to whichever past composer is credited at the moment with having possessed the Elixir of Life.

It would be a mistake, I think, to put this attitude down to a spiritual humility comparable to the quite natural inferiority complex a modern sculptor might feel in the presence of some early Chinese carving. It is more in the nature of a last refuge, comparable to the maudlin religiosity of a satiated rake. After the debauches of the Impressionist period nothing is left to the modern composer in the way of a new *frisson* save a fashionable repentance.

Unlike the experimental period of the seventeenth century the pre-war period has led to a psychological cul-de-sac. There are many explanations of this, of which the most convincing is a simple and practical one. By 1913 music had already reached the absolute limit of complication allowed by the capacity of composers, players, listeners and instrument makers. With very few exceptions in detail—such as the piano writing of Sorabji, the polytonal choral writing of Milhaud and the quarter-tone writing of Aloys Haba— there is nothing in present-day music more complicated from any point of view than what we find in the music of twenty years ago. The composer is now faced, not with further experiment but with the more difficult task of consolidating the experiments of this vertiginous period. He is like a man in a high-powered motor-car that has got out of control. He must either steer it away from the cliff's edge back to the road or leap out of it altogether. Most modern composers have chosen the latter plan, remarking, as they dexterously save their precious lives: "I think motor-cars are a little *vieux jeu*[4]—don't you?"

There is an obvious end to the amount of purely physical experiment in music, just as there is an obvious end to geographical exploration. Wyndham Lewis has pointed out that when speed and familiarity have reduced travelling in space to the level of the humdrum those in search of the exotic will have to

2. I.e., "it is in the true tradition of Gounod."
3. I.e., in it "are found the glittering graces of Scarlatti."
4. I.e., "old hat."

travel in time, and this is what has already happened in music. The Impression-ist composers vastly speeded up the facilities for space travel in music, explor-ing the remotest jungles and treating uncharted seas as though they were the Serpentine. Stravinsky, at one time the globe trotter par excellence, can no longer thrill us with his traveller's tales of the primitive steppe and has, quite logically, taken to time travelling instead. He reminds one of the character in a play by Evreinoff who lives half in the eighteenth century, half in the present.

The advantages of time travelling are obvious. The pioneer work has been done for you already and, owing to the increased facilites for moving from one century or decade to another, you can always be in the right decade at the right time, whereas in space travelling you may be delayed by a month or two, or even find that the intellectual world has gone on to the next port.

42 Leonard B. Meyer

The pluralism that was already evident in the post–World War I period, dis-cussed by Constant Lambert in the previous reading, became even more charac-teristic of music composed during the second half of the century. In this excerpt from his book *Music, the Arts, and Ideas,* the music theorist and cultural histo-rian Leonard B. Meyer (b. 1918) argues that the condition of stylistic plurality in contemporary art is not just a passing phase but will remain a permanent attri-bute, at least into the foreseeable future. Music will exist within a state of con-stant change and fluctuation, without any single compositional orientation gaining an upper hand, except perhaps for a relatively brief period. With this view Meyer was among the first to develop a theory of the "postmodern," although the term had not been coined when his book appeared in 1967. Time, moreover, seems to have supported Meyer's hypothesis, at least to date: musical developments of the subsequent quarter century have done little to refute it.

FROM *Music, the Arts, and Ideas*
(1967)

THE AESTHETICS OF STABILITY

> *And therefore I have sailed and come*
> *To the holy city of Byzantium.*
> —W. B. Yeats

INTRODUCTION

•   •   •   •   •

The present seems to be aberrant, uncertain, and baffling because the prevalent view of style change—involving notions of progress and teleology, *Zeitgeist* and cultural coherence, necessity and organic development, or some combination of these—posits the eventual establishment of a single common style in each, or even in all, of the arts. As a result, composers as well as critics and historians have come to expect that one dominant style would emerge in the arts—whether as the result of radically new developments, an accommodation of prevailing styles to one another, or the "triumph" of some existing style. Thus Winthrop Sargeant, commenting upon the works of composers who employ quite different styles, says, "The astonishing thing is that these composers all exist at the same time, and the inference to be drawn from this fact is that none of the revolutions has been definitive."[1] And, though composing in an idiom anathema to Mr. Sargeant, Boulez also tacitly assumes a monolithic model of style development, asserting, "Anyone who has not felt . . . the necessity of the 12-tone language is SUPERFLUOUS. For everything he writes will fall short of the imperatives of our time."[2]

But suppose that the paradigm which posits cumulative change and the discovery of a common style is no longer pertinent and viable? Perhaps none of the "revolutions" will be definitive; then astonishment would disappear. Suppose, too, that there are no "imperatives" of the sort that Boulez assumes (Whose imperatives? What is "our time" but the totality of actions, including art works, that take place in it?), and, consequently, that no style is necessarily superfluous. Suppose, in short, that the present pluralism of coexisting styles (each with its particular premises and even its attendant ideology) represents not an anomalous, transient state of affairs, but a relatively stable and enduring one.

I am suggesting not only that such a hypothesis is neither theoretically absurd

TEXT: *Music, the Arts, and Ideas* (Chicago: University of Chicago Press, 1967), pp. 171–75.

1. "Twin Bill," *The New Yorker* 42 (May 28, 1966), p. 88. [Au.]
2. Harold C. Schonberg, "Very Big Man of Avant-Garde," *New York Times*, May 9, 1965, sec. 2, p. 11. [Au.]

nor empirically impossible but that, once it is adopted, seemingly incompatible pieces of the puzzling present begin to form an intelligible pattern. If our time appears to be one of "crisis," it does so largely because we have misunderstood the present situation and its possible consequences. Because a past paradigm has led us to expect a monolithic, all-encompassing style, the cultural situation has seemed bizarre and perplexing. The "crisis" dissolves when the possibility of a continuing stylistic coexistence is recognized and the delights of diversity are admitted. The question then becomes not is this style going to be THE STYLE, but is this particular work well-made, challenging, and enjoyable.

THE PROFILE OF PLURALISM
THE DYNAMICS OF FLUCTUATION

What the proposed hypothesis, then, envisages is the persistence over a considerable period of time of a fluctuating stasis—a steady-state in which an indefinite number of styles and idioms, techniques and movements, will coexist in each of the arts.[3] There will be no central, common practice in the arts, no stylistic "victory." In music, for instance, tonal and non-tonal styles, aleatoric and serialized techniques, electronic and improvised means will all continue to be employed. Similarly in the visual arts, current styles and movements—abstract expressionism and surrealism, representational and Op art, kinetic sculpture and magic realism, Pop and non-objective art—will all find partisans and supporters. Though schools and techniques are less clearly defined in literature, present attitudes and tendencies—the "objective" novel, the theater of the absurd, as well as more traditional manners and means—will, I suspect, persist.

Though new methods and directions may be developed in any or in all of the arts, these will not displace existing styles. The new will simply be additions to the already existing spectrum of styles. Interaction and accommodation among different traditions of music, art, or literature may from time to time produce hybrid combinations or composites, but the possibility of radical innovation seems very remote. As will be suggested, however, the abrupt juxtaposition of markedly unlike styles—perhaps from different epochs and traditions—within a single work may not be uncommon.

Though a spectrum of styles will coexist in what is essentially a steady-state, this does not mean that in a given art all methods and idioms will be equally favored at a particular time. In music, for example, one or possibly two of the stylistic options available to composers may for a number of years prove especially attractive; and activity will be most intense in those parts of the stylistic spectrum. But this will not indicate that other traditions and idioms are no longer viable or are declining. For subsequently, fascinated by different prob-

3. Pluralism is by no means confined to the arts. Diversity and heterogeneity characterize most disciplines and subjects. Often disparate paradigms or conceptual schemes coexist within a single field. [Au.]

lems or swayed by different attitudes, composers will, by and large, turn to other traditions and other styles.

Such a succession of wavelike fluctuations may make it appear as though one style has followed or replaced another. But what will in fact have happened is that one style—or perhaps a group of related styles—will, so to speak, have "crested," becoming for a time particularly conspicuous. And at the very time most composers are riding the crest of the stylistic wave, others will have continued to follow ways and procedures temporarily less popular.

Fluctuation of this sort has, it seems to me, been characteristic of the history of the arts during the past fifty years. Various musical styles have appeared to succeed one another—late romanticism (serial as well as tonal), primitivism, neo-classicism, aleatoric and totally ordered music; but almost all have continued, in one form or another, as ways of making music. Some—for instance, serialism—have already "crested" more than once; none has really disappeared or been replaced. In the plastic arts, where learning a syntax is not involved and the resistance of performers to novelty is not a consideration, fluctuation has been both more rapid and more patent. After a long sequence of styles and movements, beginning with those that followed World War I and continuing through abstract expressionism, action-painting, Pop, Op, and so on, many painters are "returning" to more or less traditional forms of representation, to surrealism and the like. Not that the latter styles were ever really abandoned—only that for a time the majority of artists found them less provocative and exciting than other means and modes.

Though a fluctuating stasis may well be characteristic of present and future changes in the arts, I do not wish to suggest that the rate, direction, or kind of changes exhibited by them will be concurrent or congruent. Sometimes style changes in two or more arts may be simultaneous. In such a case, if the arts in question move in a similar direction—say, toward greater freedom from traditional norms or toward a more meticulous control of means—some common ideological-aesthetic tendency may be involved. At other times, such concurrent changes may simply happen by chance. More often than not, however, each of the arts will probably exhibit its own peculiar pattern of style fluctuation.

The continuing existence of a spectrum of styles is also indicated by the fact that a number of composers, artists, and writers have found it possible to move easily from one practice or tradition to another—according to their interest, taste, or humor. Thus, after developing and writing a number of works in the twelve-tone method, Schönberg found it interesting and not inconsistent occasionally to compose in the idiom of tonal music. In like manner, Picasso has from time to time returned to a neo-classicism which he first employed quite early in his career. If the repertory of available styles grows, as I believe it will, to include many of the styles of earlier Western art[4] and even some from non-

4. When the term "art" or "work of art" is used, it will generally mean all the arts. Similarly, when the term "artists" is used alone, it will refer to plastic artists, musicians, writers, and so on. [Au.]

Western civilizations, such shifts in style from one work to another will become more common.

This does not imply that all artists, or even a majority of them, will be stylistically polylingual. Many will cultivate only one of the many styles available. (Generally these will, I suspect, be the "Traditionalists" for whom art is a form of personal expression, and whose motto must, accordingly, be: One Man, One Style.) Frequently, too, there will be deep and irreconcilable differences between artists working in different traditions or espousing different ideologies.[5]

Which styles or traditions are preferred by any considerable number of artists at a particular time—and for how long—will depend upon a number of different factors. The ability of one outstanding composer—or perhaps even a group of composers—to write convincing, effective, and interesting music in a particular idiom will be important in attracting others to the style. The challenge and fascination of particular compositional methods and problems may also serve to stimulate a wave of activity in a particular part of the stylistic spectrum. Related to this is the real possibility that one style may be abandoned and another adopted simply because the composer no longer finds the problems and procedures of the first style interesting. At times a conceptual model of order (or disorder), developed in connection with some other art or one of the sciences, may also influence the direction of style change. Nor, as recent history indicates, should one underestimate the role played by theory and criticism in shaping stylistic interests and tendencies. Finally, the power of patrons, particularly institutional ones—foundations, universities, symphony orchestras, museums, and the like—to encourage or discourage stylistic movements and tendencies may be of considerable importance.

Because they may not necessarily exhibit any consistent direction or pattern, such successive waves of stylistic activity may seem little more than a series of fashions. Possibly so; but the implied value judgment is not warranted. For since in the coming years the criteria of aesthetic value will, according to the present hypothesis, be those of skill and elegance, rather than those of imitation, expression, or social relevance as they have been in the past, style fluctuations occasioned by problems to be solved would not be capricious or merely modish. Just as the scientists, for instance, tend to direct their energies toward sets of problems where developments in one field have made exciting advances and elegant solutions possible (perhaps in a different field)—yesterday in nuclear physics, today in genetics and molecular biology—so, for the composers, musical problems broached or solutions proposed in one segment of the stylistic spectrum may make elegant and fruitful activity in some other segment possible and attractive.

•   •   •   •   •

5. See Harold Rosenberg, *The Tradition of the New* (New York: Horizon Press, 1959), pp. 54–55. [Au.]

43 Umberto Eco

The Italian Umberto Eco (b. 1932), one the most prominent and versatile thinkers of the later twentieth century, has produced major work in such diverse
fields as semiology, literary criticism, cultural theory, and creative writing. (His
novel *The Name of the Rose* even achieved bestseller status.) The influential
essay from which this reading is taken appeared in the 1960s, when indeterminacy was a particularly prominent feature in artistic activities. Eco uses examples drawn from music of the time (he was then closely associated with the
Italian composer Luciano Berio) to develop his notion of the "open" work,
which, like a "construction kit," allows itself to be assembled in different forms,
producing multiple final shapes, none of which can be considered the "work
proper." Eco also questions why such structures, based upon artistic assumptions so markedly contrary to tradition, appeal so strongly to contemporary artists, noting analogies between these "works in movement" and certain
developments in modern science.

FROM The Poetics of the Open Work
(1962)

A number of recent pieces of instrumental music are linked by a common
feature: the considerable autonomy left to the individual performer in the way
he chooses to play the work. Thus, he is not merely free to interpret the composer's instructions following his own discretion (which in fact happens in traditional music), but he must impose his judgment on the form of the piece, as
when he decides how long to hold a note or in what order to group the sounds:
all this amounts to an act of improvised creation. Here are some of the best-
known examples of the process.

1. In *Klavierstück XI*, by Karlheinz Stockhausen, the composer presents the
performer a single large sheet of music paper with a series of note groupings.
The performer then has to choose among these groupings, first for the one to
start the piece and, next, for the successive units in the order in which he
elects to weld them together. In this type of performance, the instrumentalist's
freedom is a function of the "narrative" structure of the piece, which allows
him to "mount" the sequence of musical units in the order he chooses.

2. In Luciano Berio's *Sequenza for Solo Flute*, the composer presents the
performer a text which predetermines the sequence and intensity of the sounds

TEXT: *The Open Work*, trans. by Anna Concogni (Cambridge, Mass.: Harvard University Press,
1989), pp. 1–5, 17–20. Reprinted by permission of the publishers.

to be played. But the performer is free to choose how long to hold a note inside the fixed framework imposed on him, which in turn is established by the fixed pattern of the metronome's beat.

3. Henri Pousseur has offered the following description of his piece *Scambi:*

> *Scambi* is not so much a musical composition as a *field of possibilities,* an explicit invitation to exercise choice. It is made up of sixteen sections. Each of these can be linked to any two others, without weakening the logical continuity of the musical process. Two of its sections, for example, are introduced by similar motifs (after which they evolve in divergent patterns); another pair of sections, on the contrary, tends to develop towards the same climax. Since the performer can start or finish with any one section, a considerable number of sequential permutations are made available to him. Furthermore, the two sections which begin on the same motif can be played simultaneously, so as to present a more complex structural polyphony. It is not out of the question that we conceive these formal notations as a marketable product: if they were tape-recorded and the purchaser had a sufficiently sophisti-cated reception apparatus, then the general public would be in a position to develop a private musical construct of its own and a new collective sensibility in matters of musical presentation and duration could emerge.

4. In Pierre Boulez's *Third Sonata for Piano,* the first section (*Antiphonie, Formant 1*) is made up of ten different pieces on ten corresponding sheets of music paper. These can be arranged in different sequences like a stack of filing cards, though not all possible permutations are permissible. The second part (*Formant 2, Trope*) is made up of four parts with an internal circularity, so that the performer can commence with any one of them, linking it successively to the others until he comes round full circle. No major interpretative variants are permitted inside the various sections, but one of them, *Parenthèse,* opens with a prescribed time beat, which is followed by extensive pauses in which the beat is left to the player's discretion. A further prescriptive note is evinced by the composer's instructions on the manner of linking one piece to the next (for example, *sans retenir, enchaîner sans interruption,* and so on).

What is immediately striking in such cases is the macroscopic divergence between these forms of musical communication and the time-honored tradi-tion of the classics. This difference can be formulated in elementary terms as follows: a classical composition, whether it be a Bach fugue, Verdi's *Aïda,* or Stravinsky's *Rite of Spring,* posits an assemblage of sound units which the com-poser arranged in a closed, well-defined manner before presenting it to the listener. He converted his idea into conventional symbols which more or less oblige the eventual performer to reproduce the format devised by the com-poser himself, whereas the new musical works referred to above reject the definitive, concluded message and multiply the formal possibilities of the distri-bution of their elements. They appeal to the initiative of the individual perfor-mer, and hence they offer themselves not as finite works which prescribe specific repetition along given structural coordinates but as "open" works, which are brought to their conclusion by the performer at the same time as he experiences them on an esthetic plane.[1]

To avoid any confusion in terminology, it is important to specify that here the definition of the "open work," despite its relevance in formulating a fresh dialectics between the work of art and its performer, still requires to be separated from other conventional applications of this term. Esthetic theorists, for example, often have recourse to the notions of "completeness" and "openness" in connection with a given work of art. These two expressions refer to a standard situation of which we are all aware in our reception of a work of art: we see it as the end product of an author's effort to arrange a sequence of communicative effects in such a way that each individual addressee can refashion the original composition devised by the author. The addressee is bound to enter into an interplay of stimulus and response which depends on his unique capacity for sensitive reception of the piece. In this sense the author presents a finished product with the intention that this particular composition should be appreciated and received in the same form as he devised it. As he reacts to the play of stimuli and his own response to their patterning, the individual addressee is bound to supply his own existential credentials, the sense conditioning which is peculiarly his own, a defined culture, a set of tastes, personal inclinations, and prejudices. Thus, his comprehension of the original artifact is always modified by his particular and individual perspective. In fact, the form of the work of art gains its esthetic validity precisely in proportion to the number of different perspectives from which it can be viewed and understood. These give it a wealth of different resonances and echoes without impairing its original essence; a road traffic sign, on the other hand, can be viewed in only one sense, and, if it is transfigured into some fantastic meaning by an imaginative driver, it merely ceases to be *that* particular traffic sign with that particular meaning. A work of art, therefore, is a complete and *closed* form in its uniqueness as a balanced organic whole, while at the same time constituting an *open* product on account of its susceptibility to countless different interpretations which do not impinge on its unadulterable specificity. Hence, every reception of a work of art is both an *interpretation* and a *performance* of it, because in every reception the work takes on a fresh perspective for itself.

Nonetheless, it is obvious that works like those of Berio and Stockhausen are "open" in a far more tangible sense. In primitive terms we can say that they are quite literally "unfinished": the author seems to hand them on to the perfor-

---

1. Here we must eliminate a possible misunderstanding straightaway: the practical intervention of a "performer" (the instrumentalist who plays a piece of music or the actor who recites a passage) is different from that of an interpreter in the sense of consumer (somebody who looks at a picture, silently reads a poem, or listens to a musical composition performed by someone else). For the purposes of esthetic analysis, however, both cases can be seen as different manifestations of the same interpretative attitude. Every "reading," "contemplation," or "enjoyment" of a work of art represents a tacit or private form of "performance." [Au.]

mer more or less like the components of a construction kit. He seems to be unconcerned about the manner of their eventual deployment. This is a loose and paradoxical interpretation of the phenomenon, but the most immediately striking aspect of these musical forms can lead to this kind of uncertainty, although the very fact of our uncertainty is itself a positive feature: it invites us to consider *why* the contemporary artist feels the need to work in this kind of direction, to try to work out what historical evolution of esthetic sensibility led up to it and which factors in modern culture reinforced it. We are then in a position to surmise how these experiences should be viewed in the spectrum of a theoretical esthetics.

Pousseur has observed that the poetics of the "open" work tends to encourage "acts of conscious freedom" on the part of the performer and place him at the focal point of a network of limitless interrelations, among which he chooses to set up his own form without being influenced by an external *necessity* which definitively prescribes the organization of the work in hand.[2] At this point one could object (with reference to the wider meaning of "openness" already introduced in this essay) that any work of art, even if it is not passed on to the addressee in an unfinished state, demands a free, inventive response, if only because it cannot really be appreciated unless the performer somehow reinvents it in psychological collaboration with the author himself. Yet this remark represents the theoretical perception of contemporary esthetics, achieved only after painstaking consideration of the function of artistic performance; certainly an artist of a few centuries ago was far from being aware of these issues. Instead nowadays it is primarily the artist who is aware of its implications. In fact, rather than submit to the "openness" as an inescapable element of artistic interpretation, he subsumes it into a positive aspect of his production, recasting the work so as to expose it to the maximum possible "opening."

•   •   •   •   •

It would be quite natural for us to think that this flight away from the old, solid concept of necessity and the tendency toward the ambiguous and the indeterminate reflect a crisis of contemporary civilization. On the other hand, we might see these poetical systems, in harmony with modern science, as expressing the positive possibility of thought and action made available to an individual who is open to the continuous renewal of his life patterns and cognitive processes. Such an individual is productively committed to the development of his own mental faculties and experiential horizons. This contrast is too facile and Manichaean. Our main intent has been to pick out a number of analogies which reveal a reciprocal play of problems in the most disparate areas of contemporary culture and which point to the common elements in a new way of looking at the world.

2. Henri Pousseur, "La nuova sensibilità musicale," *Incontri musicali* 2 (May, 1958), p. 25. [Au.]

What is at stake is a convergence of new canons and requirements which the forms of art reflect by way of what we could term *structural homologies*. This need not commit us to assembling a rigorous parallelism—it is simply a case of phenomena like the "work in movement" simultaneously reflecting mutually contrasted epistemological situations, as yet contradictory and not satisfactorily reconciled. Thus, the concepts of "openness" and dynamism may recall the terminology of quantum physics: indeterminacy and discontinuity. But at the same time they also exemplify a number of situations in Einsteinian physics.

The multiple polarity of a serial composition in music, where the listener is not faced by an absolute conditioning center of reference, requires him to constitute his own system of auditory relationships.[3] He must allow such a center to emerge from the sound continuum. Here are no privileged points of view, and all available perspectives are equally valid and rich in potential. Now, this multiple polarity is extremely close to the spatiotemporal conception of the universe which we owe to Einstein. The thing which distinguishes the Einsteinian concept of the universe from quantum epistemology is precisely this faith in the totality of the universe, a universe in which discontinuity and indeterminacy can admittedly upset us with their surprise apparitions, but in fact, to use Einstein's words, presuppose not a God playing random games with dice but the Divinity of Spinoza, who rules the world according to perfectly regulated laws. In this kind of universe, relativity means the infinite variability of experience as well as the infinite multiplication of possible ways of measuring things and viewing their position. But the objective side of the whole system can be found in the invariance of the simple formal descriptions (of the differential equations) which establish once and for all the relativity of empirical measurement.

· · ·

This is not the place to pass judgment on the scientific validity of the metaphysical construct implied by Einstein's system. But there is a striking analogy between his universe and the universe of the work in movement. The God in Spinoza, who is made into an untestable hypothesis by Einsteinian metaphysics, becomes a cogent reality for the work of art and matches the organizing impulse of its creator.

The *possibilities* which the work's openness makes available always work within a given *field of relations*. As in the Einsteinian universe, in the "work in movement" we may well deny that there is a single prescribed point of view. But this does not mean complete chaos in its internal relations. What it does imply is an organizing rule which governs these relations. Therefore, to sum up, we can say that the "work in movement" is the possibility of numerous different personal interventions, but it is not an amorphous invitation to indis-

3. On the "éclatement multidirectionnel des structures," see A. Boucourechliev, "Problèmes de la musique moderne," *Nouvelle revue française* (December–January, 1960–61). [Au.]

criminate participation. The invitation offers the performer the opportunity for an oriented insertion into something which always remains the world intended by the author.

In other words, the author offers the interpreter, the performer, the addressee a work *to be completed.* He does not know the exact fashion in which his work will be concluded, but he is aware that once completed the work in question will still be his own. It will not be a different work, and, at the end of the interpretative dialogue, a form which is *his* form will have been organized, even though it may have been assembled by an outside party in a particular way that he could not have foreseen. The author is the one who proposed a number of possibilities which had already been rationally organized, oriented, and endowed with specifications for proper development.

Berio's *Sequenza,* which is played by different flutists, Stockhausen's *Klavierstück XI,* or Pousseur's *Mobiles,* which are played by different pianists (or performed twice over by the same pianists), will never be quite the same on different occasions. Yet they will never be gratuitously different. They are to be seen as the actualization of a series of consequences whose premises are firmly rooted in the original data provided by the author.

This happens in the musical works which we have already examined, and it happens also in the plastic artifacts we considered. The common factor is a mutability which is always deployed within the specific limits of a given taste, or of predetermined formal tendencies, and is authorized by the concrete pliability of the material offered for the performer's manipulation. Brecht's plays appear to elicit free and arbitrary response on the part of the audience. Yet they are also rhetorically constructed in such a way as to elicit a reaction oriented toward, and ultimately anticipating, a Marxist dialectic logic as the basis for the whole field of possible responses.

All these examples of "open" works and "works in movement" have this latent characteristic, which guarantees that they will always be seen as "works" and not just as a conglomeration of random components ready to emerge from the chaos in which they previously stood and permitted to assume any form whatsoever.

44 George Rochberg

Stylistic pluralism, discussed by Constant Lambert in connection with post–World War I music (see pp. 220–24) and Leonard Meyer in a more general esthetic context (pp. 224–28), became particularly prominent during the 1960s, when composers started not only evoking and parodying earlier music but actually quoting large segments of it, often constructing entire compositions by reworking preexistent material. At the same time there was a widespread move in both Europe and the Americas to "return to tonality," not merely by quotation but through reassimilation of the techniques and gestures of Western common-practice music. The Third String Quartet by the American George Rochberg (b. 1922), a leading figure in advancing both quotation and simulation, played a major role in this development, attracting considerable controversy when it first appeared in 1965. Though there is no actual quotation in the quartet, there is one lengthy movement of an almost purely Beethovenian character, along with others that combine segments sounding like Mahler and Bartók with what is presumably Rochberg's "own" contemporary style.

On the Third String Quartet
(1965)

When I wrote my Third String Quartet I had no idea it would call forth the quantity and kinds of critical comment that followed its first performances and recording. Some critics rejected the work out of hand on the grounds that its combination of tonal and nontonal musics simply did not add up to being "contemporary." Some seemed fascinated but still puzzled by the phenomenon of structural fusion of past and present. The majority of writers, however, welcomed it even though they were uncertain whether the direction that the quartet pointed to could or would be followed up.

The acceptability of such a work hinges no doubt on whether one is able to reconcile a juxtaposition of musically opposite styles. In order to effect such a reconciliation, one has to be persuaded, first, that the idea of history as "progress" is no longer viable and, second, that the radical avant-garde of recent years has proved to be bankrupt. Both conditions lay behind the impulse that generated my quartet. Both were determining factors in my choice of ideas, levels of musical action, and the structure of the work itself. Far from seeing tonality and atonality as opposite "styles," I viewed them as significant aspects of an enlarged language of musical expression with branching subdivisions of what I like to call "dialects"—a particular way of stressing or inflecting parts of the whole spectrum of Western musical language. These dialects can be presented singly or in combination depending on what one wants to say and the particular size, shape, and character of the work one wants to say it in. In the quartet the dialects range widely from diatonic, key-centered tonality to forms of chromaticism which veer toward nineteenth-century or early-twentieth-century practices (but still structurally tonal) to a more atonally oriented chromaticism; from predictable to unpredictable periodicities of phrase structure; from simple to complex metric pulsation; and from continuous to noncontinuous gestural relationships between phrases, sections, and movements.

TEXT: *The Aesthetic of Survival*, ed. by William Bolcom (Ann Arbor: University of Michigan Press, 1984), pp. 239–42. Used by permission.

By embracing the earlier traditions of tonality and combining them with the more recently developed atonality, I found it possible to release my music from the overintense, expressionistic manner inherent in a purely serially organized, constant chromaticism, and from the inhibition of physical pulse and rhythm which has enervated so much recent music. With the enlargement of this spectrum of possible means came an enlargement of perspective which potentially placed the entire past at my disposal. I was freed of the conventional perceptions which ascribe some goal-directed, teleological function to that past, insisting that each definable historical development supersedes the one that has just taken place either by incorporating or nullifying it.

In this view, the invention of classical twelve-tone methodology—and later total serialism—not only superseded everything that came before it but literally declared it null and void. Obviously, I rejected this view—though not without great discomfort and difficulty, because I had acquired it, along with a number of similar notions, as a seemingly inevitable condition of the twentieth-century culture in which I had grown up. The demanding effort to evolve and maintain a personal kind of transcendentalism still occupies me; but that effort has resulted in being able to compose whatever kind of music I feel deeply and intensely.

I am not aware that anyone has yet attempted a full-scale answer to the questions my quartet seems to have raised. Perhaps wisely—because I believe the issues involved are complex beyond imagining, and therefore certainly not susceptible to the kind of either/or, binary thinking so characteristic of the contemporary mind. To live with paradox and contradiction is not and has not been our cultural or intellectual way. I suspect that what my quartet suggests to others, and what I began to accept for myself at least fifteen years ago, is that we can no longer live with monolithic ideas about art and how it is produced. Nor can we take as artistic gospel the categorical imperatives laid down by cultural messiahs or their self-appointed apologists and followers of whatever persuasion.

On the contrary, the twentieth century has pointed—however reluctant we may be to accept it in all areas of life, social as well as political, cultural as well as intellectual—toward a difficult-to-define pluralism, a world of new mixtures and combinations of everything we have inherited from the past and whatever we individually or collectively value in the inventions of our own present, replete with juxtapositions of opposites (or seeming opposites) and contraries. In other words, not the narrow, pat, plus/minus, monoview of the rational-minded, but the web of living ideas which combine in strange and unexpected ways much as the stuff of biological matter does; not the self-conscious aesthetic or morality which excludes so much for the sake of "purity," but the sensed (if not quite yet articulate) notion that stretches to embrace everything possible to one's taste and experience, regardless of its time or place of origin. This not only makes it mandatory to see the "past" as continuously viable and alive in our "present" but also to be able to perceive large chunks of time as unities which create a vast physical-mental-spiritual web enfolding our individual lives, actions, and feelings.

I believe we are the filaments of a universal mind which transcends our individual egos and histories. The degree to which we partake of that universal mind is the degree to which we identify with the collective imagery, fate, wisdom, and tragedy of our still struggling species. By ourselves we are virtually nothing—but by opening ourselves to the transcendent collectivity of mankind and its experiences, we share in a totality which, however mysterious its sources, dimensions, and ultimate fate, sustains us.

Pluralism, as I understand it, does not mean a simplistic array of different things somehow stuck together in arbitrary fashion but a way of seeing new possibilities of relationships; of discovering and uncovering hidden connections and working with them structurally; of joining antipodes without boiling out their tensions; of resolving the natural tensions of contradictory terms on new symbiotic hierarchic levels—more than all of the above, a way of preserving the uncertainty of the artistic enterprise which itself demands that, out of the tensions and anxieties attendant upon it, we struggle for clarity and order, to gain not a permanent certainty (which is not possible anyhow) but a momentary insight into how it is possible to resolve the chaos of existence into a shape or form which takes on beauty, perhaps meaning, certainly strength. Art is a way of fighting the encroachment of the forces which diminish us. Through art we are all Don Quixotes battling Time and Death.

Granting pluralism, how is a composer to deal with it? From the inside out, i.e., from the internal psychic imagery which becomes the musical gesture to its artistic manifestation. Gesture, singly or in combination, successive or simultaneous, is the determining factor—not style, language, system, or method.

Given the very strong possibility that music is rooted in our biological structure—as are spoken language and mathematics—the gestures of music can only proceed authentically from one direction: from inside. That is where they get their energy, their power, their immediacy. The conscious effort to give voice to the vast range of these gestures becomes the act of composing, and inevitably demands not only freedom of choice but freedom of combination. If Beethoven, for example, had not felt this way, we would not have the late quartets—those glories of our civilization. There is surely no logic to a movement such as the "Heiliger Dankgesang" of Op. 132, with its combination of alternating Baroque chorale variations and eighteenth/nineteenth-century idealized dance which hides vestiges of the old courtly minuet; or to the insertion of a German folk dance in the more metaphysical surroundings of Op. 130 which Beethoven capped with the grandest fugue of them all. There's no rational way to understand Ives's placing a diatonic fugue in C major cheek by jowl with the layered musics of the other movements of his Fourth Symphony; or his juxtaposition and overlay of chromatic on diatonic, diatonic on chromatic, in his two gems, "The Unanswered Question" and "Central Park in the Dark." (Consider the juxtaposition of the intensely chromatic fugue and essentially pandiatonic last movement in Bartók's *Music for Strings, Percussion and Celesta.*)

The determination to write the Third Quartet the way I did (and other works similar in nature but cast differently, because of different gestural needs, balances, and projections) stems from my personal way of understanding composers like Beethoven, Bartók, and Ives, but is not limited to them. If, in the need to expand our sources—pluralism of gesture, language, and style—we lay ourselves open to the charge of eclecticism, we need not concern ourselves. Other and earlier forms of eclecticism may also be charged to medieval music or to early classical music or to Bach or to Mozart (who seemed thoroughly eclectic to his contemporaries), or to Stravinsky.

Some of the critics who have commented on my quartet have wondered out loud whether the work would "last." How can anyone tell? It is not important. Culture is not the additive product of a series of discrete, specific events or works. It is, like the biology that it rests on, a self-renewing, self-sustaining organism that proliferates, spreads, unites, subdivides, reunites, dies individually but lives collectively. The cultural mechanism for continuity (posterity; immortality) resides in human memory and the preservation of what is authentic and has, therefore, captured a piece of human wit or wisdom (as possible in music as in painting, as in literature). The cultural mechanism for renewal resides in the courage to use human passion and energy in the direction of what is authentic again and again. The ring of authenticity is more important than the clang of originality. Whatever is authentic about the twentieth century will be preserved, and we need not worry about it. Given that certainty, we can safely leave it alone and get back to the business of writing music without falsely institutionalizing the means we use to produce it. But we must be sure that it *is* music; i.e., that we write what we believe in, write it consummately well and that we intend it at least for the delectation and edification of the human ear and heart—beyond that, if possible, for the purification of the mind.

To quote from my notes to the recording of the Third Quartet: "I am turning away from what I consider the cultural pathology of my own time toward what can only be called a *possibility:* that music can be renewed by regaining contact with the tradition and means of the past, to re-emerge as a spiritual force with reactivated powers of melodic thought, rhythmic pulse, and large-scale structure."

45 Carl Dahlhaus

The German Carl Dahlhaus (1928–1989), one of the most far-ranging thinkers in twentieth-century musicology, wrote extensively on such diverse topics as music historiography, the evolution of harmonic tonality, the history of nine-teenth-century music, the music of Schoenberg, and music theory and esthetics. In this essay, the final chapter of his book *What is Music?* (1985), Dahlhaus discusses the ways in which even our most basic ideas about music have been affected by the changes the art has experienced in the twentieth century. Dahl-haus is particularly interested in the strains placed upon a unified concept of music in an age characterized by constant contact with the musics of other peoples and cultures. Such modern Western distinctions as those between "the musical" and "the extramusical," "serious" and "entertainment" music, and even "music" and "noise," become difficult to maintain in a world filled with such diversities. Relating the question of "music" (in the singular) to the more encompassing one of "humanity" (also in the singular), Dahlhaus concludes that "according to twentieth-century criteria . . . , humanity consists less in mak-ing the heterogeneous more homogenous than in mutual acceptance, even where differences may appear unbridgeable."

Music—or Musics?
(1985)

The idea of a world history of music—an idea behind a UNESCO project which the organizers seem disinclined to abandon despite mounting difficulties of an intrinsic and extrinsic nature—carries a double burden: the vagueness of the concept "music" and the ideological implications of the notion of a "world history." And the one difficulty is closely related to the other: the problem of whether "music," in the singular, actually exists cannot even be defined (at any rate, not in a way that invites a foreseeable solution) without a clear idea of whether and in what sense "history," in the singular, is a reality or a mere figment of the imagination.

TEXT: "Gibt es 'die' Musik," in Carl Dahlhaus and Hans Heinrich Eggebrecht, *Was ist Musik?*, ed. by R. Schaal, Taschenbücher zur Musikwissenschaft 100 (Wilhelmshaven: Heinrichshofen Verlag, 1985), pp. 9–17. Translation by Stephen Hinton.

Translated word for word, the title should read: "Does 'the' music exist?" The use of articles, both definite and indefinite, before the singular form of nouns differs between German and English. Nor is it consistent. When the definite article is used, as here, it not only lays stress on the singular but can also imply oneness. Yet German-speaking people may well wonder whether the unity of *die Musik* (at once emphasized and questioned by the quotation marks) is essential or accidental, as Carl Dahlhaus's text makes apparent. The increasingly widespread use in English of the plural "musics" seems to confirm the thrust of Dahlhaus's observations. [Tr.]

The linguistic convention that proscribes making a plural from the word "music" has been increasingly ignored in recent years, owing to difficulties that arise when one clings to the singular, although the attendant stylistic discomfort, which is also discomfort about substance, still lingers. The naïvety with which the nineteenth century either dismissed the musical "other" as undeveloped or unconsciously assimilated it has disappeared or at least diminished, and as a result (a) social, (b) ethnic, and (c) historical differences prove so huge that one feels forced to abandon a unified concept of music.

(a) For several decades a controversy has been conducted, with unvarying arguments, about the dichotomy between classical music and light music,[1] and the terminological issues associated with that socio-esthetic division are so closely bound up with notions and decisions that directly impinge on social practice as to make those issues seem like a theoretical reflection of that practice. The quarrel about the social functions and esthetic criteria of classical music and light music would not be possible if the sonic phenomena, kept separate from one another through their respective labels, were not at the same time bracketed together by the umbrella term "music." Yet it is by no means obvious that a pop song and a twelve-tone composition belong to the same category, as a comparison with other fields shows. No one describes newspapers as "literature," though since a newspaper is printed language, such an application of the term, albeit unusual, would hardly be absurd from an etymological point of view. (The linguistic umbrella term linking journalism and poetry, "text types" [*Textsorten*], has not become common parlance.) And linguistic convention is both cause and effect of the fact that it is not customary to compare the social functions and esthetic criteria of newspapers and poems. Yet twelve-tone compositions are forced to compete with products of the musical entertainment industry via listener statistics, from which practical consequences are drawn. The "spell cast by language" [*Verhexung durch die Sprache*] (Ludwig Wittgenstein)[2]—in this case, by the precarious and questionable singular "music"—precludes a differentiation that seems quite natural in the case of the printed word. (The term "text types," which has pretensions toward neutrality and is supposed to render such differentiations ideologically suspect, is itself underpinned by a "counter-ideology": commensurability instead of incommensurability.) The dissimilarity in the categorization of language and music can be explained pragmatically. Since there is no musical

1. Dahlhaus uses the conceptual pair "E-Musik" (*ernste Musik:* "serious music") and U-Musik (*Unterhaltungsmusik:* "entertainment music"), which carries more terminological weight than the various English equivalents ("classical vs. light," "serious vs. pop," "high vs. low," etc.). Not only have the terms been institutionalized, the large radio stations in Germany have two music departments, and music royalties are paid on two scales, with a distinction being drawn in each case between "E-Musik" and "U-Musik." The terms have also served as the basis for countless esthetic debates. [Tr.]

2. The Austrian philosopher Ludwig Wittgenstein, in his *Philosophical Investigations* (Oxford: Basil Blackwell, 1958), §109, describes philosophy as "a battle against the bewitchment of our intelligence by means of language."

language that serves as an everyday tool of communication, like a vernacular, pop song and twelve-tone composition, both equally removed from everyday reality, are instinctively subsumed under the same category. The convention of talking about "music" in both cases may thus be explained in historical and socio-psychological terms, but such an explanation can hardly be construed as an esthetic justification. Although it might still give one pause, the plural "musics" would be more realistic.

(b) If the consequences arising from the collective singular impinge in a direct and far-reaching way on musico-social reality—a reality defined by the dichotomy between classical and light music, whereby the neutralizing word "music" represents a more serious problem than the controversial adjectives "classical" and "light"—in the case of ethnic and regional differences, the questionable consequences of a universal and neutralizing concept of music are apparent less in practice than in scholarly debate. Sonic phenomena for which a European observer reserves the term "music"—a word for which a linguistic equivalent is often missing in non-European cultures—lose their original meaning if they are divorced from their "extra-musical" context. Strictly speaking, the context of which they are an inextricable part is neither "musical" nor "extra-musical." The former expression [that is, "musical"] stretches the concept of music, a concept of European origin, to such an extent that it can no longer correspond with European reality, while the latter ["extra-musical"] presupposes a concept of music that is not only European but specifically modern. This latter concept of music, which, in a strict sense, dates only from the eighteenth century, crudely distorts non-European musical reality—a reality not just of sonic facts but also of the consciousness of those facts.

If it is true that the category "music" (which supplies criteria for isolating certain "specifically musical"[3] features in complex cultural processes) is an abstraction made only in certain cultures and not in others, then one is faced with an unfortunate alternative: either to reinterpret and expand the European concept of music to the point of alienating it from its origins, or to exclude the sonic creations of a number of non-European cultures from the concept of music. Deciding one way would be precarious in terms of the history of ideas. Deciding the other way would invite the charge of being Eurocentric (as a rule most Africans, even when they emphasize the *négritude* of their culture, do not wish to relinquish "music" as a label of prestige). And a way out of the dilemma is to be found only by considering the ethnological problems in relation to the historical ones; by attempting to solve any difficulties by first increasing them.

(c) The differences between the epochs of European music history, however substantial they may have been, left the inner unity of the concept of music essentially intact as long as the tradition of the ancient world obtained: a tradi-

---

3. "Spezifisch musikalisch" is a phrase used by Eduard Hanslick in *Vom Musikalisch-Schönen* (Leipzig: Rudolph Weigel, 1854), p. 31. [Tr.]

tion whose essential ingredient was the principle of an unchanging tonal system [*Tonsystem*],[4] constituted by direct and indirect relations of consonance, that underpinned a multiplicity of styles. (The principle may not be specifically European, but that does not alter the fact that it formed the essential link in the chain of historical continuity from Antiquity via the Middle Ages through the Modern Age. What is specific—contrary to a prejudice fostered by the method of determination by demarcation—is not always what is essential.)

It was electronic music and "sound-composition" [*Klangkomposition*] inspired by John Cage that first provoked the question whether sonic phenomena that renounce the tonal system can still be considered music according to the European tradition. At the same time, a response to the question seemed plausible: electronic music perpetuated that tradition insofar as the issues it addressed continued a line of historical development. It is indeed possible to interpret the idea of "composing" tone colors (assembling them from sine tones or filtering them out of white noise) as an extreme manifestation of the tendency toward rationalization which Max Weber believed to be the law governing the development of European music: the tendency toward the control of nature, toward giving the compositorial subject unlimited power over its sonic material [*Tonstoff*] or, put in Hanslick's terms, toward making "spirit" [*Geist*] the undisputed master of that "matter which is capable of spirituality" [*geistfähiges Material*].[5] And guided at the outset by the axioms of serialism, one was able to establish a direct connection with the current state of development reached by avant-garde composition. That is why electronic music indubitably became a matter for composers rather than for physicists and engineers. Hence it could still be subsumed under the category of music as this is understood in modern Europe: a historically changeable category that is defined and continually redefined by the work of composers.

The social, ethnic, and historical disparities that appear to force an abandonment of the concept of music seem scarcely reconcilable. If one nonetheless refrains from completely relinquishing the idea expressed or intimated by the collective singular, then a plausible premise for "rescuing" it could be that the idea of "music" in the singular was ultimately grounded in Hegel's conception of world history: a world history which began in the Near East and made its way via Greece and Rome to the Romance and Germanic nations. Hegel's construction undoubtedly suffers from being Eurocentric; yet to make the charge 150 years later is as futile as it is easy. More germane than this manifest shortcoming is the less obvious fact that the anthropological idea which informs

4. "Tonal system" is used here in the broadest sense. It is not restricted to "functional tonality" but covers all musical systems—from Antiquity to the present day—that are organized on the basis of "an arrangement of intervals" (see Carl Dahlhaus's entry on "Tonsysteme," *Musik in Geschichte und Gegenwart*, vol. 13 (Kassel, 1966), cols. 533–47. [Tr.]

5. The word *Geist* is ultimately untranslatable. The word's usage embraces the Latin expressions *spiritus, anima, mens,* and *genius.* The original phrase alluded to here is: "Das Componieren ist ein Arbeiten des Geistes in geistfähigem Material" (Eduard Hanslick, *Vom Musikalisch-Schönen,* p. 35). [Tr.]

Hegel's Philosophy of History [*geschichtsphilosophische Konzeption*] is by no means obsolete: the idea that a culture—even a musical culture—of remote epochs or parts of the world "belongs to world history" to the extent that it participates in "education toward humanity," as that development was commonly called around 1800. The concept of history (in the singular) or world history—a rigorously selective category which excludes from "history proper" the greater part of what occurred in former times as mere detritus—is plausible only when one realizes that it was guided by the classical idea of humanity (in precarious rivalry to the development of science, technology, and industry, which similarly constitutes "a" history—in the singular—regardless of ethnic and social differences).

The concept of world history, at least with regard to earlier epochs, can scarcely be justified in pragmatic terms: the Japanese, Indian, and West European cultures of the fourteenth century scarcely permit the construction either of an external, empirical framework or of a unifying *Zeitgeist*. Their "simultaneity" was chronologically abstract, not historically concrete. Only in the twentieth century have the continents grown together, thanks to economic, technological, and political interdependence, to form a single world whose structure makes it historiographically viable to write world history in the pragmatic sense of the word: a history which also includes the history of music, since the external connection between cultures has become irrefutable, even though any intrinsic one is often questionable, as illustrated by the fad for Indian music.

On the other hand, the idealistic concept of world history need not be relinquished, as long as it is radically modified. It is no longer possible to determine in a dogmatic fashion what a step in the direction of "education toward humanity" should be—from the perspective, that is, of a "cosmopolite" of the early 1800s, who turns out to be an enlightened bourgeois masquerading as the ideal of humanity. "Humanity" in the singular no more exists than "history" in the singular. What remains is the patient effort of understanding, which not only tolerates the "other" precisely on account of its initially disconcerting otherness (tolerance can imply disparagement) but actually respects it.

According to twentieth-century criteria, which are probably not immutable, humanity consists less in making the heterogeneous more homogenous than in mutual acceptance, even where differences may appear unbridgeable. If so, the search in music esthetics (as a derivation of the idea of humanity) for an underlying foundation common to the sonic phenomena of all ages and continents is less important than an awareness and mutual recognition of utterly different principles of formation: the elements and basic patterns are less crucial than the consequences and differentiations. It may be that the principle of consonance and alternating rhythm are "innate ideas" which are merely being forever "transformed," as some historians and ethnomusicologists believe. Or perhaps one can accept as independent, irreducible, and equally valid principles the measurement of interval size alongside relations of consonance, and additive or quantitative rhythm alongside alternating [or qualitative] rhythm [*i.e.,* a succession of *arsis* and *thesis* or strong and weak beats]. Either way, such questions are less important than the appreciation of a substantial dissimilarity of formations or "transformations" [*"Überformungen"*], whether these are constructed on common or differing foundations. To ground the concept of "music" (in the singular) as some "natural given," whether as a musically objective or an anthropological structure, is a difficult and probably pointless enterprise, unless one misuses the concept of "transformation" by invoking it without naming the criteria that allow one to distinguish between "transformations" of common but unrecognizable "deep structures" on the one hand and incoherent diversity on the other. (Moreover, rather than opposing nature and history, one should adopt Fernand Braudel's suggestion and draw a distinction between structures of long, medium, and short duration.)

The driving force behind the idea of "music" (in the singular)—itself a result of "history" (in the singular)—was the classical utopia of humanity that, in Kant's *Critique of Judgment* [*Kritik der Urteilskraft*], formed the basis of an esthetics in which judgments of taste are "subjective" but nevertheless "universal," to the extent that subjectivities strive to converge in a *sensus communis,* a "common sense." If, however, humanity finds expression less in the discovery of a common substance than in the principle of respecting untranscendable difference, one remains true to the idea of "music" (in the singular) by relinquishing it as a concept of substance in order to reinstate it as a regulative principle of mutual understanding.

INDEX

Note: Numbers in boldface refer to pages where definitions for a term are found, or to the source reading passages themselves.